European Gothic

MANCHESTER
UNIVERSITY PRESS

European Gothic

A spirited exchange 1760–1960

edited by
AVRIL HORNER

MANCHESTER UNIVERSITY PRESS

Manchester and New York

distributed exclusively in the USA by Palgrave

Published by Manchester University Press
Oxford Road, Manchester M13 9NR, UK
and Room 400, 175 Fifth Avenue, New York, NY 10010, USA
www.manchesteruniversitypress.co.uk

Distributed exclusively in the USA by
Palgrave, 175 Fifth Avenue, New York, NY 10010, USA

Distributed exclusively in Canada by
UBC Press, University of British Columbia, 2029 West Mall,
Vancouver, BC, Canada V6T 1Z2.

British Library Cataloguing-in-Publication Data
A catalogue record for this book is available from the British Library.

Library of Congress Cataloging-in-Publication Data applied for

ISBN 0 7190 6063 X *hardback*
      0 7190 6064 8 *paperback*

First published 2002

10 09 08 07 06 05 04 03 02   10 9 8 7 6 5 4 3 2 1

Typeset by
Northern Phototypesetting Co. Ltd., Bolton
Printed in Great Britain by
Bell and Bain Limited, Glasgow

Contents

CONTENTS

List of illustrations

LIST OF ILLUSTRATIONS

Every effort has been made to obtain permission to reproduce copyright material in this book. If any proper acknowledgement has not been made, copyright-holders are invited to contact the publisher.

Notes on contributors

Ahlam Alaki is a doctoral student at the University of East Anglia, Norwich in England. Her areas of research interest include: *The Arabian Nights*; Arabic oral and folk literature; symbolism in Arabic artistic and architectural forms; the figure of Shahrazad in relation to women's writing and relations between women; Gothic literature. She has published articles in three major Saudi Arabian daily newspapers.

Neil Cornwell is Professor of Russian and Comparative Literature at the University of Bristol, England. He is editor of the *Reference Guide to Russian Literature* (Fitzroy Dearborn, 1998); *The Gothic-Fantastic in Nineteenth-Century Russian Literature* (Rodopi, 1999); *The Routledge Companion to Russian Literature* (2001); and (with Maggie Malone) the 'New Casebook' on *The Turn of the Screw* and *What Maisie Knew* (Macmillan, 1998). His authored books include: *The Literary Fantastic: From Gothic to Postmodernism* (Harvester Wheatsheaf, 1990); *Pushkin's 'The Queen of Spades'* (Bristol Classical Press, 1993); and *Valdimir Nabokov* (Northcote House, 1999). He is currently writing a study of the absurd in literature.

Joan Curbet is a lecturer in English Literature at the Universitat Autònoma de Barcelona, Spain. He has published widely on the subject of the transition between sacred and secular discourse from the Renaissance to Romanticism, concentrating on the work of authors such as Sir Thomas More, George Herbert, Teresa de Jesús and Edmund Spenser. He is the editor of *Medieval Travel Writing 1096–1492: an Introduction* (Peter Lang Press, 2002) and the author of a Spanish edition of Lord Byron's *Manfred* (forthcoming, 2003).

Terry Hale is currently Research Fellow in the Performance Translation Centre at the University of Hull, England. His main research interest is the relation between translation and creative writing, both with regard to prose fiction and the theatre. He has published more than a dozen translations, including anthologies of detective fiction (*Great French Detective Stories*, 1983), the Surrealist short story (*The Automatic Muse*, 1994), and *The Dedalus Book of French Horror: The Nineteenth Century* (1998). His most recent work is a new translation of J.-K. Huysmans's *Là-bas* (as *The Damned*) for Penguin Classics (2001). He has also written extensively on the history and practice of literary translation.

Jerrold E. Hogle is Professor of English and University Distinguished Professor at the University of Arizona, U.S.A. The holder of several major research fellowships, he has written widely on British Romantic literature, literary and cultural theory, and the Gothic. His best-known book is *Shelley's Process* (Oxford University Press, 1988) and he is a past president of the International Gothic Association. His latest book, *The Undergrounds of 'The Phantom of the Opera'* has recently been published by St. Martin's Press/Palgrave, and he has edited the forthcoming *Cambridge Companion to Gothic Fiction*.

Avril Horner is Professor of English and a member of the European Studies Research Institute at the University of Salford, England. Her research interests and publications focus on twentieth-century literature and in particular on modern poetry, women's writing and the Gothic. She is the co-author, with Sue Zlosnik, of *Landscapes of Desire: Metaphors in Modern Women's Fiction* (Harvester Wheatsheaf, 1990) and *Daphne du Maurier: Writing, Identity and the Gothic Imagination* (Macmillan, 1998). She is currently working, with Sue Zlosnik, on *Gothic and the Comic Turn*, forthcoming from Macmillan.

Catherine Lanone is a Professor at the University of Toulouse II, France, where she teaches nineteenth- and twentieth-century English literature. She has published two books, one on E.M. Forster and one on Emily Brontë, as well as chapters and articles on nineteenth- and twentieth-century writers such as Mary Shelley, Charles Dickens and Virginia Woolf. Her research interests include the significance of intertextual references and the rewriting of Gothic archetypes, particularly in the work of the Brontës and Angela Carter.

Robert Miles is Professor of English Studies at the University of Stirling, Scotland. His publications include *Ann Radcliffe: The Great Enchantress* (Manchester University Press, 1995); *Gothic Writing 1750–1820: A Genealogy* (1993; reprinted Manchester University Press, 2002) and *Gothic Documents 1700–1820: A Sourcebook,* ed. with E.J. Clery (Manchester University Press, 2000). From 1997–2001 he was president of the International Gothic Association.

Peter Mortensen was educated in Denmark and America and is assistant professor of English at Aarhus University, Denmark, where he teaches British literature. He has published critical essays on Wordsworth, Scott, Austen and Lawrence, and his current research centres on the interconnections between European and British writing during the Romantic period. He is currently finishing a book entitled *Acts of Appropriation: Romantic Writing in an Age of Europhobia,* in which he re-examines some Romantic writers' creative responses to continental pre-Romanticism in an attempt to revive interest in European influences on British Romantic literature.

Victor Sage is Professor of English in the School of English and American Studies at the University of East Anglia, Norwich, England. He is a novelist and short story writer, and has written extensively on the Gothic novel tradition. He is the author of *Horror Fiction in the Protestant Tradition,* 1988 and the editor of the casebook, *The Gothick Novel,* 1990. Recent publications include: *Modern Gothic: A Reader* (1997, co-edited with A. Lloyd Smith), new editions of Charles Maturin's *Melmoth the Wanderer* (2000) and J.S. Le Fanu's *Uncle Silas* (both for Penguin Classics). He is currently working on *Le Fanu's Gothic,* a critical study of J.S. Le Fanu.

John Williams is a Reader in Literary Studies at the University of Greenwich, England. His *William Wordsworth: Romantic Poetry and Revolution Politics* was published in 1989 by Manchester University Press. His *Literary Life of William Wordsworth* was published by Macmillan in 1996, and this was followed by a volume on Mary Shelley in the same series in 2000. An essay on Percy Shelley and Wordsworth was included in *Evaluating Shelley* published by Edinburgh University Press in 1996. He has recently completed a book on Wordsworth for the Palgrave Critical issues series.

Angela Wright lectures on eighteenth-century and Romantic literature and literary theory at the University of Sheffield, England. Her research is focussed on English and French Gothic literature between 1790 and 1820. She has published articles on French melodrama, comparative Gothic literature and, from the English Gothic tradition, on Clara Reeve and Sophia Lee. She is currently undertaking research on radical women novelists who published with the Minerva Press in the 1790s and 1800s.

Acknowledgements

The idea for *European Gothic: A Spirited Exchange 1760–1960* emerged from a conference entitled 'Beyond Boundaries II: New Europe ... Pan Europe? Trajectories and Destinations', organized by the European Studies Research Institute and held at the University of Salford in 1999. I would like to thank all those delegates who attended the 'Gothic' stream of this conference for the lively debates which they generated during the event and for their enthusiastic insistence that the moment had come for a book such as this. Thanks also to the anonymous reader whose constructive advice helped me make many improvements to the text. Matthew Frost, of Manchester University Press, has been – as always – a source of excellent advice and cheerful encouragement since the book's inception. Finally, many thanks to Terry Hale, Geoff Harris and Ursula Tidd, who commented on various sections of the book in draft form, and to Howard for helping me, yet again, to unravel the mysteries of information technology.

Introduction

AVRIL HORNER

European Gothic: A Spirited Exchange 1760–1960 seeks to challenge the tyranny of Anglo-American narratives of the Gothic. It offers a range of essays that demonstrate the importance of translation and European writing in the development of the Gothic novel, a vampire-like phenomenon that thrives on the blood of others. The volume thus charts the movement of Gothic themes, tropes and motifs across national and linguistic borders and boundaries; it also examines the cultural and political climates that either allowed the Gothic to flourish or dampened it down through censorship. In so doing, it offers a corrective to what has become a somewhat lopsided story of the development of the Gothic novel. All too often academic accounts of the Gothic repeat, almost mantra-like, the names at the core of the Anglo-American tradition: Walpole, Radcliffe, Lewis, Shelley, Brockden Brown, Hawthorne, Poe. Where are the comprehensive histories of French or Italian Gothic, for example? Sadly, they are not to be found in French or Italian universities, where study of the Gothic has yet to gain a secure foothold. And whilst some recent and valuable overviews of the Gothic, such as Ann Williams's *Art of Darkness* (Williams 1995) and David Punter's *A Companion to the Gothic* (Punter 2000), touch frequently on what we might call European exchanges in the Gothic, they do not focus exclusively on them. Interestingly, the more precise charting of a broader historical and cultural perspective seems to have been left to critics writing for a wider readership. Richard Davenport-Hines's *Gothic: 400 Years of Excess, Horror, Evil and Ruin* (1998) does pay proper attention to European Gothic, attributing enormous importance, for example, to the influence of Salvatore Rosa and de Sade in the development of the Gothic mode.

1

Furthermore, the academic tendency to narrow the lens when look-ing at the rise of the Gothic novel has been exacerbated by the frequent choice of psychoanalytic theory as a methodology for analysis. This is not to say, of course, that it does not have its uses: as Michelle A. Massé has recently commented: 'we *cannot* understand individual and cultural expression – or effect lasting change – without careful consideration of the hinted-at, the hidden and the denied' (Massé 2000: 230). However, it is a critical approach which, used without due care and attention, can result in the occlusion of the historical and the cultural; in this respect, its integrity as a methodology has only lately been challenged. Aware of the limitations of the psychoanalytic approach as a tool for cultural analysis, critics have recently either intelligently adapted it for their own ends (Williams 1995; Hogle 1996; Punter 1998) or resisted its seductions altogether in the pursuit of historical and cultural contexts (Mighall 1999; Baldick and Mighall 2000). However, even within this current return to the historical, academic critics are still inclined to produce an Anglo-American narrative. The promisingly entitled *The History of Gothic Fiction* by Markman Ellis, for example, concerns itself mainly with British and American Gothic writing, although the reader is offered short detours into Europe via the literary history of the vam-pire and into the Caribbean courtesy of the zombie (Ellis 2000).

The different perspectives adopted within *European Gothic: A Spirited Exchange* reveal shared and significant preoccupations that present a rather different picture. For example, several contributors concentrate on Maturin's *Melmoth the Wanderer* and, in particular, on its influence in the development of the Gothic mode in France. This suggests that a work of immense importance within the European Gothic tradition has been overshadowed, perhaps, by the excessive crit-ical attention given to Walpole's *The Castle of Otranto*. There also emerges a keen understanding of how the dual dynamic of abjection/ projection works in the construction of conflicting European identi-ties. This is very evident, of course, in the Gothic novel's representation of Catholicism by Protestant writers and vice versa, but it also applies to representations of southern Europe by northern Europeans, and of eastern Europe by writers within western Europe. Again, several con-tributors point out that an over-zealous desire to categorize texts, either generically or as 'high' culture, has led to a neglect or misun-derstanding of the presence of Gothic elements in the work of certain European 'realist' authors such as Balzac, Turgenev and Checkhov. In relation to chronology, some essayists suggest that a link between automata, mechanization and modernity informs and underpins the development of the Gothic mode from the eighteenth century onwards. Finally, all the essays recognize that translation has been vital to the survival of the Gothic novel and that the cultural transfusions and 'misappropriations' effected by the act of translation should not be dismissed simply as derivations or deviations. Rather, the increasing sophistication of translation studies now allows us to understand more clearly how translation functions to enable 'interpretative communities' (in the broadest sense) to relate to each other. For example, the inflection, censorship or augmentation of Gothic tropes within the process of translation can be seen as a means whereby national identities and ideologies are either challenged or reinforced. A better appreciation of such issues should prompt us to construct a richer and more inclusive history of the Gothic novel that will restore its proper European lineage.

This collection has been organized, therefore, to range beyond texts which are securely placed within the Gothic canon. For that reason, there are no essays focused solely on established Gothic writers such as Radcliffe or Stoker. However, such apparent omissions are remedied within the body of the book: for example, Radcliffe's portrayal of Europe and, in particular, her influence upon French and Russian authors of the Gothic are addressed by several of the contributors. Thus, the collection embraces several aims: to situate works by British writers and American writers within a European context and legacy; to offer readings of less-known works by Gothic authors (such as Coleridge's *Remorse* and Maturin's *The Wild Irish Boy*); to prompt a reconsideration of the part played by the Gothic strain within the works of certain European 'realist' writers; and, finally, to introduce the reader to a range of neglected, albeit influential, European Gothic texts which originated in Russian, Spanish, French and German. One result of this is that the volume contains many passages translated from works written in languages other than English (often for the first time, as in Curbet's essay). The issue of translation as a vehicle of ideological manipulation, representation or censorship is present as an underlying topic in nearly all the essays.

The volume's opening chapter, Terry Hale's 'Translation in distress: cultural misappropriation and the construction of the Gothic', takes this topic as its main focus. Hale's contribution is of crucial significance since it argues, somewhat contentiously perhaps, that 'the Gothic novel was not only the cause of considerable translational activity ... but that the genre was also substantially a *product* of that process' (p. 17). A neglect of this fact has led critics, Hale believes, to over-value the significance of Walpole's *The Castle of Otranto* (1764), which certainly did not immediately provoke imitations or adaptations. Indeed, the Gothic novel lay immured in silence for some years until Clara Reeve's *The Old English Baron* (1777), Sophia Lee's *The Recess* (1783–85) and Charlotte Smith's version of *Histoire de Manon Lescaut* (1785) appeared. These novels, Hale argues, were the texts that energized Gothic writing in late eighteenth-century England. All three women were translators as well as authors and Hale's assertion is that their translations of work by French writers such as the Abbé Prévost (1696–1763), Baculard d'Arnaud (1716–1805) and Gayot de Pitaval (1673–1743) fed into their own creations of Gothic fiction. In this account, the origins of the Gothic novel lie in a late eighteenth-century cross-Channel interchange marked, in particular, by English translations of the French sentimental adventure tale and by the fascinating shifts in ideological emphasis which take place during the translation process.[1] This emphasis moves the focus on Gothic origins from Walpole – an English author who *pretended* to translate 'From the Original Italian of Onuphrio Muralto' (Fairclough 1968: 37) – to three English women writers who were actual translators as well as writers of the Gothic. Perhaps, then, modern Gothic owes its beginnings more to three founding mothers than one founding father; certainly Hale's argument that the Gothic was 'forged in the crucible of translation' (p. 23) is a highly persuasive one. Such cross-cultural exchanges continued with the translation of novels by Reeve, Radcliffe, Maturin and other English writers into French; in turn, this Anglo-French legacy influenced later writers such as Baudelaire and Balzac. It is, then, as Hale points out, somewhat bizarre to find that even accounts of the Gothic by French scholars, such as Maurice Lévy (Lévy 1995), privilege the British tradition (and, to a lesser extent, the American) over that of France.[2] Hale's essay sets out to remedy this bias by offering closely attentive readings of the French translations of novels by Radcliffe and Maturin. Both the changes that occurred during the translation of *Melmoth the Wanderer*, and its importance for the development of European Gothic, are briefly examined here, as is the significance of its absence from the Spanish Gothic tradition. Developing this broader perspective, the essay charts a European trajectory for

4

the Gothic novel: whilst it fell into decline in England during the early nineteenth century, it flourished in France as French authors devoured translations of English Gothic novels. From France, the Gothic flame passed to Italy where it shone more brightly than in Spain; by the end of the nineteenth century, thanks, probably, to the importation of cheap reprints of earlier Italian translations, we find Maltese authors writing Gothic fiction. Rather than dismissing these transmutations as merely derivative, Hale suggests that we should read such texts as suggestive of possible 'histories of the Gothic in cultures where it has long been thought the Gothic had no history worth telling' and in such a way as to 'challenge our own conception in Britain and America of the nature of the Gothic canon' (p. 35).

The second essay in the volume, 'European disruptions of the idealized woman: Matthew Lewis's *The Monk* and the Marquis de Sade's *La Nouvelle Justine*', by Angela Wright, exemplifies Hale's argument in that it examines the undocumented and mutually influential relationship within which both authors' work developed. Wright argues that Lewis's experience in Paris during the summer of 1791, of reading the second edition of *Justine* (which contained much more salacious detail than the first) in Paris, radically influenced his writing of *The Monk*. The result was an English Gothic novel which was to shock many contemporary readers. Furthermore, she suggests that de Sade's third and final revision of *Justine* in 1797 seems to be have been influenced by his acquaintance with Lewis's *The Monk*, which was translated into French for the first time in that same year. In exploring this textual relationship, she notes the thematic similarities of the two works, one of which is 'the brutal collation' of the two heroines 'with idolized versions of the Madonna' (p. 41). This shared emphasis, she claims, 'launched a critique of the privileging of such iconography in religion' (p. 41). Developing her argument, Wright suggests that *The Monk* offers three models of femininity, all deriving from and intended to disrupt, previous literary representations. Antonia owes much to the portrayal of women in the works of Diderot, de Sade and Radcliffe; Agnes seems to descend directly from Diderot's Suzanne in *La Religieuse* (1780); Matilda is remarkably similar to Jacques Cazotte's devil Biondetta in *The Devil in Love* (1772). In turn, it seems likely that these inscriptions of virtue in distress influenced de Sade's revisions to the third edition of *Justine*. Wright's conclusion is that such textual interchange resulted from and sharpened both authors' attitudes to the role of sensuality and sexual desire within the ritualized ceremonies of Catholic worship. These attitudes were remarkably similar, in spite of the fact that de Sade was an atheist and Lewis an Anglican-Protestant.

In his essay, 'Diderot and Maturin: Enlightenment, automata and the theatre of terror', Victor Sage similarly challenges the received version of the relationship between a British and a French author. Rejecting Mario Praz's claim in *The Romantic Agony* (1970) that Maturin simply plagiarized parts of Diderot's *La Religieuse* (1796) when writing *Melmoth the Wanderer* (1820), he sets out to prove that the similarities and differences between the two texts indicate the complicated nature of cultural transmission during the period. In particular, he focuses on the automatic and the systematic in Maturin's novel in relation to contemporary philosophical conceptualizations of consciousness and identity. What he perceives here is a debate between Maturin and Diderot concerning the relationship between the notion of mechanism and aspects of human behaviour such as hypocrisy, acting, role playing and ritualized social behaviour. The use of dialogic form and the oblique invocations of the theatre of terror suggest an author whose 'real subject in *Melmoth* is the distortion caused to the individual psyche by "systems of belief"' (p. 67). Sage thus seeks to persuade us that the textual relationship between the two authors, one conventionally labelled as an atheist and Enlightenment thinker, the other as Protestant and Gothic, indicates a common legacy: 'a self-conscious fictional heritage whose master trope is the theatre, which shapes the different questions they ask of the novel genre in a demonstrably common manner' (p. 69). This particular reading of *Melmoth the Wanderer* also explains, in part, the novel's continuing appeal within the French literary tradition.

Catherine Lanone's essay, 'Verging on the Gothic: Melmoth's journey to France' also offers a fresh reading of Maturin's most famous work. Acknowledging the well-documented appeal of its maze-like narrative for Baudelaire and the Surrealists, Lanone turns her attention to Balzac's debts to Maturin. However, she departs from those critiques that perceive Balzac's use of the Gothic as an aberration from his realist mode, or as a textual element that is best understood metaphysically. Rather, she explores the roots of Balzac's fascination with the Gothic by examining his first 'real' piece of writing, *Le Centenaire ou les deux Beringheld* (1822; later reissued as *Le Sorcier ou les deux Beringheld*).

Most critics have ignored this as an early, imitative piece which comes close to plagiarizing Maturin's *Melmoth the Wanderer*. Rather than simply dismissing this as an apprentice work, however, Lanone argues that Balzac's attempts to modernize Maturin's plot suggest a desire to conflate a Gothic world with that of bourgeois society. She pursues this argument by offering a fresh reading of *Melmoth Réconcilié* which, published in 1835, provides evidence of Balzac's sustained interest in the Gothic and of his continuing dialogue with Maturin. Rejecting the usual interpretation of the novel as a metaphysical tale about the possibility of redemption, Lanone reads it as a fiercely ironic comment on the consumer society of Paris and the nature of modernity, within which 'the wild darkness of absolute desire can only be commodified' (p. 78). Finally, she turns her attention to *The Wild Ass's Skin* (1831), in which the pact with evil clearly indicates Maturin's influence. Again, she sees this text as working on the borderline of the Gothic and the realist modes: 'Exposing in a nutshell the erotic economy of the modern world – and the modern text – the talisman creates a gloomy Gothic spell which is doomed to shrink and vanish, as dark textual enchantment yields to the cooler "lost illusions" of the bulk of the work' (p. 80). Lanone's startling claim in this essay, then, is that Balzac's great realist project, *La Comédie humaine*, is built on the very ruins of the Gothic; that 'some of the power of the dissections of the Parisian vanity fair may well come from unconscious Gothic reminiscences' (p. 81). Balzac's recognition that Maturin's version of Gothic could not easily be transposed to Paris seems to lead him to question the nature and construction of desire and fulfilment in the world of the bourgeoisie. This, in turn, leads to the acute analysis of human behaviour which is the hallmark of *La Comédie humaine*.

Maturin is also a key reference point in Robert Miles's essay 'Europhobia: the Catholic other in Horace Walpole and Charles Maturin'. Miles here argues that the projection of certain characteristics upon the Catholic 'other' in early Gothic fiction had as much to do with the 'proto-nationalism' of the eighteenth century as it had to do with a post-Reformation Europhobia. Using Kristeva's notion of abjection to enrich our understanding of what the process of projection involves, Miles turns to David Hume's 'Of Superstition and Enthusiasm' (1741). Hume's attempt to define 'true' as oppose to 'false' religion is predicated initially on the assumption that both 'superstition' and 'enthusiasm' are equally corrupting forces. However, Miles notes that, as the

AVRIL HORNER

essay continues, a slippage evolves so that gradually the enthusiast 'becomes a token of the fierce, liberty-loving British subject' who is both reasonable and civil, whilst French Catholicism becomes the enthusiast's abject other: 'supersitition ... renders men tame and abject, and fits them for slavery' (Hume 1963: 79). What comes to the fore here, Miles suggests, is 'not the threat from without, but the threat from within, the fear that enthusiasm is "corruption" indeed, a force equally compromised by a tendency to despotism, subjugation and religious war' (p. 89).

This provides the lens with which Miles then examines Walpole's *Castle of Otranto* (1765) and two early works by Maturin. He sees the real anxiety at the heart of *The Castle of Otranto* as the matter of legitimacy, suggesting that the text is haunted by the question of the Reformation and 'the fear that the post-Glorious Revolution settlement is without legitimacy' (p. 94). Such matter is conveyed by the plot's dependence on and the author's obsession with genealogies. Maturin's two Irish tales, *The Wild Irish Boy* (1808) and *The Milesian Chief* (1812) – one a comic romance, the other tragic – reveal a similar anxiety concerning legitimacy. Both also embody dreams of nationhood and Irish aspirations; both contain Catholic elements and stereotypes. Miles's point is that, in both cases, 'Maturin's plot at once confronts these stereotypes, and succumbs to them; but the energy that propels it is not anti-Catholicism *per se*, but Irish nationalism' (p. 100). Thus the Catholic as abject European other in British Gothic writing 'is inextricably linked to questions of authority, authenticity and, finally, legitimacy' at home, 'all of which were intensified by the emergence of nationalism as an ideological force in the eighteenth century' (p. 100).

Neil Cornwell develops further the narrative of European Gothic by exploring the connections between French, English, German and Russian writers of the Gothic and by attempting to trace more precisely the genealogy of Russian Gothic fiction. Whilst acknowledging that it embraces elements of Russian folklore and medieval ingredients such as chronicles and the lives of saints, he argues that the Gothic strain in nineteenth-century Russian writing derives from a fascinating amalgam of European influences. These include the English Gothic novel, the French *fantastique* and *frénétique* traditions and the works of Schiller and Hoffmann. Clara Reeve's *The Old English Baron*, for example, had been translated into Russian by 1792 and Ann Radcliffe's novels appeared in Russian by the early 1800s. However, many English

Gothic novels were relayed into Russian via French, since this was the language of the educated Russian elite. Briefly sketching out the trajectories of French and German Gothic, Cornwell notes that certain authors (such as Jacques Cazotte, de Sade, Schiller) had a direct influence on Russian writers. He claims, however, that the most important figure in the development of Russian Gothic writing was E.T.A. Hoffmann. Charting the impact of *The Ghost-Seer* by Schiller (the writing of which had been influenced by Cazotte's *The Devil in Love*) on Hoffmann's *The Devil's Elixirs* (1816), the essay suggests that many subsequent works in the Gothic mode by Russian writers such as Gogol and Dostoevsky (who had read Radcliffe's novels in translation as a child) would seem inconceivable without Hoffmann. Tracing the roots of Gothic Russian back to *The Island of Bornholm* (1794) by Nikolai Karamzin, and acknowledging Vatsuro's work on the Gothic in Russian and that of Izmailov and Todorov on the fantastic, Cornwell claims that the heyday of Russian Gothic fiction fell in the second quarter of the nineteenth century, during which Aleksandr Pushkin (1799–1837) wrote *Queen of Spades* – an undisputed masterpiece of Russian Gothic. Moving into the second half of the century, Cornwell notes that many Russian 'realist' writers embraced an element of the Gothic in their works: Dostoevsky (1821–81), like Balzac, 'opened his career with a strong Gothic flourish' (p. 118), Turgenev produced some Gothic-fantastic tales and Checkhov 'turned his hand to Gothic phantasmagoria' in his late work (p. 120). Throughout the nineteenth century, then, the eastward spread of European influences mingled with local currents in Russian fiction and a rich process of cross-fertilization ensued. The broad perspective of Cornwell's essay is particularly valuable in showing how such spirited exchanges fuelled, throughout the whole of Europe, 'subsequent Gothic revivals and Neo-Gothic movements' (p. 121). It also usefully detaches the history of Russian Gothic from those Russian critical traditions which have subsumed it within the fantastic or Russian romanticism.

Cornwell's mention of Schiller as an important figure in the development of European Gothic is developed by Peter Mortensen in the following essay, 'The robbers and the police: British Romantic drama and the Gothic treacheries of Coleridge's *Remorse*'. Mortensen here analyses Coleridge's 'misappropriation' of Schiller's *Die Räuber* (1780) in the context of 'the large-scale invasion of closets and stages, both in London and the provinces, by European Gothic spectacles and bourgeois tragedies' (p. 128). Whilst criticizing the emotionalism and sensationalism of French and German plays, British Romantic dramatists nevertheless manipulated their Gothic elements, 're-deploying them as ... focal symbolic ingredients'. Mortensen sets out to prove that Coleridge did precisely this when adapting the plot of *Die Räuber* for his own purposes, a venture which had its seeds in the year 1794 but which did not result in publication until 1813. In particular, he draws attention to the way both plays seem obsessed with techniques of control and correction. Although *Remorse* is set in sixteenth-century Spain, there are clear parallels, Mortensen suggests, with the Regency Britain of Coleridge's own experience. Drawing on Foucault's work, he argues that the way Coleridge adapts Schiller's plot of fraternal conflict 'allegorizes the transition from a pre-modern, overt form of discipline, which operates from without on the body of the condemned person, to a modern, discrete form of discipline, which is all the more pervasive and efficient in that it enlists the subject in the project of his or her own domination' (p. 141). Thus, where Schiller's play uses the language of seduction and excess, Coleridge's vocabulary is that of enclosure and decorum; whereas Schiller's tragedy is about disenfranchisement and celebrates revenge, Coleridge's *Remorse* actually offers a moral critique of revenge. Coleridge's play, then, conveys a very different political message from Schiller's *Die Räuber*. In rewriting the German transgressive plot, Coleridge exploited the success of 'this dangerously un-English genre, even whilst using it to solidify a national culture and buttress a national identity in the period of the Revolutionary and Napoleonic Wars' (p. 143). Mortensen thus sees *Remorse* as a revisionist work that seeks to correct the pre-Romantic cult of the wilful ego (a feature explicitly recognized in contemporary reviews).

John Williams's 'Translating Mary Shelley's *Valperga* into English: historical romance, biography or Gothic fiction?' keeps us with the topic of Romantic 'misappropriations' of continental narratives. In this essay, Williams investigates the relationship between the political, biographical and autobiographical content of Mary Shelley's second published novel, *Valperga* (1823), which is set in medieval Italy and concerned with the struggle for power between the Guelph and Ghibelene factions. In writing this work, Shelley researched the life of Castruccio, a fourteenth-century Tuscan warrior politician, with the intention of producing a Gothic novel that would address the political issues of her own day, both in Italy and England. One of her main sources for this was

INTRODUCTION

Sismondi's *Histoire des républiques italiennes du Moyen Age* (1809–18). This analysis of Italian history massaged the past in order to celebrate the medieval Italian Republics in a manner that left little doubt about the author's 'abhorrence of the way autocratic rule was sweeping across Europe in the wake of the Napoleonic wars' (p. 148). Shelley also looked carefully at how Scott had blended historical fact with fiction in producing his Waverley novels (*Ivanhoe* seems to have been of particular interest to her). As Williams points out, recent research has documented Shelley's intense and life-long interest in the cause of Italian unity (her authorship of 'Modern Italian Romances' (1838), for example, has now been proven). As the daughter of William Godwin and a member of an influential intellectual set, Mary Shelley shared the belief that intellectuals formed a social elite whose duty it was to educate the masses in the ways of political justice. It is therefore not surprising to find Shelley allowing herself author's licence in the representation of Castruccio's life in order to produce a novel that functioned as a critique of contemporary British political life. Her Castruccio is less the portrait of a Tuscan warrior than a picture of the repressive forces that continued to oppose the champions of Italian nationalism in her own time. Her husband consequently found *Valperga* problematic, a fact which resulted in his taking great pains to reassure his publisher that the book was merely a harmless historical romance. Analysing in particular Shelley's adoption and subversion of Gothic tropes, Williams notes her ambivalence concerning the social function of Gothic writing. He also examines the novel as a *roman à clef* and, in so doing, argues that the identification of the novel's characters with people in the Shelley circle and beyond crucially informed Shelley's reading of European history, even as her sense of history informed her 'reading' of the individuals around her. In particular, Williams relates the problems of Shelley's life to her fictional representation of the corruption that can be wrought by idealism and the struggle for power:

> It was but a short step from the high ideals of Godwin's *Political Justice* to the Byronic Castruccio: arrogant, cynical, and worldly ... The Castruccio who would be Percy Shelley ... is all too influenced by the powerful personality of his Byronic alter ego, even to the point where he becomes obsessed with Byron's woman, Beatrice/Claire. (p. 157–8)

Thus the boundaries between private and public worlds, fact and fiction, biography and autobiography, become destabilized in a novel which projects a narrative of Italian history onto an English present. Despite its parodically self-conscious use of Gothic tropes, its focus on power and its dissolution of boundaries mark *Valperga* as a quintessentially Gothic novel. Indeed, its very status as a work of fiction allowed Shelley to articulate her personal and political sense of disaffection from both her husband and certain European political strategies without too much risk of censorship.

From censorship within the private world we move to Catholicism as an institutionalized form of censorship. Joan Curbet's essay, '"Hallelujah to your dying screams of torture": representations of ritual violence in English and Spanish Romanticism', examines the representation of ritual violence, as sanctioned by the Catholic Church, in English and Spanish pictorial and literary texts between 1796 and 1834. Taking a passage from Maturin's *Melmoth the Wanderer* as a key reference point, Curbet explores how Gothic writing manages to offer an Enlightenment intellectual perspective on sacrificial acts whilst drawing the reader into an emotional experience that embraces a flux of wild desires – including fear, horror, excitement, sadism and masochism. It thus simultaneously offers, Curbet argues, both objective and subjective perspectives on the act of torture. Whilst Maturin was free to explore the connection between the importance of sacrifice within Catholicism and the culture of religious violence generally, the dominance of the Catholic Church in Spain made it more difficult for Spanish writers to examine these issues. Thus the essay sets out to compare and contrast English primitivist representations of Spain (especially those which dwell on the Catholic Church and religious violence) with the restricted manner in which Spanish writers and artists expressed the same subject matter. In so doing, Curbet focuses on the writings of the Europhile republican intellectual, José María Blanco-White and the paintings of Goya. Whilst acknowledging that political conservatism and the censoring powers of the Catholic Church prevented the development of the Gothic in Spain during this period, Curbet suggests that we can, nevertheless, discern Gothic elements in the work of such Spanish writers and painters and that these should be seen as 'key examples of the difficult progress of the Enlightenment in Spanish cultural history'. (Significantly, both Blanco-White and Goya eventually chose to live in exile.) Concluding with an analysis of some of Goya's murals, Curbet suggests that in these late works we see the Spanish painter questioning the very nature of human rationality: that is, moving beyond the Gothic aesthetic towards an essential nihilism.

INTRODUCTION

Nihilism and the sublime, as evoked by the constant deferral of meaning, are important elements in Ahlam Alaki's essay, 'Potocki's Gothic Arabesque: embedded narrative and the treatment of boundaries in *The Manuscript Found in Saragossa* (1797–1815)'. Alaki here examines the narrative technique of embedding and the representation of the Other in this complex work, which was written in French by a Polish Count and which drew on eighteenth-century interest in oriental tales. *The Arabian Nights*, translated into French by Antoine Galland (1704–77), influenced both the writing of Beckford's *Vathek* and Potocki's *Manuscript* and thus becomes a central reference point in the essay, particularly in relation to the idea of the labyrinthine text and the Arabesque. The narrative technique of embedding tales within tales derives, Alaki argues, from the oriental tradition and leads the reader to experience a sense of sublime infinity. This occurs because the lack of final closure signifies a constant deferral of meaning or endpoint and results in (to use Burke's phrase) a sense of 'delightful horror'. Metaphorically, the text evades death by opening endless gates onto a series of repetitions; this image of repeated death and revival resembles the Eastern art of the Arabesque and also offers the reader an interesting variation on the Gothic sublime. Furthermore, the Arabesque of narrative embedding creates a maze in which even the storyteller becomes lost, reflecting the Eastern notion that the created is more important than the creator. The novel's various representations of the Gothic Other are also explored and Alaki relates these to the location of Potocki's story in a Spanish setting which itself suggests a divided culture – Arabic, Moorish and Muslim on the one hand, European and Christian on the other. This is indicated by the novel's structure which gives us a master narrative continually competing with various subnarratives, reflecting a divided society fraught with conspiracies and subversions. Thus, Alaki concludes, *The Manuscript Found in Saragossa* clearly draws on the central European traditions of the Gothic and novel writing but at the same time it is enriched by the cultural perspectives and narrative techniques of the East. The result is a novel in which 'the indefinite nature of narrative subordination is a source of sublime and uncanny horror' (p. 201).

The volume's penultimate chapter, Jerrold E. Hogle's, 'The Gothic crosses the Channel: abjection and revelation in *Le Fantôme de l'Opéra*', returns us to the Anglo-American/French dynamic. Not only did Leroux draw on a host of American and English Gothic tales (including those of Poe and Stoker) when writing his novel but, in turn, his own work has crossed both the Channel and the Atlantic via various stage adaptations, the most famous of which is Andrew Lloyd-Webber's 1986 version, *The Phantom of the Opera*. Hogle suggests that Leroux's most famous work draws not only on the *conte fantastique* but also on that sub-genre's anticipation of Freudian representations of the unconscious. Using Kristevan theory, Hogle argues that *Le Fantôme de l'Opéra* (1910) enacted the classic abjective function of middle-class Gothic in relation to issues of class, race and 'high'/'low' culture as they manifested themselves in Paris at the turn of the twentieth century. In tracing the novel's early stage adaptation into very successful theatre, the essay also examines the origins and architecture of the Opéra Garnier (where the play was first staged) and the socio-economic roots at the core of early twentieth-century middle-class pretensions to cultural supremacy in France. In this context, the phantom's mask, or disguise, is seen to represent a middle-class ambivalence about both facing and abjecting matters of origin, status and contamination. Hogle thus argues that Leroux's work also explores the 'new Europe' of its day. In his extensive use of the real Paris Opera (opened in 1875) and its actual history, Leroux both unearths and conceals several ironic foundations of a capital city that had by 1910 become a model for urban redevelopment throughout much of Europe. In order for this new 'palace of the people' to be built, many old buildings and alley-ways of central Paris had been ruthlessly demolished, forcing the poorer and working-class inhabitants of the city to its margins. The phantom's skull-face set on top of a nearly skeletal body can, then, be read as representing a 'haunting' of the 'new Paris' by the skeletons of the lower classes who have been 'othered' as undesirable residents. The novel thus anticipates and predicts the empty heart at the centre of the twentieth-century European city. Conventional middle-class aspiration, Leroux's work reveals, so needs its otherings to establish its difference from them, that those very confusions of categories turn out to be the deepest foundations of this new sense of identity. Suggesting that Leroux's book 'vividly continues the ... interplay of the psychological and the deeply cultural that has always been a part of the English Gothic', Hogle nevertheless finds a distinctiveness in the way that Leroux recuperates earlier French transformations of the Anglo-American Gothic 'into dark psychological fantasies or descriptive devices within bourgeois hyper-realism' (p. 213).

INTRODUCTION

My own essay, '"A detour of filthiness": French fiction and Djuna Barnes's *Nightwood*', continues Hogle's examination of the Anglo-American/French dynamic within the Gothic and maintains his focus on Paris. I argue here that Barnes's most famous novel reveals its author's adherence to a particular French literary tradition of intellectual pessimism, described by Kristeva as 'a black lineage' and represented for her by the works of Lautréamont and Artaud (Kristeva 1982: 137). There is clear biographical evidence that Barnes became acquainted with the works of many European authors in translation whilst a child, and that she read much French fiction during her long residence in Paris between 1921 and 1931. A few critics have begun to speculate on her debts to Rabelais, Huysmans and Breton; my own contribution to this picture is to suggest strong links between *Nightwood* and two French texts that shocked contemporary readers – Lautréamont's *Les Chants de Maldoror* (1868–69) and Céline's *Voyage au bout de la nuit* (1932). Reworking the parodic Gothic elements of Lautréamont's disturbing book and adopting Céline's tone of comic lyricism in the face of the abject, Barnes's novel celebrates transgression and non-conformity. Published in 1936, as the clouds of fascism were gathering in Europe, *Nightwood* presents the Beast and filthiness as forms of cultural integrity in the face of social hypocrisy and institutionalized cruelty. Using Kristeva's analysis of the role of 'filth' as a vital boundary in the construction of subjectivity, I conclude that *Nightwood*'s cynicism and Gothic humour derive from Barnes's detour into such French 'filth'. This detour was also to influence, in turn, the development of certain Anglo-American writers of the Gothic, including Carson McCullers, William Faulkner and Angela Carter. The final essay in the volume, then, confirms the argument of Hale's opening piece, which calls for – amongst other things – a re-assessment of the importance of Anglo-French exchanges in the development of Gothic writing.

Notes

1 See Terry Hale's entry on the *roman noir* in Marie Mulvey-Roberts's *The Handbook to Gothic Literature* (1998) for a fuller investigation of these links.
2 See, however, Lévy 1974.

AVRIL HORNER

References

Baldick, C. and Mighall, R. (2000) 'Gothic Criticism', in D. Punter (ed.), *A Companion to the Gothic*, Oxford, Blackwell, pp. 209–228.

Davenport-Hines, R. (1998) *Gothic: 400 Years of Excess, Horror, Evil and Ruin*, London, Fourth Estate.

Ellis, M. (2000) *The History of Gothic Fiction*, Edinburgh, Edinburgh University Press.

Fairclough, P. (ed.) (1968) *Three Gothic Novels*, Harmondsworth, Penguin.

Hogle, J.E. (1996) 'The Gothic and the "Otherings" of Ascendant Culture: The Original Phantom of the Opera', *South Atlantic Quarterly*, 95:3, 157–171.

Hume, D. (1963) *Essays Moral, Political and Literary*, Oxford, Oxford University Press.

Kristeva, J. (1982) *Powers of Horror: An Essay on Abjection*, trans. L.S. Roudiez, New York, Columbia University Press.

Lévy, M. (1974) 'English Gothic and the French Imagination: A Calendar of Translations, 1767–1828', in G.R. Thompson (ed.), *The Gothic Imagination: Essays in Dark Romanticism*, Washington,Washington State University Press, pp. 150–176.

—— (1995), *Le Roman 'Gotique' anglais, 1764–1824*, Paris, Albin Michel [1967].

Massé, M.A. (2000) 'Psychoanalysis and the Gothic', in D. Punter (ed.), *A Companion to the Gothic*, Oxford, Blackwell, pp. 229–241.

Mighall, R. (1999) *A Geography of Gothic Fiction: Mapping History's Nightmares*, Oxford, Oxford University Press.

Mulvey-Roberts, M. (1998) *The Handbook to Gothic Literature*, Basingstoke, Macmillan.

Punter, D. (1998) *Gothic Pathologies: The Text, the Body and the Law*, Basingstoke, Macmillan.

—— (2000) (ed.) *A Companion to the Gothic*, Oxford, Blackwell.

Williams, A. (1995) *Art of Darkness: A Poetics of Gothic*, Chicago and London, University of Chicago Press.

1

Translation in distress: cultural misappropriation and the construction of the Gothic

TERRY HALE

'Translation has to do with authority and legitimacy and, ultimately, with power', wrote the late André Lefevere, 'which is precisely why it has been and continues to be the subject of so many acrimonious debates' (Lefevere 1992a: 2). For Lefevere, translation – all translation – implies a process of rewriting, a conscious or unconscious manipulation of the text, which is either the consequence of the translator's own ideological motivations or, should the translator be unsympathetic to the dominant ideology of his or her time, a reaction against the prevailing ideological constraints.[1]

This chapter seeks to apply such a view of translation to the realm of the late eighteenth-century and early nineteenth-century horror novel, specifically with regard to its British manifestation (where it was known as the Gothic novel) and its various French forms (i.e. the *roman noir*, which flourished from the 1790s through to around 1820; and the related *roman frénétique*, which flourished during the 1820s and early 1830s), arguing that the level of ideological manipulation which occurred as texts were translated, mistranslated, appropriated, misappropriated, altered and adapted from one language to another was so considerable, and so systematic, that generic mutations were occasioned. Indeed, it will be argued here that the Gothic novel was not only the cause of considerable translational activity (this much is well known even if the point is generally not thought worthy of remark) but that the genre was also substantially a *product* of that process: that is, many of the conventions which we associate with the British Gothic novel today arose as a by-product of the translation process. Similarly, it will be argued that many aspects of the French *roman noir* and *roman frénétique*, genres with close links not only with the Gothic but also with the *Schauerroman*, were also initially the quasi-accidental result of generic mutations which occurred as British and German texts made their way into French.

This is an ambitious programme for a short essay and it is not so much intended here to demonstrate the incontestable correctness of such a far-reaching hypothesis as to establish its viability as a line of inquiry. Indeed, we shall examine in detail but three texts: Charlotte Smith's 1785 translation of the Abbé Prévost's 1731 *Histoire du Chevalier des Grieux et de Manon Lescaut*; the anonymous 1797 French translation of Ann Radcliffe's *A Sicilian Romance* (1790); and Jean Cohen's 1821 translation of Charles Maturin's *Melmoth the Wanderer* (1820). In the concluding section of this chapter we shall, however, further examine such related issues as the dissemination of translated Gothic, *noir* and *frénétique* novels across Europe during the course of the nineteenth century and the implications for future research into the Gothic.

Some time in the course of 1785 the London publisher Thomas Cadell brought out a translation by Charlotte Smith of the Abbé Prévost's 1731 novel *Histoire du Chevalier des Grieux et de Manon Lescaut* under the title *Manon L'Escaut: Or, The Fatal Attachment. A French Story*. Although hardly a turning point in British literary history, the events surrounding this troubled publication shed a certain amount of light on the status of the translator in the late eighteenth century, especially when the translator happened to be female. 'Translation was a form of literary business favoured by women authors', comments Loraine Fletcher, Charlotte Smith's most recent biographer, 'especially as a first step to professional authorship; but it was the more incumbent on a woman to choose an uncontroversial text' (Fletcher 1998: 83).

Charlotte Smith's problems only started when the publisher sent a copy to the influential but irascible critic George Steevens. It was Steevens, apparently, who first began to voice reservations about the moral tone of the book. These reservations carried so much weight with the publisher that he immediately withdrew the book from sale. At the same time, Steevens sent a letter signed with the sobriquet 'Scourge' to the *Public Advertiser* couched in the following terms: 'Literary frauds should be made known as soon as discovered; please to acquaint the public that the novel called *Manon L'Escault*, just published in two volumes octavo, has been twice before printed in English, once annexed to *The Marquis de Bretagne*, and once by itself, under the title *The Chevalier des Grieux* – it was written by the Abbé Prévost about 40 or 50 years ago' (cited by Fletcher 1998: 82).

Steevens's paradoxical behaviour – on one hand condemning the moral tendency of the work and on the other hand admitting to having earlier published a translation himself (though it was probably not until sixteen years later that Mrs Smith learned that Steevens and 'Scourge' were, in fact, one and the same person) – elicits no comment from Loraine Fletcher other than that he might have been 'less energetically hostile had there been a man's name on the title page' (Fletcher 1998: 83). This may well be so, but one cannot help but suspect that the issue of morality was more by way of a pretext for his conduct than a valid reason for it. After all, was Steevens's own translation only intended for male readers? In fact, this minor skirmish was but one of many in a continuing battle of the sexes which was really about the rights of women to the financial remuneration and intellectual prestige of authorship in the widest sense. That Steevens intended to protect his own literary preserve (not to mention potential sales) from interlopers is beyond doubt, but by framing the argument in moral terms he was seeking to marginalize not only Charlotte Smith as a competitor but women authors and translators as a class. It is an appropriate epigraph to this story that, some two hundred or so years later, the British Library still does not possess a copy of Charlotte Smith's translation of *Manon Lescaut*, even though this represents the second published work of a major late eighteenth-century/early nineteenth-century author.[2] Needless to say, Steevens's translation is well in evidence.

But what of Charlotte Smith's textual practices as a translator? Loraine Fletcher provides us with the following extract, in which the narrator describes his first sight of Manon, who is in chains on her way to New Orleans:

> Such was the beauty and elegance of her face and form, that neither the deep depression she appeared to be under, nor the dirt and dust with which she was cover'd, could conceal it; and she inspired me at once with pity and respect. While she turn'd from the gaze of vulgar curiosity as much as her chain would admit, there was in her countenance and attitude such an air of dignity and modesty, that it was difficult to believe she could ever have deserv'd the terrible punishment under which she was suffering; and the expression of grief and terror impressed on features

delicate, regular and animated, made her the most interesting figure I had ever seen. (Fletcher 1998: 73; Smith 1785: I, 3–4)

The original passage in Prévost's novel reads as follows:

> Sa tristesse et la saleté de son linge et de ses habits l'enlaidissaient si peu que sa vue m'inspira du respect et de la pitié. Elle tâchait néanmoins de se tourner, autant que sa chaîne pouvait le permettre, pour dérober son visage aux yeux des spectateurs. L'effort qu'elle faisait pour se cacher était si naturel, qu'il paraissait venir d'un sentiment de modestie. (Prévost 1967: 34)

As Fletcher notes, Smith is at even greater pains than Prévost to present Manon in a favourable light in this opening encounter. However, the textual changes go much further than this, as might be suspected given that the English translation of this passage is almost twice as long as the French original. In Prévost's version, there is little distinction, except perhaps a qualitative shift, made between the narrator's gaze (referred to in the first sentence) and the vulgar gaze of the public (the subject of the second sentence). But in Charlotte's Smith's version, any voyeuristic element on the part of the narrator is eliminated. It is Manon herself who inspires the narrator with pity, unmediated by any reference to his sight of her (which therefore becomes, at most, implicit).

The subject of the male gaze has, of course, given rise to considerable academic discussion in recent years. If one applies to this passage Laura Mulvey's concept of scopophilia, involving as it does the subjection of the object of desire to what she terms the 'controlling gaze', Smith's different narrative strategy is surely indicative of a decision, whether deliberate or unconscious, to rewrite the text from a feminist stance. Scopophilia, in Mulvey's view, is, moreover, primarily sexual in intent: 'using another person as an object of sexual stimulation through sight'. (Mulvey 1976: 10). In Prévost's text, the eroticism of the narrator's gaze in this opening sentence concentrates initially on, indeed is perhaps stimulated by, Manon's dirty clothes ('la saleté de son linge et de ses habits').

This involves a double psychological element, both largely absent in the translation: firstly, the fetishization of the object of the narrator's gaze through reference to her clothes; and, secondly, the additional element of social topography contained in the information that these clothes were dirty. With regard to the latter, Stallybrass and White (1986) have provided detailed analysis of the fascination which dirt and

women of low social status held for the nineteenth-century male bourgeois adolescent (and it is surely no accident that *Manon Lescaut*
would become one of the privileged texts of the nineteenth century
both in France and Britain).[3] All this is lost in Charlotte Smith's version. The opening part of the sentence presents a stylish eighteenth-
century set of parallels ('Such was the *beauty and elegance* of her *face
and form*'), continues by introducing an entirely new element concerning the subject's mental condition ('that neither the deep depres-
sion she appeared to be under'), refuses to fetishize the subject by
completely eliminating reference to her clothes ('nor the dirt and dust
with which she was cover'd, could conceal it') and concludes by making
a direct link between the female subject and the male narrator ('and she
inspired me at once with pity and respect').

If these changes are interesting in themselves, the Gothic elements
that Charlotte Smith incorporates into the second half of the final sentence of the extract are even more remarkable: 'the expression of *grief
and terror* impressed on *features delicate, regular and animated*, made
her the most interesting figure I had ever seen'. Here again we find a
peculiarly eighteenth-century contrast ('features delicate, regular and
animated'[4] versus 'the expression of grief and terror'). In many respects
the phrase 'grief and terror' comes close to expressing the experience of
works belonging to what has sometimes been called the English sentimental Gothic period prior to the publication, with its much cruder
emphasis on horror, of M.G. Lewis's *The Monk* in 1796. Truth be told,
many of the terrors of the Ann Radcliffe school are mild enough, as the
following extract, from *The Mysteries of Udolpho*, testifies.

> While she [Emily] paused, the music ceased; and, after a momentary hes-
> itation, she re-collected courage to advance to the fishing-house, which
> she entered with faltering steps, and found unoccupied! Her lute lay on
> the table; every thing seemed undisturbed, and she began to believe it was
> another instrument she had heard, till she remembered, that, when she
> followed M. and Madame St. Aubert from this spot, her lute was left on a
> window seat. She felt alarmed, yet knew not wherefore; the melancholy
> gloom of evening, and the profound stillness of the place, interrupted only
> by the light trembling of leaves, heightened her fanciful apprehensions.
> (Radcliffe 1980: 9)

As with Charlotte Smith's translation of *Manon Lescaut*, it is the
extreme vulnerability of the heroine which gives rise to and sustains
the suspense. Prévost's wild and criminal heroine will not be as wild

and criminal in Mrs Smith's version, nor will the Chevalier des Grieux behave quite so much like a desperado. In one important scene, des Grieux cynically shoots a porter, who attempts to prevent his escape, in the stomach, presumably killing him. 'C'était un puissant coquin,' recounts Prévost's narrator, 'qui s'élança sur moi sans balancer. Je ne le marchandai point; je lui lâchai le coup au milieu de la poitrine'[5] (Prévost 1967: 101). In Charlotte Smith's version, the man is only wounded and the translator makes it clear that he recovers.

From the point of view of the future development of the Gothic novel, however, it is the reference to the 'grief and terror' impressed on Manon's features which is most worthy of remark. At the moment Charlotte Smith's version of *Manon Lescaut* was published in 1785, the Gothic novel did not exist as a genre. Certainly, Horace Walpole's improbable masterpiece *The Castle of Otranto* had been published as early as 1764. But it had had few successors except for Clara Reeve's *The Old English Baron* of 1777 and, some years later still, Sophia Lee's *The Recess* of 1783–85. Significantly, both Reeve and Lee may be considered as author–translators.[6] It is also curious to note that Sophia Lee and Charlotte Smith shared the same publisher, Thomas Cadell. The Gothic would not become a recognizable genre until some time in the very late 1780s or early 1790s. Smith herself was among the earliest group of authors of this new wave of Gothic sensibility, her first novel (also published by Cadell), *Emmeline, the Orphan of the Castle*, being brought out in 1788.

Yet these words 'grief and terror' – which do not have even the remotest equivalent in the original – indicate beyond any doubt that Charlotte Smith's translation of *Manon Lescaut* should be considered as a proto-Gothic novel. The link, of course, is provided by Edmund Burke's *A Philosophical Enquiry into the Origin of our Ideas of the Sublime and Beautiful* (1757) which has long been recognized as a major influence on Gothic aesthetics.[7] Indeed, Burke provided the psychological basis for the late eighteenth-century horror novel with its preoccupation with sublime passions. Appropriately, Burke identifies fear as the mainspring of the sublime, the source of which is attributed to the subject's concern for his or her self-preservation. Both grief and terror are provided with separate entries in Burke's 1757 study. With regard to the former he writes:

> It must be observed, that the cessation of pleasure affects the mind in three ways. If it simply ceases, after having continued a proper time, the

effect is indifference; if it be abruptly broken off, there ensues an uneasy sense called disappointment; if the object be so totally lost that there is no chance of enjoying it again, a passion arises in the mind, which is called grief. (Burke 1992: 34)

It is presumably within this Burkian aesthetic that Charlotte Smith seeks to relocate her version of *Manon Lescaut*. Thus, Smith's translation of Prévost's *Manon Lescaut* (and the subtitle, *The Fatal Attachment*, should be noted in this context) would seem to shift the genre from one which might be called the French sentimental adventure story to something closer to the English Gothic novel. In order to achieve this, she imports a considerable range of social, psychological and aesthetic ideas as well as entirely re-engineering the poetics of the text. Surely, in this case, it might be truly said that the Gothic is being forged in the crucible of translation.[8]

The popularity of the English Gothic novel – whether in its early incarnation as the sentimental Gothic or its later, more physically horrific form – in France has long been noted. Indeed, the first three sections of the influential *De Horace Walpole ... à Jean Ray* catalogue issued by the Librairie Gérard Oberlé in 1972 are devoted to 'Les Maîtres anglais' (Walpole, Reeve, Radcliffe, Mary Shelley, Lewis, Sophia Lee, Godwin, Maturin, Mrs Roche, George Moore,[9] and, somewhat unexpectedly, Smollett); 'L'Evolution du genre noir en Angleterre' (e.g. Chatterton, Fielding, Scott, Mrs Inchbald); and 'Des Romantiques anglais aux maîtres modernes' (e.g. Bulwer-Lytton, G.P.R. James, Wilkie Collins, Rider Haggard, Lord Dunsany).

This, however, is but to follow in a tradition of scholarship which has privileged British (and, to a lesser extent, American) texts over French texts. This is a process which began with Alice Killen's 1924 doctoral dissertation (Killen 1967); continued with Reginald Hartland's less known *Walter Scott et le roman 'frénétique': Contribution à l'étude de leur fortune en France* (1928); and is still clearly in evidence in Maurice Lévy's *Le Roman 'gothique' anglais, 1764–1822* (1967). In each case, two research strategies may be detected: firstly, the author, aware that translated texts are frequently corrupt, relies exclusively on the original edition (even when that edition is unlikely to have been widely known outside Britain); secondly, French texts, whether derivative of English texts or otherwise, are systematically ignored or their interest minimized.

This, of course, is perfectly understandable given the scholarly criteria which prevailed at the time (and, indeed, outside the new discipline of Translation Studies, still generally prevail). Translation has long been considered a somewhat disreputable practice, especially with regard to light literature. Moreover, the French interest in the Gothic has tended to exist in the context of English literary studies. The consequence, however, is a tendency to believe that the French experience largely mirrored that of Britain in terms of which writers are given canonical status and an assumption that the texts were read in very much the same way across cultures. In the light of the preceding analysis of Charlotte Smith's translation of *Manon Lescaut*, it is clear that such tendencies and assumptions cannot be taken for granted.

Among the French writers who appropriated the Gothic, in whatever degree, for purposes of their own one must count the Vicomte d'Arlincourt (1789–1856), François Guillaume Ducray-Duminil (1761–1819), and Jean Joseph Regnault-Warin (1775–1844). Indeed, detailed investigation of the motivations informing the work of such writers might well provide a very different view of the nature of the *roman noir* than an examination of British texts, however popular they might have been at the time in translation. Certainly, in the case of the Vicomte d'Arlincourt, the pro-monarchical content of his work meant that there were occasional reprints in French and Spanish until quite late in the nineteenth century; in the case of Regnault-Warin, a Spanish translation of *Le Cimetière de la Madeleine* (1800), a novel which employs a narrative structure of a kind used by Edward Young in his *Night Thoughts* (1742–46), was reprinted as late as 1920.[10] Yet such authors have received significantly less attention than, say, Ann Radcliffe or M.G. Lewis both in the French and Spanish context.

None the less, it is important to note how rapidly many key texts found their way into French. *The Castle of Otranto* (1764) was available in French by 1767;[11] if Clara Reeve's *The Old English Baron* (1777) had to wait a decade before a French version came out, when at last it did appear there were two different translations almost simultaneously; Radcliffe's *The Romance of the Forest* (1791) was available by 1794, *A Sicilian Romance* (1790) came out as *Julia, ou les souterrains du château de Mazzini* in 1797, the same year as *The Castles of Athlin and Dunbayne* (1789) and *The Mysteries of Udolpho* (1794) made their way into French, while *The Italian; or, the Confessional of the Black Penitents* (1797) gave rise to two different French versions the same year as the English edition.[12]

The rapidity of the translation process does not necessarily indicate that the translations themselves were textually very faithful, however. Thus, as the anonymous translator of *A Sicilian Romance* noted in the *Avertissement du traducteur* to the French edition:

> Nous nous sommes permis d'élaguer quelques épisodes, de raccourcir quelque longues descriptions, auxquelles madame Radcliffe paraît se livrer avec plaisir, et qui ne ferait pas fortune ici.
> A Londres, le peuple exige que l'étranger prenne, des pieds à la tête, l'habit et les formes anglaises. En France, nous faisons grace [sic] aux Anglais sur ce chapitre; nous adoptons même leurs formes et leurs usages; mais sur l'article de la littérature, nous sommes un peu plus sévères, et les détails minutieux sur lesquels aime peut-être à s'appesantir la morosité brittanique, déplaisent à la vivacité française, épuisent sa patience, et l'amènent promptement au dégoût. (Radcliffe 1798: iii–iv)

> (We have allowed ourselves to prune certain passages, to shorten certain long descriptions, which Mrs Radcliffe would seem to delight in, and which will not be well received here.
> In London, the population demands that the foreigner adopts, from head to foot, the customs and the costume of the English. In France, we humour the English on this point; we even adopt their forms and usages ourselves; but on the subject of literature, we are rather stricter, and the minute details, over which the British tendency towards moroseness perhaps likes to linger, are displeasing to French vivaciousness, wears out its patience, and quickly leads to repugnance.) (My translation)

In the case of *Julia, ou les souterrains du château de Mazzini* the translator is as good as his or her word. Thus, a number of long descriptive passages are removed, including, for example, a 25-line disquisition on the differences between a 'familiar' and a 'sentimental' conversation.[13] Elsewhere, short descriptive passages, which add to the mood of the novel, but do little to develop the plot, are likewise eliminated.

Such practices were common at the time, and perhaps indicate that the French readership was not as culturally sophisticated as the initial English readership. This impression receives further support from the tendency of the translator to move from the rather abstract language of the original, especially when dealing with the supernatural, to less complex structures and ideas:

> They all returned to the hall, without having witnessed any extraordinary appearance; but though their fears were not confirmed, they were by no means dissipated. The appearance of a light in a part of the castle which

had for several years been shut up, and to which time and circumstance had given an air of singular desolation, might reasonably be supposed to excite a strong degree of surprise and terror. In the minds of the vulgar, any species of the wonderful is received with avidity; and the servants did not hesitate in believing the southern division of the castle to be inhabited by a supernatural power. (Radcliffe 1993: 9–10)

The French version of this passage, which is considerably expanded, reads as follows:

Ils reviennent après une longue perquisition, sans avoir rien rencontré, ni vu d'extraordinaire.
Mais les personnes crédules ne se rassurent pas facilement. Une impression de frayeur était restée dans tous les esprits. Que pouvait être cette lumiere [sic] apparue dans un lieu inhabité? Quel était l'homme sorti de la tour? Par quel charme s'était-il dérobé à tous les regards? De toutes ces observations répétées, grossies et commentées par les habitans subalternes du château, il en résulta l'opinion générale que les bâtimens du midi, et particulièrement la tour, était habités par des puissances surnaturelles, telles que des fées, des esprits, des magiciens ou des revenans. (Radcliffe 1798: I, 15–16)

(They returned after a long perquisition, without having met anything, nor seen anything unusual.
But the credulous are not easily reassured. A sense of fear had remained in everyone's mind. What could this light which had appeared in an uninhabited place be? Who was the man who had come out the tower? By what magical trick had be avoided the gaze of all? As a result of all these remarks, repeated, expanded, and commented upon by all the resident servants in the castle, the general consensus was that the southern parts of the building, and particularly the tower, were occupied by supernatural powers, such as fairies, spirits, magicians, and ghosts.) (My translation)

Here the translator considerably expands the original, recapping the nature of the mystery in the crudest terms, and offering a number of common superstitions to account for it. This is surely indicative of a considerable displacement of the central interest, which in the English version depends largely on the reader's initial rejection of, or at least doubts about, anything other than a rational explanation for what is happening. The French text, on the other hand, barely suggests any possibility other than some form of supernatural intervention. Note also that, in the original text, there is a clear separation of the system of beliefs of masters and servants. The ruling elite will barely credit any explanation which defies the laws of nature; superstition serves as a class marker which categorizes the holders of such beliefs as belonging to the 'lower orders'. This is not the case in the French text: 'Une impression de frayeur était restée dans *tous* les esprits' (my emphasis). This *tous* is extremely ambiguous. At the very least it serves to shift the focus of the text from 'above stairs' to 'down stairs', a potentially considerable relocation if this is repeated elsewhere; more generally, though, it suggests a common set of values shared by masters and servants alike.

In both instances, one can clearly see the considerable effect of the reinscription of the text within the French revolutionary context. Thus, one effect of the Revolution of 1789 was a breakdown in traditional Catholic patterns of belief. As Schama notes, 'by decimating the clergy the Terror ... destroyed the only reliable (and cheap) source of teaching personnel available for elementary education' (1989: 828). But the consequence of this was that, rather than inaugurating a culture founded on the principles of enlightened scepticism (as the leaders of the Revolution might have hoped), the county was plunged into a state of intellectual chaos which would continue well into the nineteenth century. More particularly, the decline in the influence of the Church did not result in the uninstructed abandoning of orthodox religious practice and beliefs but rather a turn 'to an unorthodox mixture of pagan and Christian forms' (Berenson 1984: 37).

This intellectual confusion is demonstrated by the dramatic increase in the number of works – mainly hastily assembled compendiums drawing on sources as diverse as the French fairy tale, German romantic poetry, the Gothic novel, and folklore – published in the early nineteenth century dealing with the different forms of supernatural agency. Thus, one might find, thrown together higgledy-piggledy in the pages of a single work, a collection of short anecdotes concerning imps, demons, gremlins, alchemists and vampires. Of course, this was a tradition which, in the hands of an author such as the Abbé Nicolas Lenglet-Dufresnoy (whose work was regularly plundered), dated back to the mid-eighteenth century. But such compendiums proliferated after the French Revolution, and were still thriving as late as 1820. In that year, a certain J.P.R. Cuisin published a collection of such tales under a title which clearly exposes the confused generic and intellectual resources at work: *Les Ombres sanglantes, galerie funèbre de Prodigues, Evénemens merveilleux, Apparitions nocturnes, Songes épouvantables, Délits mystérieux, Phénomènes terribles, For-*

faits historiques, Cadavres mobiles, Têtes ensanglantées et animées, Vengeances atroces et combinaisons du crime (1820).[14]

Naturally, the philosophical and intellectual system underlying Radcliffe's novels, a system largely deriving from rational empiricism and theories such as Burke's work on aesthetics, begins to crumble in the translation owing to the transformations taking place in French society. In *A Sicilian Romance*, the translator routinely sentimentalizes terms such as 'awe' into '*mélancholie*' while the supernatural effects are highlighted throughout. More generally, Radcliffe's translators throughout the period in question substantially lighten – again unaware of the significance of such passages, or unwilling to trust to their reader's patience – the descriptive passages relating to the countryside. Thus, paradoxically, if the English Gothic novel was the product of the application of a set of philosophical and aesthetic criteria to the French sentimental adventure story, the *roman noir* marks the point at which those same criteria are filtered out as English texts make their way in turn to France.

On occasion, the transformation which could occur when a text was translated into French could take on an even more radical nature. This was the case with Jean Cohen's translation of Charles Maturin's *Melmoth the Wanderer*, which appeared the year after the novel was first published.[15] By this time, a more politically sophisticated variety of horror novel was beginning to emerge in France, a genre for which Charles Nodier is said to have coined the expression *roman frénétique* in the course of a review of a new French translation (1820) by Henri de Latouche of Christian Spiess's *Das Petermännchen* (1791).[16] Significantly, Spiess's novel concerns two tutelary demons, thus locating the work in the French tradition of supernatural agency discussed above, who are at war over the soul of a certain Rodolphe of Westerbourg. However, in de Latouche's translation at least, Spiess's novel explores a considerable range of political issues linked with the notion of aristocratic privilege, another major concern of the period.

In 1820, the political situation in France was very different to what it had been when *A Sicilian Romance* had been translated. The restoration of the French monarchy in 1815 brought to an end a long period of revolution and war, even if there was relatively little enthusiasm for the Bourbons. But if the Constitutional Charter, which underwrote many of the fundamental principles of 1789, was to be guaranteed by an independent judiciary, the downside of the restoration was an increased reliance on the Church to provide a spiritual and moral bolster for the new regime. When Louis XVIII's younger brother, Charles X, was crowned in 1825, it was in accordance with a ceremony suggestive of divine right which dated back to the Middle Ages.

During the course of these ten years between 1815 and 1825, France underwent a Catholic reaction. Consequently, 1821 was not a propitious year for the French publication of *Melmoth the Wanderer*, a work with a virulent anti-Catholic bias. Rather than provide the English and the French versions of key passages from these two works, it is more appropriate here to give just the former, the main excisions being marked by square brackets.

I was overpowered with congratulations, blessings, and embraces. I received them with trembling hands, cold lips, a rocking brain and a heart that felt turned to stone. Everything passed before me as in a dream. [(1) I saw the pageant move on, without a thought of who was to be the victim.] I returned to the convent – I felt my destiny was fixed – I had no wish to avert or arrest it [(2) – I was like one who sees an enormous engine (whose operation is to crush him to atoms) put in motion, and, stupefied with horror, gazes on it with a calmness that might be mistaken for that of one who was coolly analysing the complications of its machinery, and calculating the resistless crush of its blow. [A further thirteen lines omitted.]] I repeated to myself, 'I am to be a monk,' and there the debate ended.
[...]
My voice was good, and my profound melancholy gave an expression to my tones, which these men [i.e. the Jesuits], [(3) always on the watch to grasp at any thing that may aggrandize them, or delude their victims,] assured me were like the tones of inspiration.
[...]
[(4) At these words, which I suppose I uttered in a tone unlike that of the usual chaunt of monastic conversation, another interposed, and asked what I was uttering in so loud a key? 'I am only saying,' I replied, 'that I must be a monk.' 'Thank God it is no worse,' replied the querist, 'your contumacy must long ago have wearied the superior and the brethren – thank God it's no worse.' At these words I felt my passions resuscitated, – I exclaimed, 'Worse! what have I to dred? – am I not to be a monk?']
[...]
I did not perceive they were treating me as a lunatic, yet certainly my foolishly reiterated expressions might have justified them in doing so, [(5) – they had their own plans in concert with the Director, – my silence went for proof.] The Director came often to visit me, [(6) and the hypocritical wretches would accompany him to my cell.]
[...]

[(7) It seems the reverent fathers were as anxious as their old enemies the Moors, to convert an idiot into a saint. [A further thirteen lines omitted.]] Luckily, [(8) during all this uproar of imposture, fear, falsehood and misrepresentation,] the Superior remained steady. He let the tumult go on, to aggrandize his importance; but he was resolved all the time that I should [(9) have sanity enough to enable me to] take the vows.[17]

Unlike the case of *A Sicilian Romance*, where alterations to the text would seem to be based largely on a misunderstanding of the intentions of the original and an analysis of the level of sophistication of the potential audience, the translation of *Melmoth* has a clear ideological agenda to it. The nine abridgments noted above (together with a number not noted for reasons of space) account for a total of some 60 lines of text out of a total of 125. Overall, this level of censorship is not maintained throughout the entire work (which is perhaps reduced by no more than twenty per cent). However, the passages excised above clearly turn a powerful anti-Catholic novel in English into, at best, a work critical of the administration and workings of the Church in the French version. More particularly, Maturin's intense dislike of the Jesuits is not only toned down but, in many details, removed altogether. Thus, a sentence such as: 'A son – the eldest son of the Duke de Monçada, taking the vows, was a glorious triumph for the *ex-Jesuits*, and they did not fail to make the most of it' (Maturin 1984: 144; my emphasis) becomes: 'Un fils, le fils aîné du duc de Monçada, promonçant ses voeux, était un grand triomphe *pour le couvent*, qui ne manquait pas de s'en glorifier' (Cohen 1984: 682; my emphasis).

As a whole, the translator has removed passages in which the Church is portrayed as acting tyrannically (1, 2, 4, 9), or the conduct of members of the religious community is perceived as being underhand (3, 5, 6, 7, 8). Some of these cuts, of course, serve also to drive on the narrative, a common concern of translators of such works. None the less, it cannot but be affirmed that this French version of *Melmoth*, arguably the most disseminated of the four French translations, serves to re-encode the text in a manner radically different to that intended by the original author.

In the case of *Melmoth*, it is particularly important to examine the translation as this is undoubtedly the version that an author such as Balzac – who wrote a short continuation of the novel, as *Melmoth réconcilié*, in 1835 – would have known. In Balzac's sequel, Melmoth easily persuades a cashier, in urgent need of money, to take over his pact with the Devil. He, in turn, manages to pass it on, such that it eventually makes its way around the stock exchange. Balzac's intention is, of course, half-satirical, and the work is perhaps not among the author's most successful tales. The point is this, however: as a text *Melmoth reconcilié* is plausible in French, in the light of a translation such as that by Jean Cohen, in a way that it simply is not in English.

That translation in the late eighteenth century and early nineteenth century could be – indeed, generally was – extremely unreliable has long been recognized. However, instead of treating the proliferation of texts which occurred as a result of translation (not to mention imitation, stage adaptation and parody) as evidence of separate cultural systems giving rise to independent cultural artefacts worthy of study in their own right, in the interest of academic rigour commentators have preferred to fall back on the original source texts.

Translation, on the strength of the evidence provided by Clara Reeve, Charlotte Smith and Sophia Lee, was one means by which women had access to the literary marketplace in the Britain of the mid-1780s; but in order to achieve this it was necessary for the texts to be re-gendered during the translation process. More or less at the same moment, the French *roman noir* was largely the creation of a massive programme of translation, though that programme of translation may have led to the British aesthetic tradition being replaced by local political and social issues. Finally, in the 1820s, the *roman frénétique* was a genre which likewise was a product of the market for translations, though those translations reflected the politics and concerns of post-Restoration France and could give rise to sequels not immediately possible in the source language.

Scholars have not previously had the conceptual tools at their disposal to make sense of the shifting patterns of genres such as the Gothic as they moved backwards and forwards across cultural boundaries. More recently, however, the emerging discipline of Translation Studies has supplied a number of concepts which allow for a more sensitive analysis of the textual practices of forms of writing which have previously been considered inferior or derivative.[18]

Thus, in addition to the massive paradigm shifts which can occur during the translation process, the very choice of which works are translated can, and frequently does, play a major role in the construction of local literary canons. Maurice Lévy may be able to point to more than a hundred English Gothic novels translated into French, but as the Gothic novel radiated out across Europe, the range of translated works became considerably restricted.

In the case of Spain, prior to 1850, the few Gothic novels which were translated belonged to the sentimental variety: Mrs Helme was among the first authors to be translated with *Louisa; or, the Cottage on the Moor* (1787; trans. *Luisa o la cabaña en elle valle*, 1803), followed by Mrs Roche with *The Children of the Abbey* (1796; trans. *Los niños de la Abadia*, 1808). Ann Radcliffe was not translated until 1819, when *Julia o los suterráneos del castillo de Mazzini* (*A Sicilian Romance*) was published in Valencia. Given that all these works had been subject to prior translation into French, and given the relatively low status of English as a European language at the time, it would be safe to assume that some, if not all, were translated into Spanish on the strength of the French edition, thus allowing for a potential second layer of ideological manipulations to occur.

With regard to Mrs Radcliffe, moreover, it would appear that she never enjoyed tremendous popularity in Spain. The unique edition of *Los misterios de Udolfo*, for example, was not published until 1832, and even that edition was printed in Paris. A number of works falsely attributed to her, such as Catherine Cuthbertson's *The Romance of the Pyrenees* (1803), did manage to find a Spanish imprint, however (indeed, on the strength of the numerous translations into languages as diverse as French, Italian, Spanish and Portuguese, this novel is unjustly neglected by modern scholars). Generally speaking, the more dangerous works tended to be published in Paris where, as a result of political upheaval in Spain, there must have been a sufficiently large number of Spanish exiles to make the such ventures financially viable. Such was the case with the sole Spanish translation of M.G. Lewis's *The Monk* (1796; trans. *El fraile o historia del Padre Ambrosio y de la bella Antonia*, 1821). The following year, the first of several Spanish editions of W.H. Ireland's *The Abbess* (1799; trans. *La abadesa*, 1822) was brought out by the same Parisian publisher.[19]

But if when, where and how a text is translated raises important questions, equally important are the questions raised by what was *not* translated. For obvious reasons, there was no nineteenth-century Spanish edition of *Melmoth the Wanderer*, thus blocking off an important line of possible development of the genre within a Spanish context. More generally, it is quite obvious that French *frénétique* texts vastly outnumber English works as the century progresses. Montesinos

(1973), whose bibliography is a convenient starting point for analyses of this kind, lists dozens of texts by authors such as Eugène Sue and Frédéric Soulié. In the cultural marketplace of the mid-nineteenth century, French translations squeezed out English translations just as in the present marketplace British and American works tend to dominate international bestseller lists.

Elsewhere, a similar pattern of French cultural hegemony may be seen in operation. It would seem that the vogue for the Gothic came to the Maltese Archipelago some time in the 1890s and continued to hold sway for some 30 or so years into the twentieth century. Typical titles, when translated into English, included works such as the prolific Arturo Caruana's *Carlo de Von Hove or the Atrocities of the Public Executioner* (1899) and P. De Alex Portanier's *Lazzarino the Robber, Captain of the Assassins* (1902).[20] As late as 1930 Caruana was responsible for a substantial 900-page novel, entitled *Il misterji tal Uardija* (i.e. *The Mysteries of Guardia*), which seem to conjure the departed shades of, in equal measure, Ann Radcliffe and Eugène Sue.

The catalogue of the National Library of Malta at Valetta contains no works (either in English or in translation) by M.G. Lewis or Charles Maturin. However, there are to be found a number of Italian translations of English Gothic novels, including two editions of *Le visioni del castello dei Pirenei*, attributed to one Anna Radcliffe, and an odd volume of a work, with a similar attribution, entitled *Lo scheletro vivente, o la terrible vendetta*. In fact, both these attributions are probably false. *Le visioni del castello dei Pirenei* is, no doubt, an Italian translation of the French translation of Catherine Cuthbertson's *Romance of the Pyrenees* (1803). The Italian version follows the French title: *Les Visions du château des Pyrénées*. It was this 1809 French translation which first attributed the work to Ann Radcliffe, a tradition apparently continued by the Italian editions of 1827–28 (described as a 'Nuoava traduzione', hence implying that there was an earlier version), 1847 (the earlier of the two editions in the Valetta library), 1858, 1864, 1882 and 1888. *Lo scheletro vivente, o la terrible vendetta* is more difficult to identify but it may well prove to be an Italian translation of André Cantwell's French translation (as *Le Château d'Albert, ou le squelette ambulant*, 1799) of an anonymous Minerva Press novel called *The Animated Skeleton* (1798). The copy in the Valetta library, apparently the only Italian edition, is dated 1868.

From this brief, and somewhat haphazard, bibliographical tour it is clear that already in the late eighteenth century the English Gothic novel had met with a favourable reception in France, and that this reception continued for some time after the Gothic vogue had fallen into decline in Britain. From France, the Gothic flame would appear to have passed to Italy, where it continued to shine long after its moment had passed in more northern climes. Finally, by the turn of the century, probably at least in part as a result of the importation of cheap reprints of earlier Italian translations, local Maltese authors began to write Gothic fiction on their own account. Even here, though, the competition with the *roman frénétique* would have been intense, for authors such as Sue and Soulié were widely translated into Italian.

On the basis of the manner in which the Gothic had slowly travelled southwards through Europe over the course of a century, one might be tempted to hypothesize that the genre may have undertaken other journeys, perhaps eastwards, again through French, to Russia and Poland; perhaps northwards, here the relay language may have been (at least in part) German, through the Scandinavian countries. The genre may even have undertaken a number of perilous sea crossings – one route which would suggest itself would be towards the Indian sub-continent; another might be (via French and Spanish) to South America. Indeed, there is evidence that this is exactly what did occur. But at each stage of the journey, local publishing strategies will have given rise to different corpora of translated texts; and differing translation strategies will have made available very divergent texts to the ones we know in English. In the case of countries such as Russia and Brazil, moreover, the extent of French cultural hegemony was such that the Gothic remained, until recently, a marginal genre in comparison with French cultural productions.

But no act of translation is ever arbitrary. Each act of translation implies not only a translator, a publisher, a printer and a bookseller but also, in the best of all cases, a reader – in short, the act of publishing a translation denotes the application of very considerable resources, both intellectual and economic. More importantly still, such texts provide us with evidence of how literary translators and writers of genre fiction (as we have seen, in some cases the groups are identical) act as an interpretive community struggling to construct cultural meaning. As we have also seen, the textual strategies employed are frequently the very reverse of passive. Indeed, it is in their very insistence on resisting the most compelling interpretations of the texts that they retell or invent in favour of new meanings which is of primary interest. The act of learning to read translations makes possible histories of the Gothic in cultures where it has long been thought the Gothic had no history worth telling. Ideally, such histories may also challenge our own conception in Britain and America of the nature of the Gothic canon.

Notes

1   Lefevere would seem to have drawn a distinction between ideological motivations and 'poetological' motivations (cf. Lefevere 1992b: 7). This distinction, in the light of the work of commentators such as Venuti, which seeks to link poetical and rhetorical forms to ideological issues, seems to me to be redundant. Thus, in the case of Sir John Denham, for example, who was a translator of Virgil and was closely bound up with the royalist cause at the time of the English Civil War, Venuti notes how the selection of particular words and terms transformed the story of the fall of Troy into an allegory of the defeat of the English monarchy. Significantly, Denham employed a recognizably English word-order and, in the heroic couplet, a recognizably English verse form – a clear example of the relationship between an aesthetic form (used here both to disguise the ideological issues and as a cultural vehicle) and power (cf. Venuti 1995: 44–65).
2   I am grateful to the library of the University of Pennsylvania for making a microfilm of the 1786 edition available. This is, presumably, identical in every way to that of 1785.
3   See, for example, their analysis of the voyeuristic nature of the diary entries of the mid-nineteenth-century poet and barrister Arthur Munby in relation to Hannah Cullwick, his maid of all work (Stallybrass and White 1986: 154–156).
4   One might also point to the manner in which three adjectives are used here to form a stylistic closure to a passage which is otherwise dominated by pairs of counterbalancing nouns and adjectives.
5   See Fletcher 1998: 72. A modern idiomatic translation of this passage, one which would not disgrace a hard-boiled detective story of the 1940s, might read: 'He was a big bloke and he came straight at me. There was no point in talking with him so I let him have it right in the stomach'.
6   For a brief analysis of how Sophia Lee seeks to rewrite Prévost's *Le Philosophe anglais: histoire de Cleveland* (1732–39), a process which involves changing the entire historical location of the novel and transforming the gender of the principal characters, see Hale 1998: 189–195. Montague Summers notes that Clara Reeves' *The Exiles, or Memoirs of the Count de Cronstadt* (1789) is a fusion of two stories by Baculard d'Arnaud (Summers 1968: 188). Charlotte Smith was also responsible for a translation of selected tales from Gayot de Pitaval's *Les Causes célèbres* entitled *The Romance of Real Life* (1787). Finally, it might also be mentioned that Ann Radcliffe herself cites Gayot de Pitaval as a source for *The Romance of the Forest* (1791), even if the one commentator who has sought to follow up this lead fails to positively locate the precise text (McIntyre 1920: 57).
7   See, for example, Milbank 1998: 226–232.
8   For an analysis of another passage in Smith's translation of *Manon Lescaut* in which the import of aesthetic concepts deriving from Thomas Burke seems to play a central role, see Hale 2002.
9   Author of *Grasville Abbey* (1797).
10 *Del trono al cadalso* (i.e. *From the Throne to the Scaffold*) (Regnault-Warin 1920).

Regnault-Warin's novel represents a visionary account of the excecution of Louis XVI in 1793. More generally, it is quite obvious, on the basis of the work of J. Fernandez Montesinos, especially on the evidence of the bibliography he provides, that all three French authors were vastly more important in Spain than any British Gothic novelist in the first half of the nineteenth century (Montesinos 1973). For a discussion of the Vicomte d'Arlincourt, see Hale 2000.

11   The famous bookseller's catalogue of *Romans noirs – contes de fées* issued by Marc Loliée in 1952 contains an intriguing reference to a French pseudotranslation called *Roseide et Valmor ou les victimes de l'orgueil* of 1800. Loliée provides the following information (my translation): 'First French edition of this extremely rare and little-known novel by Walpole. There are two very unusual frontispieces by Blanchard. One recalls the gravures of the early editions of [Sade's] *Nouvelle Justine* and depicts a flagellation scene with monks whipping young girls in a chapel.' Here we would seem to have an excellent example of the process of cultural appropriation at work, including such elements as: genre shift (from the Gothic to the pornographic); false attribution both as to author and source language; ideological manipulation; and delay (Walpole's *Otranto* was know in French as early as 1767).

12   A convenient listing may be found in Lévy 1974.

13   This is the paragraph beginning 'Conversation may be divided into two classes', pp. 7–8 in the 'World's Classics' edition of *A Sicilian Romance* (Radcliffe 1993).

14   i.e. Blood-drenched Ghosts, Funeral Gallery of Prodigies and Marvellous Events, Nocturnal Apparitions, Fearful Dreams, Mysterious Crimes, Freaks, Historic Murders, Moving Corpes, Animated Heads After Decapitation, Terrible Vengeances, and Criminal Conspiracies.

15   (Maturin 1821b). I have not seen the other translation of the same date, though judging by the fact that it was published in only three volumes, the abridgement must be even more considerable (Maturin 1821a).

16   Milner 1960: I, 269. Significantly, Nodier reviewed a considerable number of translations of late Gothic novels and related works in the French press around 1820, and was also responsible for a variety of stage adaptations, sequels and continuations. A decade later, one of Nodier's most remarkable texts – *L'Histoire du roi de Bohême et de ses sept châteaux* (1830) – would represent an attempt to conclude an episode from Laurence Sterne's *Tristan Shandy* purposely left unfinished in the original. Sterne's influence (via Nodier and others) on the experimentalism of the *roman frénétique* of the same period was considerable, but has hitherto been largely unremarked.

17   Maturin 1984: 143–146. Jean Cohen's 1821 translation, as *Melmoth ou l'homme errant*, is reprinted in *Romans terrifiants* (no editor specified), Paris, Robert Laffont ('Bouquins'), 1984, pp. 682–683. This is currently the most common edition available in French. Maria de Fos's 1867 translation (*Melmoth, l'homme errant*) was available in an undated edition published by Marabout (Verviers, Belgium) for many years prior to the 'Bouquins' edition. Although Fos's translation is notably different from that of Cohen, consisting almost entirely of paraphrase, it abbreviates the passage cited on pp. 29–30 above to an even greater extent (pp. 86–87). A more complete translation, by Jcqueline Marc-Chadourne, was published as *Melmoth ou l'homme errant* (Maturin 1988).

18   For an overview of current issues in translation studies, see Baker 1998.

19   For a description, see Summers 1968: 344–345.

20   Both these works are cited by Friggieri 1996: 629–630. For the convenience of readers not fluent in Maltese, I have taken the liberty of rendering the titles in English.

References

Baker, M. (ed.) (1998) *Routledge Encyclopedia of Translation Studies*, London, Routledge.

Berenson, E. (1984) *Populist Religion and Left-Wing Politics in France, 1830–1852*, Princeton, Princeton University Press.

Burke, E. (1992) *A Philosophical Enquiry*, ed. Adam Phillips, Oxford, Oxford University Press.

Cuisin, J.P.R. (1820) *Les Ombres sanglantes, galerie funèbre de Prodigues, Evénemens merveilleux, Apparitions nocturnes, Songes épouvantables, Délits mystérieux, Phénomènes terribles, Forfaits historiques, Cadavres mobiles, Têtes ensanglantées et animées, Vengeances atroces et combinaisons du crime*, 2 vols, Paris, Mme Vve Lepetit.

Fletcher, L. (1998) *Charlotte Smith. A Critical Biography*, Basingstoke, Macmillan.

Friggieri, O. (1996) 'Rumanz gotiku', in *Dizzjunarju ta' Termini Letteravji*, Malta, San Gwann, pp. 629–630.

Hale, T. (1998) 'Roman Noir', in M. Mulvey-Roberts (ed.), *The Handbook to Gothic Literature*, Basingstoke, Macmillan, pp. 189–195.

—— (2000) 'A Forgotten Best Seller of 1821: *Le Solitaire* by the Vicomte d'Arlincourt', *Gothic Studies*, 2:2, 185–204.

—— (2002) 'Continental Gothic: From Terror to Horror in France and Germany, 1730–1830', in J. Hogle (ed.), *The Cambridge Companion to Gothic Fiction*, Cambridge, Cambridge University Press (forthcoming).

Hartland, R. (1928) *Walter Scott et le roman 'frénétique': Contribution à l'étude de leur fortune en France*, Paris, Champion.

Killen, A. (1967) *Le Roman terrifiant ou roman noir de Walpole à Anne Radcliffe*, Paris, Champion.

Lefevere, A. (1992a) *Translation/History/Culture. A Sourcebook*, London, Routledge.

—— (1992b) *Translation, Rewriting, & the Manipulation of Literary Fame*, London, Routledge.

Lévy, M. (1967) *Le Roman 'gothique' anglais, 1764–1822*, Toulouse, Association de la Faculté des Lettres et Sciences Humaines de Toulouse.

—— (1974) English Gothic and the French Imagination: A Calendar of Translations, 1767–1828', in G.R. Thompson (ed.), *The Gothic Imagination: Essays in Dark Romanticism*, Washington, Washington State University Press, pp. 150–176.

Librairie Gérard Oberlé (1972) Bookseller's catalogue: *De Horace Walpole ... à Jean Ray*.

Loliée, M. (1952) Bookseller's catalogue: *Romans noirs – contes de fées*.

Maturin, C. (1821a) *L'Homme du mystère, ou l'histoire de Melmoth le Voyageur*, trans. E. Bégin, 3 vols, Paris, Delaunay.

—— (1821b) *Melmoth, ou l'Homme errant*, trans. J. Cohen, 6 vols, Paris, G.C. Hubert.

—— (1867) *Melmoth, l'homme errant*, trans. M. de Fos, Paris, Librairie intern.

—— (1984) *Melmoth the Wanderer*, ed. A. Hayter, Harmondsworth, Penguin.

—— (1988) *Melmoth ou l'homme errant*, trans. J. Marc-Chadourne, Paris, Pauvert.

McIntyre, C.F. (1920) *Ann Radcliffe in Relation to Her Time*, New Haven, Yale University Press.

Milbank, A. (1998) 'The Sublime', in M. Mulvey-Roberts (ed.), *The Handbook to Gothic Literature,* Basingstoke, Macmillan, pp. 226–232.

Milner, M. (1960) *Le Diable dans la littérature française de Cazotte à Baudelaire*, 2 vols, Paris, Corti.

Montesinos, J.F. (1973) *Introducción a la historia de la novela en España en el siglo XIX, seguido del esboza de una bibliografía de traducciones de novelas (1800–1850)*, Madrid, Castalia.

Mulvey, M. (1976) 'Visual Pleasure and Narrative Cinema', *Screen*, 16:3 (Autumn), 6–18.

Prévost, A.F. (1967) *Histoire du Chevalier des Grieux et de Manon Lescaut*, ed. H. Coulet, Paris, Garnier-Flammarion.

Radcliffe, A. (1798) *Julia, ou les souterrains du château de Mazzini*, trans. anon., 2 vols, Paris, Maradan.

—— (1980) *The Mysteries of Udolpho*, ed. B. Dobrée, Oxford, Oxford University Press.

—— (1993) *A Sicilian Romance*, ed. A. Milbank, Oxford, Oxford University Press.

Regnault-Warin, J. (1920) *Del trono al cadalso* [i.e. *Le Cimetière de la Madeleine*], trans. anon., Barcelona, La Hormiga de Oro.

Schama, S. (1989) *Citizens. A Chronicle of the French Revolution*, Harmondsworth, Penguin.

Smith, C. (1785) *Prévost: Manon L'Escaut: Or, The Fatal Attachment. A French Story*, 2 vols, London, T. Cadell.

Stallybrass, P. and White, A. (1986) *The Politics and Poetics of Transgression*, London, Methuen.

Summers, M. (1968) *The Gothic Quest*, London, Fortune Press.

Venuti, L. (1995) *The Translator's Invisibility. A History of Translation*, London, Routledge.

2

European disruptions of the idealized woman: Matthew Lewis's *The Monk* and the Marquis de Sade's *La Nouvelle Justine*

ANGELA WRIGHT

Matthew Gregory Lewis and the Marquis de Sade are, in their own rights, well-researched authors. Lewis is rightfully accorded a prominent position in critical surveys of the English Gothic novel due to his notorious production *The Monk* (Miles 1993; Kilgour 1995; Botting 1996; Punter 1996); the Marquis de Sade has also recently been afforded a great deal of critical and biographical attention (Lever 1991; Schaeffer 1999). What is less well documented, however, is the mutually influential relationship under which both authors' work flourished.

The tracing of Matthew Lewis's numerous 'borrowed' sources in *The Monk* began swiftly after the novel's publication. In 1797, for example, an article in the *Monthly Review* took pleasure in identifying in *The Monk* a number of plot motifs taken from, amongst other sources, Smollett's *Ferdinand Count Fathom*, Cazotte's *Le Diable amoureux* (1772), and numerous German romances. The review, however, was surprisingly favourable of these 'borrowings'. It argued:

> This may be called plagiarism, yet it deserves some praise. The great art of writing consists in selecting what is most stimulant from the works of our predecessors, and in uniting the gathered beauties in a new whole, more interesting than the tributary models. This is the essential process of the imagination, and excellence is no otherwise attained. All invention is but new combination. To invent well is to combine the impressive. (Anon. 1797b: 451, n. 23)

Such accusations of lightly veiled plagiarism, coupled with the extensive documentation of Lewis's familiarity with and translations of German terror literature, have haunted the publication history of *The*

Monk to such an extent that we are now inclined to read it as a Barthe-sian tissue of other stories, rather than search for coherency of themes. This chapter, however, will begin by tracing the mutual influences which the texts of de Sade and Lewis shared, and conclude by charting the reciprocity of themes and ideas between Lewis and de Sade.

Matthew Lewis published *The Monk* in 1796, subsequent to some time spent in Paris. While he was in Paris in the summer of 1791, he acquired and read the second edition of the Marquis de Sade's novel *Justine, ou les malheurs de la vertu*, published in that same year. The reading of *Justine* undoubtedly influenced Lewis's subsequent novelis-tic creation, for *The Monk* sent the English Gothic novel in a radical new direction, on account of the terrors to which its pious female char-acters are subjected. *The Monk*, indeed, bears far more comparison with de Sade's libertine novels than with the English Gothic novel form because, as many critics have noted, it is a novel that focuses entirely upon the revelatory aspect of narrative. In this way, it clearly maps on to de Sade's project of *'tout révéler'*, or 'the revelation of all'. Having acknowledged that de Sade's creation *Justine* was undoubtedly a source of inspiration for Lewis, the latter part of this chapter will chart how, in return, Lewis's novel appears to have influenced de Sade's third and final reprise of the story of *Justine*. Significantly, Lewis's *The Monk* was translated into French for the first time in 1797 under the simple title of *Le Moine*.[1] The publication date of this first translation is significant, for 1797 also marked the year in which, after a lapse of six years, de Sade revised the notorious *Justine, ou les malheurs de la vertu*, into a third and final edition entitled *La Nouvelle Justine*. Crucially, Lewis's novel lies between the second and third editions of de Sade's creation, and, I would argue, provided a stimulus for de Sade's comprehensive thematic revisions.

The first edition of de Sade's novel, *Les Infortunes de la vertu*, was written during his imprisonment in the Bastille between 1787 and 1788. *Les Infortunes* recounts the story of a pious and innocent girl named Justine, who, upon the death of her parents, is thrown out onto the streets from the convent where she has been living. She has an older sister called Juliette who is licentious by nature and who resolves to maintain herself by prostitution; to the fervently religious Justine, how-ever, this is a fate worse than death. She resolves to earn her living through honesty and charity, but in the cruel world that de Sade depicts, she soon discovers that honesty and virtue are worthless commodities.

Her starkly depicted naivety make her a victim of constant rape and torture from the figureheads of the institutions in which she places her faith.

This first edition of de Sade's novel was a modest two hundred pages in length and was described by its author as a *'conte philosophique'* or 'philosophical tale'. De Sade never published *Les Infortunes* and it did not see the light of day until 1930, when it was edited by Maurice Heine. De Sade's second edition, *Justine, ou les malheurs de la vertu*, published in 1791, retained the first-person narrative of the previous edition but redoubled the narrative of the heroine's distresses, and embodied much more salacious detail. It is this second edition of the novel that Lewis would have bought and read in Paris. Both Maurice Heine and Béatrice Didier have described the evolution between these first two versions as the progression from a simple tale to that of a romantic Gothic novel due to the subsequent additions of underground cells, macabre moments and reveries (Didier 1976: 106). In addition, Heine has drawn parallels between the trope of the 'explained supernatural' in Ann Radcliffe's novels, and de Sade's frequent and abrupt alternations between Gothic scenarios and their rational explanations (Heine 1973: III 36).

Such Gothic additions to de Sade's novel clearly influenced some of the scenarios in Lewis's novel. For example, the sepulchral location of Antonia's rape by Ambrosio in *The Monk* bears a strong resemblance to the underground seraglio in the Sainte-Marie-des-Bois monastery where Justine is raped and tortured. Besides locational and atmospheric resemblances, there are also clear thematic parallels between *Justine, ou les malheurs de la vertu*, *The Monk*, and de Sade's subsequent *La Nouvelle Justine*. One of the most striking themes which is shared by both authors lies in the brutal collation of their novelistic heroines with idolized versions of the Madonna. It was through this key coupling of their heroines with the Madonna that Lewis and de Sade launched a critique of the privileging of such iconography in religion.

In *Ways of Seeing*, John Berger has famously commented on the portrayal of women as visions that: 'Women watch themselves being looked at ... The surveyor of woman in herself is male: the surveyed female. Thus she turns herself into an object – and most particularly an object of vision: a sight ... ' (1972: 47). According to Berger, then, there is little or no distinction between this 'sight', conjured by the female to flatter the male, and becoming an 'object of vision'. The word 'vision' is of vital importance in the way that the heroines of both *The Monk* and

ANGELA WRIGHT

the various versions of *Justine* are portrayed. At the beginning of their novels, Lewis and de Sade both establish a discourse of spectacle in which both characters and readers are compelled to participate.

Lewis's novel *The Monk* signals its participation in this complicitous spectatorial discourse on the very first page, where an audience is gathered at the Church of the Capuchins to hear the eponymous monk Ambrosio preach:

> Scarcely had the Abbey-Bell tolled for five minutes, and already was the Church of the Capuchins thronged with Auditors. Do not encourage the idea that the Crowd was assembled from motives of piety or thirst of information ... The Women came to show themselves, the Men to see the Women: Some were attracted by curiosity to hear an Orator so celebrated; Some came because they had no better means of employing their time till the play began; Some, from being assured that it would be impossible to find places in the Church; and one half of Madrid was brought thither by expecting to see the other half. (Lewis 1980: 7)

By establishing at the very beginning of this novel unstable connections between female beauty, male desire and religion, the novel immediately establishes the themes that it wishes to undermine. The narrator's stark honesty at the beginning of the novel provides a sharp contrast to the characters' own lack of motivational awareness. It also, however, forces the reader into a passive position where there is no mystery to be worked out. Everything is on display in *The Monk*: sexual desire, hypocrisy and naivety are all presented to us, forcing us into a spectatorial position.

Such a revelatory beginning to *The Monk* bears comparison with de Sade's second edition of *Justine* in 1791. In *Justine, ou les malheurs de la vertu*, Justine as first-person narrator is coaxed by her otherwise silent auditors at one point in the narrative to continue her revelation of all the horrors that have been forced upon her. Her delicacy makes her pause and consider the effects of the story on her audience. However, the audience, being comprised of her libertine sister Juliette and her lover de Corville, urges her to recount all:

> Mais comment abuser de votre patience pour vous raconter ces nouvelles horreurs? N'ai-je pas déjà trop souillé votre imagination par d'infâmes récits? Dois-je en hasarder de nouveaux?
> Oui, ... dit Monsieur de Corville, oui, nous exigeons de vous tous ces détails, vous les gagez avec une décence qui en émousse toute l'horreur; (de Sade 1986: III 240)

42

(But how can I abuse your patience by relating these new horrors? Have I not already more than soiled your imagination with infamous recitations? Dare I hazard additional ones?

'Yes, ... ' Monsieur de Corville put in, 'yes, we insist upon these details, you veil them with a decency that removes their edge of horror;' (Seaver and Wainhouse 1991: 670)[2]

Every tiny detail of libertinism, horror and misfortune must be recounted in this novel, and contrary to de Corville's justifications, Justine's narrative does not gloss over the horror of the repeated violations. Although the first-person narrator, Justine, has reservations about revealing all, in contrast to Lewis's later anonymous narrator, the reader of both tales is none the less compelled to adopt the same prurient role, having duly been warned by the narrators of the horrors that await. In relation to The Monk, David Punter has demonstrated how Lewis 'tries constantly to challenge his audience, to upset its security, to give the reader a moment of doubt about whether he may not himself be guilty of the complicated faults attributed to Ambrosio' (Punter 1996: I 79), and Punter's argument here is equally applicable to de Sade's *Justine*.

If de Sade's and Lewis's narrative techniques are both brutally revelatory, then their portrayal of their heroines are similarly so. Berger's use of the term 'vision' is of vital importance in the way that the heroines of both The Monk and the various versions of Justine are characterized. At the beginning of their novels, Lewis and de Sade both immediately create very pictorial images of their heroines. These images establish the heroines as modest, virginal, religiously devout and naive. Such textual characterizations are knowingly situated within an eighteenth-century literary tradition which equated feminine beauty and distress. In *Les Malheurs de la vertu*, for example, there is a moment when Justine describes the effect that her distress has on the monk Antonin:

La violence de mes mouvements avait fait disparaître les voiles qui couvraient mon sein; il était nu, mes cheveux y flottaient en désordre, il était inondé de mes larmes; j'inspire des désirs à ce malhonnête homme (de Sade 1986: III 291)

(The violence of my movements had disturbed what veiled my breast, it was naked, my dishevelled hair fell in cascades upon it, it was wetted thoroughly by my tears; I quicken desires in the dishonest man) (Seaver and Wainhouse 1991: 720)

Here, Justine's self-depiction creates a tableau of distressed beauty which is, however, knowingly eroticized, revealing the tale's French literary heritage. For example, in Diderot's earlier novel *La Religieuse* (1780), the heroine Suzanne Simonin is similarly aware of the effect that she has on her male persecutors.[3] This earlier heroine does, however, admit to some possible complicity on her own part, stating: 'Je suis une femme, peut-être un peu coquette, que sais-je?' (Diderot 1961: 178) or 'Perhaps I am slightly flirtatious, who knows? I am a woman' (my translation). Diderot's Suzanne appears in many ways to be the French literary precursor to de Sade's Justine in her knowing admission of the desire she inspires in her persecutors. As such, she provides literary inspiration for both de Sade's and Lewis's critique of religion in her persecution by monks, and also in her confused couplings of her own beauty and distress with the desire that they inspire.

Such equations of beauty and distress inform, in turn, the construction of the English Gothic novel. The opening chapter of Ann Radcliffe's 1791 *The Romance of the Forest* (Radcliffe 1992) contains a similar scene. Here, through the focalization of a Monsieur La Motte, the heroine Adeline's features are described as having 'gained from distress an expression of captivating sweetness' and her clothes are described as having been 'thrown open at the bosom, upon which part of the hair had fallen in disorder' (Radcliffe 1992: 7). However, the crucial difference lies between the knowing eroticization provided by the female first-person narrators in the French novels, and the male-focalized third-person narratives that create these tableaux in the English Gothic novels.[4]

Our introduction to one of the principal female victims of The Monk, Antonia, confirms the spectatorial role into which Lewis's narrator forces us. When Antonia's veil is dislodged as she passes in the Church, we discover 'a neck which for symmetry and beauty might have vied with the Medicean Venus' (Lewis 1980: 9). What is more, through the focalization of the hero Lorenzo, she is also compared to an 'Hamadryad'. This choice of comparison is particularly telling and ironic: in Greek mythology, the Hamadryad is a tree nymph who dies when the tree dies. Inextricably bound in a symbiotic relationship, there is no autonomous existence for this creature. Desire is ineffably linked to the dual commodities of beauty and virginity in The Monk. Antonia is awarded attributes by her several admirers which can only be associated with purity. Therefore, once she is raped towards the end of the novel, she must die. Stripped of her perfect virginity, her most precious commodity in the eyes of the male, Antonia becomes as nothing.

Later in the novel, when Antonia has been fatally raped by the Monk Ambrosio, who claims that he has been seduced into violently raping her because of her perfect virginal beauty, she becomes simply a mirror who reflects his crimes. Ambrosio reproaches Antonia for his crime as follows:

> What seduced me into crimes, whose bare remembrance makes me shudder? Fatal witch! Was it not thy beauty? Have you not plunged my soul into infamy? Have you not made me a perjured Hypocrite, a Ravisher, an Assassin! Nay, at this moment, does not that angel look bid me despair of God's forgiveness? Oh! When I stand before his judgement throne, that look will suffice to damn me! You will tell my Judge, that you were happy, till I saw you; that you were innocent, till I polluted you! (Lewis 1980: 385)

Once Antonia's virginal integrity is shattered, her fragmented image mirrors Ambrosio's crime alone. The reproaches with which he loads her here are reminiscent of the blame that both Diderot's Suzanne and de Sade's second Justine inflict upon themselves. In all three cases, it is not the male authority figure to blame, but the female's irresistible beauty. Antonia's 'angel look' reminds Ambrosio of his irrecoverable sin, and shame and remorse subsume his previous identity as the pious, confident and irreproachable monk.

Antonia cannot survive the loss of her innocence in the textual space that this novel offers her precisely because of the unreality of her construction. In the eyes of the male characters, she is attributed solely the properties of virginal beauty, and, when this is taken from her, she mirrors only what passion has led Ambrosio to. Her death is a direct indictment of her textual establishment as an icon of modesty in the eyes of the male characters. Maggie Kilgour has commented that in the cases of both Ambrosio and Lorenzo, 'the attainment of sexual fantasies produces disgust, while the enlightened attempt to demystify only produces a deeper darkness' (1995: 160). This 'deeper darkness', as Robert Miles has suggested, is a consequence of the 'taboo territory' that their desire inhabits (1993: 27). This 'taboo territory' lies in the sublimation of their sexual fantasies within artistic representations of women.

Thus far, Lewis's novel has not really destabilized the connections between femininity, modesty and religion. If anything, it has reinforced them with the brutal death of Antonia. However, bearing in mind

Teresa de Lauretis's point that 'to perform the terms of the production of woman as text, as image, is to resist identification with that image' (1984: 36), we will now turn our attention to the second female image in *The Monk*, offered by the demon lover Matilda. Matilda is important in this novel precisely because she seduces Ambrosio through his own constructions of the idealized female. By this, I refer to his key idealization of femininity as being necessarily equated with the Virgin Mary. When he has preached a particularly pious sermon, the monk Ambrosio returns to his cell to worship a portrait of the Madonna that hangs there. He congratulates himself on being above fleshly temptation:

> 'I must accustom my eyes to Objects of temptation, and expose myself to the seduction of luxury and desire. Should I meet in that world which I am constrained to enter some lovely Female, lovely … as you Madona … !'
>
> As he said this, He fixed his eyes upon a picture of the Virgin, which was suspended opposite to him: This for two years had been the Object of his increasing wonder and adoration. He paused, and gazed upon it in delight.
>
> 'What beauty in that countenance!' He continued after a silence of some minutes; 'How graceful is the turn of that head! What sweetness, yet what majesty in her divine eyes! … Oh, if such a creature existed, and existed but for me! …
>
> Fool that I am! Whither do I suffer my admiration of this picture to hurry me? Away, impure ideas! Let me remember, that Woman is for ever lost to me. Never was mortal formed so perfect as this picture … What charms me, when ideal and considered as a superior being, would disgust me, become Woman and tainted with all the failings of Mortality. (Lewis 1980: 41)

Ambrosio's use of the words 'charm' and 'disgust', in reference to the Virgin and Woman, indicate his differing perceptions of the iconized Madonna and the reality of Womanhood. Women to him are tainted and impure: their presence threatens to taint him. It is gradually revealed to Ambrosio, however, that the image of the Madonna that hangs in his room, a painting that he venerates, is in fact a portrait of Matilda. Matilda herself, hitherto disguised as a novice, effects this shattering revelation. Matilda's declaration of love for Ambrosio occurs in parallel with her revelation of her true gender to him: she controls Ambrosio's responses and interests, just as she has controlled his desire for this portrait of the alleged Madonna. Equally, the gender-switch which she effects also disrupts Ambrosio's 'normative', heterosexual, desire for the portrait.

When Matilda, having nursed the dying Ambrosio back to health,' gradually reveals her true identity as the woman portrayed in the portrait, Ambrosio's confusion over the idolized Madonna and the sexualized female is complete, and he falls prey to her desire. Ambrosio and Matilda embark upon a passionate sexual relationship where the monk's lust is given full vent upon her willing body. Their sexual relationship also involves their collusion in order to conceal it from the rest of the monastery. However, when Matilda begins to dominate their machinations, and coldly to plan their hypocrisy, Ambrosio begins to become disillusioned with her:

> Left to himself He could not reflect without surprize on the sudden change in Matilda's character and sentiments. But a few days had past, since She appeared the mildest and softest of her sex, devoted to his will, and looking up to him as a superior Being. But now she assumed a sort of courage and manliness in her manners but ill calculated to please him ... what she gained in the opinion of the Man, She lost with interest in the affection of the Lover. (Lewis 1980: 231–232)

In order to remain sexually appealing to Ambrosio, Matilda should remain 'submissive' and, consequently, in his eyes, feminine. Ambrosio desires a reinforcement of the distinctions between male and female: he looks for someone to affirm his ideal of himself as a 'superior being' and confirm his elevated status in society. Matilda initially secures Ambrosio to herself by her very self-positioning as gentle and submissive. In order to continue to remain in his favour, such posturing should be maintained, but Matilda discards it once she has secured Ambrosio. It is only when Matilda discards submission that she, as the double of the Madonna portrait, no longer satisfies.

This thematic enjambment is fully explored by Julia Kristeva in her essay 'Stabat Mater' where she questions the supremacy of images of the Madonna in Western culture. She locates Mary and the Lady as: 'the focal point of men's desires and aspirations. Moreover, because they were unique and thus excluded all other women, both the Lady and the Virgin embodied an absolute authority the more attractive as it appeared removed from paternal sternness' (1986: 170). When Matilda transgresses the boundary of ideal, feminine behaviour and becomes masterful, she no longer doubles the Madonna portrait and consequently no longer mirrors Ambrosio's desires. She ceases to represent his image of an ideal love, and is thus replaced with Antonia, another virginal object.

None the less, it is Matilda who is responsible in this novel for destabilizing the equation of woman and modesty, and, as such, she occupies an important space. By portraying Ambrosio's fatal passion as being so linked to his love of the Madonna, Lewis also effectively critiques the location of the Virgin Mary as an icon in Western culture.

This critique offered by Lewis seems to be supported by a significant addition that he made to the ending of the second edition of the novel. Following the outraged reception of the first edition of The Monk in 1796, Lewis added an extra passage to the ending of the second, third and fourth editions of the novel.[5] In the first edition, the villainous monk Ambrosio is dashed to pieces and left to rot at the foot of a mountain by Lucifer, as a suitable punishment for his various crimes. The second edition kept that conclusion, but added a more moral note as the final closure to the tale:

> Haughty Lady, why shrunk you back when yon poor frail one drew near? Was the air infected by her errors? Was your purity soiled by her passing breath? Ah! Lady, smooth that insulting brow: stifle the reproach just bursting from your scornful lip: wound not a soul, that bleeds already! She has suffered, suffers still. Her air is gay, but her heart is broken: her dress sparkles, but her bosom groans.
>
> Lady, to look with mercy on the conduct of others, is a virtue no less than to look with severity on your own. (Lewis 1796: III 314–315)

Recent editors of *The Monk* have chosen largely to ignore this addition, only acknowledging its existence in a note upon the text. However, if we take into consideration the themes that we have just been exploring, it appears to offer a thematically tighter conclusion. By dwelling on the external appearances of two seemingly diametrically opposed female characters, named only 'Haughty Lady' and 'yon poor frail one', the author himself has cast two nameless women into stereotypical positions. However, Lewis has at the same time undermined this by his appeal for our compassion, and for external appearances to be mistrusted.

In this novel, a critique of the masculine tendency to veil the reality of the female presence is offered on several levels. One of these levels is the equation of the female form with artistic, religious representations of it. As Jerry Hogle has argued, 'all passionate desire in this book is really aroused, intensified, and answered by images more than objects or bodies, by signifiers more often than by signifieds or referents.' (1997: 1) The 'Haughty Lady' of this second edition, contrasted with the 'poor frail one' does not need a specific identity. Rather, she appears to signify the idealized versions of the Madonna, offered throughout this novel in various images, portraits and representations of women. She is also specifically contrasted with the 'poor frail one' who may represent the wronged heroines of this novel, wronged because of their unwitting similarities to the Virgin Mary.

In all, *The Monk* offers three core models of femininity that are both indebted to previous literary representations and intended to disrupt them. The first, Antonia, is a clear embodiment of previous literary representations drawn from, amongst others, Diderot, de Sade and Radcliffe. The second model, Agnes, who like Diderot's Suzanne is a nun who cannot disentangle herself from her orders, provides a remarkable representation of what happens when the flesh-and-blood reality of motherhood is neglected. The tale of her illegitimate baby, left to die on her chest as a 'suitable' punishment by her convent for fornication, is grotesquely realized. Finally, although Matilda is, as the *Monthly Review* noted in 1797, remarkably similar to Jacques Cazotte's devil Biondetta in *The Devil in Love,* she remains none the less a remarkable and unique indictment of the roles played by male desire in the previous models. Her ability to gender-switch, to posture submission when required, and her mimicry of the Madonna all undermine previous literary constructions of femininity. The character of Matilda incorporates Suzanne Simonin's knowledge of her effect on men and parodies the earlier Justine's naivety in Lewis's endeavour to untangle the links between femininity, desire and the Madonna.

In his critical work 'Idée sur les romans', first published in 1800 as a preface to *Les Crimes de l'amour,* the Marquis de Sade praised Lewis's *The Monk* for being superior, in every respect, to the brilliantly imaginative novels of Ann Radcliffe. Paradoxically, however, it was also in this same work that de Sade famously disclaimed his authorship of *Justine,* an assertion which he persisted in repeating throughout his life. In this essay, he protested, 'I have never written any such immoral works, and I never shall' (1970: 63, my translation). Given that de Sade had only recently published his third edition of his Justine tale, *La Nouvelle Justine,* his critical and literary personae appear to be clearly at odds with each other. De Sade the public author, who writes with such authority in 'Idée sur les romans' on Richardson, Lewis and Radcliffe, clearly wanted to dissociate himself from his own literary efforts. Perhaps such vehement denial was due to the fact that Alexandre-Louis de Villeterque identified the Justine novels as de Sade's and subsequently calumniated them in the *Journal des arts, des sciences et de littérature* (de Villeterque 1800). However, de Sade's very obvious admiration of Matthew Lewis in his own critical essay does appear to undermine his self-distancing from the immoral works of *Justine*.

La Nouvelle Justine, ou les malheurs de la vertu, suivi de l'histoire de Juliette, sa soeur was a work of ten volumes, with a hundred obscene engravings. It was supposedly printed 'in Holland' in 1797, although it was actually typeset in Paris by de Sade's publisher Nicolas Massé. However, Jean-Jacques Pauvert, one of the co-editors of de Sade's complete works, has raised justifiable questions about the date, 1797, and the order of publication of *La Nouvelle Justine* and *L'Histoire de Juliette*. He argues that the third *Justine* followed an earlier 1796 version of *Juliette* in August 1800 (de Sade 1986: VIII 18). This third reprisal of the story tripled the length of the second edition, and added yet more persecution and torture.

Given Pauvert's correction of the dates of *La Nouvelle Justine*, it appears highly probable that some of the much-admired Matthew Lewis's methods of inscribing virtue in distress had an impact on de Sade's revisions. In this third edition, for the first time the character Justine is denied the first-person narrative voice and the entire story is told in the third person. It is equally as important to note that this third version of the novel is not a Gothic novel. As Didier has noted, with this third Justine we witness an 'explosion' of the Gothic novel (1976: 106). Whereas in the previous two editions we had some sympathy for the unfortunate heroine, here, instead, the third-person narrator makes us entirely complicit in his mockery of Justine. Like the narrative voice at the beginning of *The Monk* which urges us not to encourage the idea that piety attracts people to church, de Sade's narrator in this final edition mocks the ineffectual piety of Justine. At one point, for example, he castigates religion for promoting self-interest (1986: 100); later he relentlessly pursues Justine for crying when her religious consolation is revealed to be illogical by the Comte du Bressac, stating that tears are 'la ressource du faible, en se voyant ravir la chimère qui le consolait', or 'the resource of a weak person, when they have their last source of consolation torn away' (1986: 141, my translation). In this final, more picaresque edition, de Sade finally achieved exactly the disruption of the idolized feminine form which he wished.[6] What his libertine characters pursue with such violence are females who idolize the Madonna with such force that they are unwittingly seen to dress like her, and shown to act with a concomitant naivety that is breathtaking.

Why was de Sade so haunted by this tale that he revised it twice over the space of ten years? As with Lewis's novel, some of the answers lie in the portrayal of virtue in distress, and with the essential linkage of that virtue to religious piety. The narrator himself justifies this assumption on the very second page of this third edition, where he states that 'Il est essentiel que les sots cessent d'encenser cette ridicule idole de la vertu, qui ne les a jusqu'ici payés que d'ingratitude' (1986: IV 26). 'It is essential that fools stop worshipping this ridiculous idol of virtue, which until now has only repaid them with ingratitude' (my translation). What is interesting here is the deliberate confusion about the subject of de Sade's attack. Virtue as a concept is what he most wishes to denigrate for his readers; but equally, one could conclude that the 'ridiculous idol of virtue' could be his character Justine, made famous through the previous two editions of the novel, and clearly associated with both purity and religion. In all three editions, Justine's beauty is compared to that of Raphael's beautiful virgins. Like Lewis, then, de Sade makes implicit connections between Justine, virginity and painting. However, in contrast, his project is clearly stated at the very beginning of the tale. He wishes to use the character Justine to teach moralists a violent lesson about idolizing virtue. The subsequent linking of this virtue to specifically Catholic institutions such as monasteries display a disgust with the artifices and ornaments of the Catholic Church. De Sade's atheistic castigation of the ritualistic worship of artifices in the Catholic Church is remarkably similar to Lewis's Anglican-Protestant condemnation of the sensuality of this worship.

The trajectory of the unfortunate adventures of Justine involves successive encounters with different institutions. The foremost of these institutions in each edition is a monastery called Sainte-Marie-des-Bois where Justine goes to confess and be comforted by the monks. Justine's naivety, coupled with her religious fervour, makes her a desirable prey for the libertine monks who run this monastery, and want to admit her to their seraglio. A very detailed passage in the third edition, *La Nouvelle Justine*, describes Justine's confession:

> Justine, éblouie par les illusions de son ardente piété, n'entend rien, ne voit rien, et se prosterne; ...

Justine, immobile, fermement persuadée que tout ce qu'on lui fait n'a d'autre but que de la conduire pas à pas vers la perfection céleste, souffre tout avec une indicible résignation; pas une plainte ... pas un mouvement ne lui échappe; son esprit était tellement élevé vers les choses célestes, que le bourreau l'eût déchirée sans qu'elle eût seulement osé s'en plaindre. (de Sade, 1986: IV 249–250)

(Overcome by the illusions of her boundless piety, Justine hears nothing, sees nothing and kneels down; ... motionless, certain that everything that she is subjected to has no other aim than to lead her step by step to celestial perfection, Justine suffers everything with an ineffable resignation; not one complaint passes her lips ... not one movement comes from her; so much was her spirit transported on to a higher plane that her tormentor might have ripped her to pieces without her once even daring to protest.) (my translation)

This description situates Justine firmly on the side of innocence and piety, whilst simultaneously destroying this picture of innocence by describing the libertine monks' desecration of her. Thus fixed in her adoration of the Virgin Mary, Justine becomes blind to the immediate danger posed by the monks who lasciviously watch her devotions and undress her. De Sade firmly makes the point in this edition of the novel that it is precisely Justine's obsession with the Virgin Mary, her fervent piety, which delivers her so easily to the cruelties of the monks of Sainte-Marie-des-Bois. Justine adopts the posture of the Virgin Mary, and the posturing incites the monks' violent desires. What the monks wish to attain, apart from sexual gratification, is the violent destruction of this virginal image by reminding Justine of her all too mortal qualities. Her innocence here appears to owe more to Lewis's portrayal of Antonia (who is shrouded in both a 'bandage of ignorance' as well as a 'veil of innocence' (1980: 264)) than to the more wordly wise characterizations of Justine in the two previous versions of de Sade's own text.

Both Matthew Lewis and the Marquis de Sade embarked upon disrupting the collation of the venerated Madonna and women. They both used fairly brutal methods to destabilize these connections in their texts. Lewis portrayed one lascivious monk who falls prey to a lustful demon who deliberately postures herself as the Madonna. De Sade's relentless destabilization comes through the successive and ever-more-brutal revision of a rape scene in a monastery where the heroine becomes so lost in her devotions to the Madonna that she forgets the real dangers which surround her. In de Sade's *La Nouvelle Justine* we, as readers, are brutally taught of the follies of Justine's posturing by being forced to laugh at both her innocence and devotion. Lewis's *The Monk* conveys its message in slightly different terms – one of these terms, as I have argued, lies in the addition of the 'Haughty Lady' to the subsequent editions, the other term is by teaching Ambrosio through damnation that the ideal and the real, such as the Madonna, doubled by Matilda and Antonia, must remain forever separate. In the words of Angela Carter: 'Even if it is the dream made flesh, the real, once it becomes real, can be no more than real' (Carter 1982: 201).

Notes

1   Anon. 1797a. Although this four-volume edition is translated anonymously, it has been identified, and is widely acknowledged on library catalogues, as having been translated by four different translators: namely, Jacques-Marie Deschamps, Jean-Baptiste Desprès, Pierre Vincent Benoist and Pierre Bernard Lamare.

2   Where available, I have used authoritative translations of de Sade's works. However, in the case of *La Nouvelle Justine* and 'Idée sur les romans', where no translations have been available, I have used my own. These instances are marked in the body of the text.

3   As Peter France has documented, Diderot in fact wrote *La Religieuse* in 1760. However, it was published in the *Correspondance littéraire* in 1780, though a teasing set of letters, which describe the circumstances of composition, had been made public in 1770 (France 1983: 37). The *Monthly Magazine* noted in December 1797 the translation of *La Religieuse*: 'Two novels have been translated from the French of Diderot, with considerable vivacity, "The Nun" and "James the Fatalist": in each of these works are some masterly delineations of character, but the pen of Diderot is not remarkable for its chastity' (Anon. 1797c: 518).

4   For a fuller exploration of the similarities and differences between *The Romance of the Forest* and de Sade's second *Justine*, see Clery 1994. Clery discusses the similar plot motifs of both novels, but demonstrates the two novels' entirely different philosophical approaches.

5   Lewis, of course, reserved the most significant changes to the text for the fourth edition of the novel, *Ambrosio, or The Monk: A Romance* (1798). However, the crucial addition to the ending is present from the second edition. The British Library carries an annotated copy of the third edition owned by Lewis where he wrote in the vital changes to be made. The copy makes for interesting reading not only because of the corrections, but also because of the bitter asides that Lewis has scribbled in. For example, a scribbled footnote to his 'Imitation of Horace' epigraph 'And when you find, condemned, despised,/Neglected, blamed, and criticised.' bitterly records of the novel's reception 'Neglected it has not been, but criticised enough of all conscience' (BL: C.28. b 4–6: iv).

6   I would justify my use of the term 'picaresque' for this final edition of the novel because the overarching am of the novel, thanks to the editorial inventions, is to satirize virtue, and its embodiment in the naive character of Justine, whose travels take her from master to master.

ANGELA WRIGHT

Anon. (1797a) *Le Moine, traduit de l'anglais*, 4 vols, Paris, Maradan.
Anon. (1797b) *Monthly Review*, 23.
Anon. (1797c) *Monthly Magazine*, December.
Berger, J. (1972) *Ways of Seeing*, Harmondsworth, Penguin.
Botting, F. (1996) *Gothic*, London, Routledge.
Carter, A. (1982) *The Infernal Desire Machines of Doctor Hoffman*, Harmondsworth, Penguin [1972].
Cazotte, J. (1772) *Le Diable amoureux. Nouvelle espagnole*, Naples and Paris, n.p.
Clery, E.J. (1994) 'Ann Radcliffe and D.A.F. de Sade: thoughts on heroinism', *Women's Writing*, 1:2.
Diderot, D. (1961) *La Religieuse*, Paris, Armand Colin [1780].
Didier, B. (1976) *Sade: Une écriture du désir*, Paris, Denoel/Gonthier.
France, P. (1983) *Diderot*, Oxford, Oxford University Press.
Heine, M. (1973) 'Le Marquis de Sade et le roman noir', in A. Le Brun and J.-J. Pauvert (eds) *Oeuvres complètes du Marquis de Sade*, 16 vols, Paris, Société Nouvelle des Editions Pauvert.
Hogle, J. 'The Ghost of the Counterfeit – and the Closet – in *The Monk*', in *Romanticism on the Net* 8 (November 1997) <http://users.ox.ac.uk/~scat0385/ghost.html>
Kilgour, M. (1995) *The Rise of the Gothic Novel*, London, Routledge.
Kristeva, J. (1986) 'Stabat Mater', trans. L. Roudiez, in T. Moi (ed.) *The Kristeva Reader*, Oxford, Blackwell.
de Lauretis, T. (1984) *Alice Doesn't: Feminism, Semiotics, Cinema*, Bloomington, Indiana University Press.
Lever, M. (1991) *Donatien Alphonse François, Marquis de Sade*, Paris, Fayard.
Lewis, M.G. (1796) *The Monk; a Romance*, 2nd edn, 3 vols, London, J. Bell.
—— (1797) *The Monk; a Romance*, 3rd edn, annotated copy: BL c.175. 113. 3 vols, London, J. Bell.
—— (1798) *Ambrosio, or The Monk; A Romance*, London, J. Bell.
—— (1980) *The Monk; a Romance* ed. H. Anderson, Oxford, Oxford University Press [1796].
Miles, R. (1993) *Gothic Writing: A Genealogy*, London, Routledge.
Punter, D. (1996) *The Literature of Terror*, 2nd edn, 2 vols, London and New York, Longman.
Radcliffe, A. (1992) *The Romance of the Forest: Interspersed with Some Pieces of Poetry*, ed. C. Chard, Oxford, Oxford University Press [1791].
de Sade, D.A.F. (1970) 'Idée sur les romans', Paris, Ducros.
—— (1986) *Oeuvres complètes du Marquis de Sade*, eds A. Le Brun and J.-J. Pauvert, 16 vols, Paris, Société Nouvelle des Editions Pauvert [1800].
—— (1991) *Three Complete Novels and Other Writings*, trans. R. Seaver and A. Wainhouse, London, Arrow.
Schaeffer, N. (1999) *The Marquis de Sade: A Life*, London, Hamish Hamilton.
de Villeterque, A.-L. (1800) *Journal des arts, des sciences et delittérature*, 22 October.

3

Diderot and Maturin: Enlightenment, automata, and the theatre of terror

VICTOR SAGE

The case of the relation between Diderot and Maturin appears to be a relatively simple one: we have textual evidence of contact. It seems Maturin simply copied out passages of Diderot's *La Religieuse* after it was published in 1796, and used them in the extended anti-Catholic diatribe of his *Melmoth The Wanderer* (1820) (Praz 1930: 429–436). The book was translated immediately and became all the rage in France. After his death in 1824, a variety of French writers both revered and enthusiastically plundered Maturin, regarding him as a great author on a par with Goethe in poetry and Beethoven in music (Clapton 1930: 66–84, 97–115). Interesting indirections appear at this point in the zig-zag, but the original cultural transmission from Diderot to Maturin appears to be the most direct possible: a simple transposition, amounting to plagiarism. Although Maturin changed the gender of his narrator and apparently added Calvinist theology to what he originally took from Diderot, judging by the silence of commentators after Praz on this point, there seems to be a general assumption that there is nothing more to it than that (Praz 1930: 429–436; 1970: 177, note 72).

But cultural transmission between Britain and Europe in the period tends to be a complicated business, and there are many surrounding determinants that are hidden or underestimated. Mario Praz pointed out long ago that a great boost was given to the representation of 'superstition', perversity and vice by the Enlightenment attitude that these things needed to be explored, represented and catalogued, and he includes Diderot as a great anticipator of de Sade in this respect (Praz, 1970: 99–100). This open, enquiring attitude, in its turn, is open to ironical exploitation by writers and readers alike, and is a contributory factor in the narrative shapes of the Gothic tradition: Christopher Frayling in *Vampyres* has exposed the rich theologico-political stew of motives which led to those 'scientific' journeys to the Levant and Bohemia under the auspices of various imperial administrations in Western Europe – journeys which helped to create the documentary form of the vampire stories (Frayling 1992: 87–88; 92–93). Le Fanu's lesbian vampire Carmilla, in a witty parody of 'materialism', uses the Enlightenment naturalist Buffon to justify her own existence (Bleiler 1964: 297). Those repositories of Enlightenment values, Dictionaries of Superstition, are rich source materials for the Gothic tradition; the format has unpredictable effects of 'authority' on a readership, and can give room for parody or hoaxing, as we know from the example of Poe's horror story, 'The Facts in the case of M. Valdemar', which was published as a scientific article about mesmerism in several quite respectable places, including one such dictionary in France (Sage 1988: 188–196). Enlightenment scepticism has its rhetorical uses.

I want in this chapter to examine the relations between Diderot and Maturin in a broader context than just the simple source-text idea, because it seems to me that, while Diderot is in some respects nearer to the 'uncanny' and the Gothic than one might have thought, Maturin sees many more things in Diderot's novel than a few diatribes about convents and monasteries, absorbing a relation between scepticism and aesthetics into the distinctive form of his own text.

When Hamlet, in Act II, Scene ii of Shakespeare's play, signs his letter to Ophelia: 'Thine evermore, most dear lady, whilst this machine is to him' (Alexander 1951: 1041), he alludes fashionably to a new tradition of philosophical and theological obsession with the machine, later to be boosted by Descartes, and carried on through Locke's opposition to Descartes, a passionate concentration of thought which becomes a strong element in both English and French writing of the eighteenth century. The interest goes far beyond technology. Thus Hoffmann's later, Gothic rendering of the metaphors of this tradition in 'The Sandman' (1816) as 'uncanny', can be read as an equivocal parody of the romantic egotism of the artist – but also of the opposite: the Pygmalion-like, Enlightenment drive towards the reduction of mind–body relationships to abstract first principles, concretized in the image of the automaton, Olympia, as a demonic actress ('We have come to find this Olympia quite uncanny ... it seems to us that she is only acting like a living creature.') (Hoffmann 1982: 116–117).

It is a commonplace that Diderot displayed an interest in machines, mechanisms and 'systems'. But his attitude towards determinism of all kinds is to celebrate it in a dialogic fashion, rather than simplify it. Diderot's sceptical attack on the fiction of the isolated, Cartesian self means that he is concerned to preserve the notion of self-consciousness whenever any analogy between the human and the material is made; but that he will also turn to the machine, whenever the account of the 'human' has reached the point of isolating that idea of the self and confining it in a spiritual vacuum apart from the system of nature.

An obvious general example of this dialogical 'reconciliation' between matter and consciousness is the clavichord metaphor from *Le Rêve de D'Alembert* (translated as *D'Alembert's Dream*: Diderot 1994). The two speakers of this dialogue, who are partly fictional and partly historical entities, I shall designate 'Diderot' and 'D'Alembert'. They have been debating the old question (something Voltaire also liked to think about) of sentience (*sensibilité*), and whether matter could have 'sensitivity' (again: *sensibilité*). This leads to the famous analogy (also very common in the period) of 'vibrating or sensitive strings'. Having been accused by 'D'Alembert' of letting in a separate category of 'observer' or 'listener' (*un on*), and of thus separating mind and matter in a latently Cartesian fashion, 'Diderot' replies:

> I may have laid myself open to that objection, but perhaps you would not have raised it if you had considered the difference between the instrument called philosopher and the instrument called clavichord. The philosopher-instrument is sensitive [sensible], being at one and the same time player and instrument [en même temps le musicien et l'instrument]. As a sensitive being he has momentary consciousness of the sound he is producing, as an animal he remembers it. This organic faculty, by linking together the sounds in his own mind, makes a melody out of them and preserves it. Assume that the clavichord has both sensitivity and memory, and then tell me whether it won't know and repeat on its own the tunes you will play on its keys. (Diderot 1987: 102–103; 1966: 157)

Each level of mechanism gives rise to a level of consciousness so that instrument implies player as much as player needs instrument. 'Diderot' even imagines a clavichord with solipsistic doubts. 'D'Alembert's sarcastic reply, that no doubt these machines give birth to sensitive little clavichords, provokes a magnificent diatribe in which a canary (*serin*) is compared to a bird-organ (*serinette*) which is portrayed as growing and hatching from the egg in a mechanical but 'sensitive' fashion:

Now the wall is breached and the bird emerges, walks, flies, feels pain, runs away, comes back again, complains, suffers, loves, desires, enjoys, it experiences all your affections and does all the things you do. And will you maintain, with Descartes, that it is an imitating machine pure and simple [une pure machine imitative]? Why, even little children will laugh at you, and philosophers will answer that if it is a machine you are one too! (Diderot 1987: 104; 1966: 158–159)

The riposte that Diderot is making here is to the idea of what Furbank calls 'scandalous materialism', an idea which he traces back to Descartes (Furbank 1992: 327). No doubt he has La Mettrie's *L'Homme machine* (1748) in mind as the most grotesque point that the Cartesian tradition of mechanical materialism had reached. It is at this point, the exposure of the 'imitating machine', that we can see the potentiality for the uncanny opening up. Here is Furbank's suggestive summary of the impact of Descartes:

No one before Descartes had made matter or the body seem so descralised and dead – nor so eerily so, for not only did he represent animals, for lack of a soul, as mere hydraulic mechanisms, he likened them to *automata*, or machines deliberately designed to simulate life and to deceive. (Furbank 1992: 327)

And yet this is the doctrine which was quickly adopted as orthodoxy by the Church and the Doctors of the Sorbonne. The debate rapidly becomes a life and death struggle in France and has some very far-reaching consequences in politics and religion.

It is this context which informs the narrative of the earlier text, *La Religieuse* (translated as *The Nun*), the novel which Diderot started in 1760, but which was not properly published until the revolutionary period, when it was needed for propaganda against the Church. *La Religieuse* has, of course, long been recognized a source text for the Gothic Romance, even though, not having come out in French until 1796, it could not have influenced Ann Radcliffe's *Mysteries of Udolpho* (1794) (Praz 1930: 496). In Diderot's novel, the notion of the automaton is linked to the system of an anti-society of isolated Cartesian cells, and becomes associated with horror and superstition, a phalanstery of mastery and slavery which anticipates the rigorous automatism of de Sade. Diderot himself had been imprisoned in Vincennes and had been unnerved by the experience to the point of apparent capitulation to the authorities, so he had studied at first hand the condition he writes about.

Suzanne, the narrator of *La Religieuse*, articulates this link between automatism and the enforced isolation and habitual obedience of the convent quite early on in her account of life at Longchamp. On the morning of taking her vows, she is undressed by the novice-mistress and her fellows:

> She had hardly gone out before the novice-mistress and my fellows entered; my religious habit was taken off and I was dressed in secular clothes – you know the custom. I heard nothing of what was being said round me, I had almost reached [J'étais presque reduite] the state of an automaton [à l'état d'automate]. I was told what to do, and often it had to be repeated because I did not understand the first time, and I did it. It was not that I was thinking of anything else, but I was absorbed, and my head was weary as though exhausted after hard thinking. (Diderot 1972: 51; 1975: 123)

'You know the custom' is the only sign of the text's dialogic frame – it is addressed, as an extended piece of testimony, to Suzanne's ally, the Marquis de Croismare. This is one of the most important, fateful moments of Suzanne's life. Up to this point, we have seen her protest vigorously. But now she has become an imitating machine; as she goes on, the related trope of the marionette is introduced by the Penguin translator, who has entered fully into the spirit of the overall conceit:

> The sermon may have been good or bad, I didn't hear. I was merely a puppet [On disposa de moi] all through that morning, which was non-existent in my life, for I never knew how long it lasted, what I did or what I said. Presumably I was questioned, presumably I replied. I pronounced vows, but I have no recollection of them, and I found I had become a nun as passively as I was made a Christian, for I understood no more about the ceremony of my profession than about my baptism; with this difference, that the one confers grace and the other presupposes it. (Diderot 1972: 51–52; 1975: 123–124)

By the end of the novel, having escaped from the convent of Arpajon, Suzanne finds some relief, working as a laundress. If her past is discovered, she will languish in a prison cell forever. But, despite her terror, she is still an automaton, and, like many a prisoner, she is afraid that her automatic behaviour will unconsciously give her away:

> I have never had the spirit of the cloister, and that is clear enough from what I am doing now, but I have become accustomed in the monastic life to certain behaviour which I go through automatically [machinalement]. For example, if a bell happens to ring I either make the sign of the cross

or kneel down. If somebody knocks on the door I say *Ave*. If I am asked a question I nearly always end my answer with yes or no, Reverend Mother or dear Sister. If a stranger approaches my arms fold themselves across my breast, and instead of curtseying I bow. My companions start laughing and think I am imitating a nun for a joke [que je m'amuse à contrefaire la religieuse], but they cannot go on and on making this mistake, and my absentmindedness will give me away and be my undoing. (Diderot 1972: 187–188; 1975: 286)

But Suzanne is also aware of her own automatism and that makes her not just an imitating machine, but an actor in her own drama and a ventriloquized *ingénue*. She is the subject and the object of her own narrative, the very papers of which have been held by Sister Ursule and preserved so that she can give this account to the Marquis de Crois-mare, who is both a real historical person and a fictionalized addressee. Suzanne is the framer and the framed and to that extent there is an open, 'present' level to the text which indicates its self-consciousness and opens it to its own history at the same time.

There are many subtle touches in this novel. The dialogic structure clearly allows Diderot the anti-clerical propagandist to have his say, while, at the same time, we glimpse the 'Gothic' aspect of the theatre of horror in the notion that there is a 'wild beast' lurking in every cell. The power of Mother de Moni, the Mother Superior and Suzanne's favourite, is absolute, except, ironically, where sin protects the slave from becoming an imitating machine:

How many times have I recalled the words of my saintly Mother de Moni: 'Among all these creatures you see around me, so docile, so innocent, so gentle, indeed, my child there is scarcely one I could not turn into a wild beast, and the likelihood of this strange metamorphosis happening is the more marked the younger they go into a cell and the less they know of social life. This strikes you as a strange thing to say, and God save you from ever experiencing the truth of it. Sister Suzanne, the good nun is the one who brings with her into the cloister some grievous sin [quelque grande faute] to expiate.' (Diderot 1972: 82; 1975: 160)

The subtlest and most ambiguous aspects of this argument are in the scenes of sexual oppression which Suzanne tells us about at Arpajon. Here the master is also the slave; the Reverend Mother of Arpajon is an automaton. She is a bad actress, whose performance is purely mechanical, because she is wholly and absolutely caught up in it. On one level, by Diderot's standards, it is not a performance at all. The transference of automatic behaviour between the two is signified by a transparent ploy worthy of Cleland:

> 'How comes it that all these fragile limbs were not broken? And that delicate mechanism [cette machine délicate] destroyed? Why was the lustre of those eyes not dimmed for ever by tears? What cruel women ! Fancy crushing those arms with ropes !' And she took my arms and kissed them. 'Drawing groans and wailing from that mouth !' She kissed that too. 'Condemning that charming, serene face to be constantly clouded by sadness !' She kissed it. 'Making the roses of those cheeks wither !' She stroked them with her hand and kissed them. 'Robbing that head of its beauty! tearing out that hair! loading that brow with sorrow!' She kissed my head, brow, hair. 'Fancy daring to put a rope round that neck and tearing those shoulders with sharp points !' She pushed aside my collar and coif, opened the top of my dress and my hair fell loose over my bare shoulders; my breast was half uncovered and her kisses spread over my neck, bare shoulders, and half-naked breast. (Diderot 1972: 142; 1975: 232–233)

The text, by its thematizing of 'delicate mechanism', and by its exaggerated repetition, insists on the automatism of the performance. This is hypocrisy, or bad acting, literalized. The actor has forgotten her audience. This gap is plainly visible to the reader. But the text is also both slightly comic, and rather disturbing, because its use of the crude conventions of pornography challenges the reader to find a position uncontaminated by sado-masochistic fantasy. The real power of this scene lies in its close study, through the ventriloquized reportage of the mesmerized victim, Suzanne, of the automaton that is laying its hands and lips on her in the name of love and reducing her to an imitating machine herself in a gross, vampiric parody of 'sympathy':

> The trembling that began to come over her, the confusion of her speech, the uncontrolled movements of her eyes and hands, her knee pressing against mine, the ardour of her embraces and the tightness of her arms as she held me, all showed me that her malady was about to come over her again. I don't know what was going on inside me, but I was seized with panic, and my own trembling and faintness justified the suspicion I had had that her trouble was contagious. (Diderot 1972: 142; 1975: 233)

Suzanne's doubled, mock-ignorant viewpoint is at once a source of clarity, satirical amusement, euphemism, and outraged terror. The 'sympathy' of her 'delicate mechanism' is beginning to betray her into imitation, even though she is not sexually aroused herself. Or is she, despite 'herself'? Of course, this tabooed (but contagious) 'malady' is a subtle challenge to what the reader is prepared to admit in the speaker's words. No wonder Diderot derived such intense pleasure from the writing of this novel. But my point is a different one: it is not the sexual content of scenes like this which is of primary importance, so much as the eerie, humiliating reduction of the human to the automatic.

But let me draw back from the socio-cultural context for the moment. This notion of the 'imitating machine' projects into several other contexts in Diderot's thought and I want to consider these now. One of these contexts is aesthetics: just as the 'philosophical' solution is dialogical, so the aesthetic one tends to have this form too. There's a striking example in *Jacques le fataliste* (translated as *Jacques The Fatalist*, 1986), which has some interesting consequences for questions of narrative self-consciousness. After an outrageously Sternean series of interruptions and digressions, the narrator of this novel teasingly registers the importunate presence of the naive reader:

> I understand, you've had enough of this and you want to return to our two travellers. Reader, you're treating me like an automaton [Lecteur, vous me traitez comme un automate]. That's not polite. 'Tell the story of Jacques' love life', 'Don't tell the story of Jacques' love life', 'I want you to tell me about Gousse', 'I've had enough ... '
>
> It is no doubt necessary that I follow your wishes, but it is also necessary that I sometimes follow my own. And that is without considering the fact that anyone who allows me to begin a story commits himself to hearing it through to the end.
>
> I told you in the first place ...
>
> Now, when a person says: 'In the first place ... ' it is a way of announcing at least a second place ...
>
> So, in the second place ... listen to me ...
>
> All right then, don't listen to me ... I'll speak to myself ... [Ecoutez-moi, ne m'écoutez pas ... je parlerai tout seul ...] (Diderot 1986: 74; 1981: 84)

The conventions here of low mimetic form, anchored in the lowest expectation of readerly appetite for the 'love story' (what Sterne calls 'reading straight forwards' – Sterne 1967: 43) are explicitly linked here with narrative automatism. The spectre is raised, and mocked, of a vanished relationship between narrator and reader, automatized into a text which is silenced by the greed of linear appetite and no longer knows it is a text. Instead, the narrator makes the text into an anti-Cartesian social space in which the narrator can 'talk to himself', in a parody of the transparent solipsism that would apparently act as a guarantee of consciousness, a joke which patently depends on the presence of the reader to apprehend it, and which thus defeats itself ('Ecoutez-moi, ne m'écoutez pas ... ').

Narrative here is clearly conceived of as a laboratory in the manner of Brecht. As soon as dialogue is silenced, the text becomes automatized. Culturally, this arises from a direct transmission. We know that Diderot derives this effect from Sterne's critique of Locke and Aristotelian aesthetics. Sterne's teasing invention of 'the Hypercritick' (Sterne 1967: 75) is the creation of an automaton-like Authority who measures the distances and times of his narrative with a pendulum and who stands in for the real reader's worst tendencies (naive linear expectations, passive reading), against which, dialogically, Sterne can expose the concidental miracles of the improbable and the true which form the actual process of his narrative.

This (comic) notion of the text as a 'noisy' social space for Diderot has a strong relation to his anti-Cartesianism. The philosopher–clavichord is both player and instrument, and this principle is discernible in several of his major pronouncements on aesthetics, including the *Le Paradoxe sur le comédien* (1773; translated as *The Paradox of the Actor*, Diderot 1994). This dialogue contains the subtext of the 'phantom' that lurks inside the 'imitating machine', which lends a Gothic tinge to all acting and seems at first as if it might be capitulating to the very different Cartesian ghost-in-the-machine. But the climax of the discussion, explicitly linking 'superstition' to the actor's art, has a wonderful sting in the tail which reasserts the dialogic principle, just at the very point of identification:

> My friend, there are three models, natural man, the poet's man, the actor's man. The natural man is not as great as the poet's man, and the poet's man is not as great as the actor's man, the most exaggerated of all. This last climbs on the shoulders of the poet's man and shuts himself inside a huge wicker mannequin [mannequin d'osiers] and becomes the soul within it [dont il est l'âme]. He moves this dummy in a terrifying way [d'une manière effrayante], terrifying even for the poet [même pour le poète] who no longer recognizes himself, and he frightens us [il nous épouvante], as you so rightly said, as children frighten each other by lifting their little short jackets over their heads, dancing about and imitating as best they can the hoarse, lugubrious voice of the phantom they pretend to be [d'un fantôme qu'ils contrefont]. But haven't you ever chanced to see engravings of children's games? Haven't you seen one of a little scallywag [un marmot] coming towards you covered from head to foot in the

frightful-looking mask of an old man [un masque hideux de vieillard]? Beneath this mask he's laughing at his little playmates who are fleeing in terror. This scallywag is the true symbol of the actor; his playmates are the symbols of the audience. (Diderot 1994: 154; 1995: 123–124)

This is a wonderful description of the theatre of horror – the ghastly, terrifying monstrous automaton – except for the last sentence. Acting is allied here by analogy with the uncanny mimetic power of ritual, with childhood nightmares, and ancient superstitious terror: Diderot's editors do not say so, but I take the 'wicker mannequin' to be an allusion to Julius Caesar's description of the Druidic practice of human sacrifice amongst the Celts (Caesar 1963: 340–341). The audience, as we say, 'identifies with' (that is, structurally, imitates) the actor's pretence – that is, his sacrifice of his humunculoid self (see Figure 1). But Diderot also uses the idea of counterfeiting or fiction (*contrefont*) to oppose automatism, as he did with Suzanne's account of her companions' very

Figure 1 'The Wicker Man': a visualization
of Caesar's 'wicker man'

healthy assumptions about her automatism. Terrified, the audience automatically delivers the complementary part of the ritualistic bargain by fleeing. But the point of view is doubled: this is precisely not ritual, the 'phantom' is a fiction, not the actor's self, and the uncanny picture of automatic behaviour is only part of the analogy. The actor who is laughing behind his mask, like the philosopher-clavichord, is both player and instrument.

So the standard account of the relation between Maturin's *Melmoth* (1820) and Diderot's *La Religieuse*, propagated by Mario Praz in 1930, and repeated in a somewhat tempered form in *The Romantic Agony* (1970), is rather reductive. This account claims that Maturin simply plagiarized certain passages of Diderot, particularly the visit of the Vicar-General to the Convent in *La Religieuse*, and 'Gothicized' them – by, for example, changing the gender, and adding a rather Grand Guignol sort of tone to accord with his own anti-Catholic prejudice and that of his audience. But the picture of this cultural transmission is more complicated and indirect than Praz implies. There is also an interest in mechanism, automatism, and 'system' in Maturin's novel, which is more like a piece of rewriting, an appropriation, even a debate, than plagiarism. Praz, however, does not mention this subtext in *Melmoth*, which forms a set of variations on Suzanne's 'J'étais presque reduite à l'état d'automate!' Let us begin with the most obvious example, the first time this idea of automatism is mentioned, in Alonzo Moncada's description (in chapter 30) of his life in the monastery:

> My life was a sea without a tide. The bell did not toll for service with more mechanical punctuality than I obeyed the summons. No automaton, con- structed on the most exquisite principles of mechanism, and obeying those principles with a punctuality almost miraculous, could leave the artist less room for complaint or disappointment, than I did the Superior and the community. I was always first in my place in the choir. I received no visits in the parlour, – when I was permitted to go, I declined the per- mission. If penance was enjoined, I submitted; if relaxation was permitted, I never partook of it. I never asked a dispensation from morning prayers, or from vigils. I was silent in the refectory, – in the garden, I walked alone. I neither thought, nor felt, nor lived, – if life depends on consciousness, and the motions of the will, I slept through my existence like the Simorgh in the Eastern fable. (Maturin 2000: 111)

The dramatic reversal from Diderot is that Moncada is not believed – he is thought by the Jesuits to be acting. Although it is as real as

Suzanne's, so inured are the occupants of the monastery to their automatism, that his fellow-inmates interpret Moncada's behaviour as a piece of impersonation and complain to the Superior:

> They stated to him my abstraction, my mechanical movements, my automaton figure, my meaningless words, my total alienation from the spirit of monastic life, while my scrupulous, *wooden, jointless*, exactness in its forms was only a mockery. (Maturin 2000: 112)

The monastery is a system that cannot see itself. It is in fact a kind of theatre which Moncada unconsciously satirizes by passively adopting its models. Here ritual and superstition occur so much as part of the social surface that Moncada's automatism seems like bad acting.

Automatism is indeed part of the theatre of terror here, too, and the relation between hypocrisy, acting and ritualized behaviour is also part of Maturin's meditation. The link is present in the theatrical allusion that Moncada makes as he sneaks a glimpse of the diabolical Director, the moment after the man has smiled acknowledgement that it is he who has had Alonzo's brother Juan killed:

> I raised my head a few moments after, and saw him, with an habitual motion (it could not have been more), make the sign of the cross, as a clock in some distant passage struck. This sight reminded me of the play so often acted in Madrid, and which I had seen in my days of liberation, – El diablo Predicador. You smile, Sir, at such a recollection operating at such a moment, but it is a fact; and had you witnessed that play under the singular circumstances I did, you would not wonder at my being struck with the coincidence. In this performance the infernal spirit is the hero, and in the disguise of a monk he appears in a convent, where he torments and persecutes the community with a mixture of malignity and mirth truly satanic. One night that I saw it performed, a groupe of monks were carrying the Host to a dying person, the walls of the theatre were so slight, that we could distinctly hear the sound of the bell which they ring on that occasion. In an instant, actors, audience, and all, were on their knees, and the devil, who happened to be on the stage, knelt among the rest and crossed himself with visible marks of a devotion equally and edifying. You will allow the coincidence to be irresistibly striking. (Maturin 2000: 246–247)

The analogy is a complicated one, and the relation between ritual and acting, automatism and theatrical representation, is a carefully constructed tautology. The text is layered, so that the speaker, the Spaniard Moncada, is consciously digressing from his narrative and drawing attention to his role as a speaker in the text, to an audience in the text, the Irishman, Young John Melmoth. One level of representation opens onto the next. This text literalizes the Greek root of hypocrisy as acting (*ypocritos* is Greek for an actor). The Devil, the ultimate hypocrite – the ultimate actor – unconsciously acts out his real nature when he stops acting, because the actor is already acting in a greater drama which converts the play (in which he performs the role of the Devil) into a play-within-a-play. The condition of forgetting himself in one play is to remember himself in another. Drama is satirically assimilated to ritual, and the effect of the latter is doubled and made into a contradiction. Then, it is reflected by Lockeian 'coincidence' in the dialogue of the speaker, and made into an analogy for something else. The level of representation is 'noisily' (that is, redundantly) insisted on all the way down through the layers.

The aesthetic self-consciousness of the dialogic text coexists in the same frame with an anti-clerical propaganda point, as it does in Diderot's *La Religieuse* (though it is not the same one). But we should be clear here: Maturin's real subject in *Melmoth* is the distortion caused to the individual psyche by 'systems of belief'. As a Huguenot, he is often thought of as a Calvinist and then this is reductively fed into his text. But even in his early work, *The Wild Irish Boy* (1808), we find him putting ironical speeches into the mouth of his narrator Ormesby about the Calvinist 'system' and the automatic nature of belief (Maturin 2000: xxiv). The subtext of mechanism returns to the text when Maturin describes Elinor's Puritan aunt in Chapter 30:

> and that figure that walks beside her, so stiff and rectangular, that it seems as [if] its motion was regulated by mechanism, whose sharp eyes are directed so straight forward, that they see neither tree on the right hand, or glade on the left, or heaven above, or earth beneath, or anything but a dim vision of mystic theology for ever before them, which is aptly reflected in their cold contemplative light, that is the Puritan maiden sister of her brother, with whom Elinor had fixed her residence. Her dress is arranged with as much precision as if a mathematician had calculated the angles of every fold. (Maturin 2000: 526)

When the aunt attempts to recover power over her niece, the connection between the imitating machine and the isolating 'system' of belief is explicit in the text:

> About this time, her Puritan aunt made a strong effort to recover Elinor out of the snare of the enemy. She wrote a long letter ... adjuring her apostate

> niece ... to return to the guide of her youth, and the covenant of her God ...
> and to flee to the city of refuge while its gates were yet open to receive her.
> She urged on her the truth, power and blessedness of the system of Calvin,
> which she termed the gospel. (Maturin 2000: 540–541)

The tart irony of this final comment subjects the mechanism of Calvinism to the same satirical metaphor as Catholicism. Moncada's formulation meets both cases of 'system':

> I was like a clock whose hands are pushed forward, and I struck the hours
> I was impelled to strike. When a powerful agency is thus exercised on us,
> – when another undertakes to think, feel, and act for us, we are delighted
> to transfer to him, not only our physical, but our moral responsibility. We
> say, with selfish cowardice and self-flattering passiveness, 'Be it so – you
> have decided for me', – without reflecting that at the bar of God there is
> no bail. (Maturin 2000: 200)

The tone of the last remark is hardly Diderot's, though I like to think he would have recognized and approved of the ethical thrust and the metaphorical logic of this passage, with perhaps the rider: 'if he exists'. Diderot feels equally able to satirize Jansenism and Jesuitism in *La Religieuse* and both novelists refer to the controversy over grace between Molinism and Jansenism, but it is the necessity of invoking and refuting the horrific and disturbing nature of the 'imitating machine' which matters most, not these sectarian conflicts.

What I have been arguing here is the case for a partial overlap between two writers who are conventionally labelled Enlightenment and Gothic. I am not trying to minimize the differences between the Protestant appropriation of the Enlightenment, evident in Maturin's text, and Diderot's arguments against the existence of God. But there are some evident continuities between the texts which derive from a particular conjunction between scepticism about 'superstition' and aesthetic form, which Praz's charge of a rather transparent 'plagiarism' tends to distract us from, I feel. Rather, it is a question of more being appropriated by Maturin, and at a higher level of generality than one might have suspected. Both writers are committed to dialogic form, and insist on subjecting linear narrative and mimetic form to noisy dialogic scrutiny. Their texts are laboratories; but in Maturin's case, as Kathleen Fowler's excellent work on the allusions to The Book of Job in *Melmoth* has proved (Fowler 1986: 133–147), the dialogic space of his Faustian text makes it a laboratory of faith, its scornful irony full of doubt and challenge to the reader. Diderot's aesthetic theory also links the theme of self-consciousness and dialogic form to the laboratory of belief, ironically using the gothic forms of superstition and ritual as modes of doubt.

The transmission of these metaphors of mechanism and automatism is a complex one when one looks at the broader context. Diderot gets much of his dialogic form, his teasing of the reader's linear expectations, and even his meditation on the 'vibrating strings', from Sterne's parodies of Locke, but also from Locke himself. The emotional concentration and the claustrophobia in *La Religieuse* derive from the work of Richardson, which is another story and another connection with the Gothic tradition that limited space forbids proper treatment of here (Praz 1970). Maturin gains much from Sterne, too, with Swift in the foreground and Cervantes in the background. Garrick, who inspired Diderot directly with his ability to pass instantly from a portrayal of happiness to fear and grief, is an important element in the work of Sterne, and Maturin quotes from Garrick's adaptation of *Romeo and Juliet* in *Melmoth* (Maturin 2000: 645, note 1). Maturin and Diderot thus independently share a self-conscious fictional heritage whose master trope is the theatre; this shapes the different questions they ask of the novel genre in a demonstrably common manner.

References

Alexander, P. (ed.) (1951) *Shakespeare: Complete Works*, London and Glasgow, Collins.

Bleiler, E.F. (ed.) (1964) *Best Ghost Stories of J.S. Le Fanu*, New York, Dover Inc.

Caesar, J. (1963) *The Gallic War*, trans. H.J. Edwards, Cambridge MA: Harvard University Press.

Clapton, G.T. (1930) 'Balzac, Baudelaire, and Maturin', *French Quarterly*, 12:2 and 3 (June and September), 66–84 and 97–115.

Diderot, D. (1966) *Rameau's Nephew and D'Alembert's Dream*, trans. L. Tancock, Harmondsworth, Penguin.

—— (1972) *The Nun*, trans. L. Tancock, Harmondsworth, Penguin.

—— (1975) *Oeuvres complètes*, eds H. Diekman and J. Varloot, Tome XI, Paris, Hermann.

—— (1981) *Oeuvres complètes*, eds H. Diekman and J. Varloot, Tome XXIII, Paris, Hermann.

—— (1986) *Jacques The Fatalist* (1986), trans. M. Henry, Harmondsworth, Penguin.

—— (1987) *Oeuvres complètes*, eds H. Diekman and J. Varloot, Tome XVII, Paris, Hermann.

—— (1994) *Selected Writing on Art and Literature*, trans. Geoffrey Bremner, Harmondsworth: Penguin.

—— (1995) *Oeuvres complètes*, eds H. Diekman and J. Varloot, Tome XX, Paris, Hermann.

Fowler, K. (1986) 'Hieroglyphics in Fire', *Studies in Romanticism*, 25, 133–147.

Frayling, C. (1992) *Vampyres: Lord Byron to Count Dracula*, London, Faber & Faber.

Furbank, P.N. (1992) *Diderot*, London, Secker and Warburg.

Hoffmann, E.T.W. (1982) *Tales of Hoffmann*, trans. R.J. Hollingdale *et al.*, Harmondsworth, Penguin.

Maturin, C. (2000) *Melmoth The Wanderer*, ed. V. Sage, Harmondsworth, Penguin.

Praz, M. (1930) 'An English Imitation of Diderot's *La Religieuse*', *Review of English Studies*, VI, 429–436.

—— (1970) *The Romantic Agony*, Oxford, Oxford University Press.

Sage, V. (1988) *Horror Fiction in the Protestant Tradition*, London, Macmillan.

Sterne, L. (1967) *The Life and Opinions of Tristram Shandy*, ed. G. Saintsbury, London, Dent.

4

Verging on the Gothic:
Melmoth's journey to France

CATHERINE LANONE

Often considered to be the last true Gothic novel,[1] *Melmoth* was translated into French as early as 1821, first by Mme E.F. Bégin under the
title *L'Homme du mystère, ou histoire de Melmoth le voyageur*, then
by J. Cohen under the title *Melmoth ou l'homme errant*. But the text
was cut and altered; only in 1965 was a full translation given by Jacque-
line Marc-Chadourne. Jean-Jacques Pauvert chose to publish this with
André Breton's famous 1954 preface, which praised its influence on
French literature. Not surprisingly, the leader of Surrealism considered all the hallucinatory desires, the dark castles and visions found in
Gothic novels as a potent 'drug'; indeed, Breton compared the visual
impact of *The Castle of Otranto* to the cinematic thrill caused in 1929
by Bunuel's eerie image of the razor cutting through the eye in *Un
chien andalou*. But Breton seems to find *Melmoth* particularly compelling, describing it as a great meteorite flashing through the frame of
the Gothic window, an endless shower of ashes mysteriously suspended
for a brief moment ('On doit attendre jusqu'à 1820 pour qu'un nouveau
météore se détache du cadre rituel de la fenêtre ogivale, suspendant son
interminable pluie de cendres' (Breton 1996: 15)). I wish to pursue
here the motif of the shower of ashes, and discuss the way *Melmoth*,
itself influenced by Diderot's *La Religieuse* (Lévy 1995: 579), crossed
the Channel to spark fresh inspiration in France at the precise moment
when the great Gothic fires of damnation were yielding to the ashen
precision of realism in both countries.

For Annie Le Brun, nineteenth-century French literature defines
itself in terms of its relationship with the Gothic – especially with
Melmoth the Wanderer – whether this influence is acknowledged or not

(Le Brun 1982). At a time when France was still scarred by the violence of the Revolution and of Napoleonic wars, and a new bourgeois order was emerging, the sheer darkness of *Melmoth* was bound to trigger fear and fascination, especially since the novel glosses over the circumstances which lead Melmoth to surrender his soul; it focuses on the aftermath, the long quest for someone who might sell a soul and free the tempter. Maturin becomes 'a practitioner of psychopathological taxonomy' (Punter 1996: 128), but the taxonomy is curiously unstable, as cruel religious institutions (Sage 1988) and everyday evil outdo the arch villain, whose death eventually fails to provide secure catharsis.

Thus *Melmoth the Wanderer* darkly conveys the disturbing forces plaguing society, and depicts potential disruption and the violence inherent in humanity. Baldick defines the Gothic as a 'sickening descent into disintegration' (Baldick 1992: xix). In this case, we have several descents into degradation and abjection; the pattern of claustrophobic enclosure occurs both symbolically – through poverty and lack of love – and literally – in the cells of the Inquisition or the subterranean labyrinth of convents. This core of darkness was bound to appeal to Romantics and Surrealists, who were fascinated by the apparition of Melmoth on a lonely rock towering above the stormy sea, or by the play on nightmares and dreams – those dreams which magically take Immalee back to her island every night.

Indeed, the text builds claustrophobic boundaries which it challenges, through the figure of the ubiquitous eponymous character whom no walls can stop; who appears quietly at the bottom of a hidden cell in Spain or in the middle of a wild, luscious island; who appears unchanged from one century to the next. Just as we share the sense of entrapment which shatters all secondary characters, we are fascinated by the dreamlike, bewildering erasure of all spatial boundaries as the powerful protagonist switches effortlessly from tale to tale.

The most subversive element in *Melmoth the Wanderer* may well be the structure of the text itself. Balzac especially was fascinated by Maturin's daring energy, calling him, in the Preface to *La Peau de chagrin*, the most original writer in contemporary Britain. Indeed, *Melmoth* plays obsessively with textual boundaries, embedding narrative layers to create a fractal set of Chinese boxes. Centuries go by while the focus switches from one sorry plight to another, weaving an ironic rosary of evil, as Monçada warns his listener: 'have patience, and you will find that we are all beads strung on the same string' (Maturin 2000: 332).

Thus the novel metatextually exposes its own devices, foregrounding gaps rather than excusing them, the way in which the Gothic text seeks both to establish and challenge boundaries, subverting systematic claustration into an exploration of emptiness, discovering a dark, giddy void at the heart of life. The novel delights in its literally amazing structure. The traditional witness account, which is faithfully reported, is mocked by the totally illogical discovery of an old Jew's cabinet of curiosities, in which Monçada must sit by skeletons and copy the wondrous tales of Melmoth, including the tediously slow courtship of Immalee, though no possible explanation can ever be found for such a text. The oral repetition of the written copy of the mysterious illogical text (which paradoxically allows a straight heterodiegetic approach to the Wanderer's own love story) creates a dizzy narrative structure. Victor Sage points out 'the relentless fragmentation of the process of transmission' (Sage 2000: xviii). Rosemary Jackson also emphasizes the way in which *Melmoth* deconstructs the very notion of representation, equivocating over interpretation, interrogations and evasions: 'Its relentlessly fragmented structure permits the reader little security. One scene spirals and merges into another, each tale breaking off to lead to another tale, equally truncated, incomplete' (Jackson 1988: 104). The tainted palimpsest expands yet shrinks, the tales which are read, copied, told and retold or burnt, weave a cancerous texture, as if the text were eroded by an uncertain disease.

Thematically the reader must enter this deterritorialized, wandering text in order to share, not the story of the wanderer, but his bitter, inconclusive experience, along a dark line of flight which leads nowhere. As the narratives function as screens, we follow descent after descent towards anger and despair, but the object of temptation, the lure of the pact with the devil, is supposedly barred from language, only to reappear repeatedly elsewhere, sometimes through slips of the tongue. In Deleuzian terms, what we have here is a rhizome, a subterranean set of ramifications connecting at random. Melmoth's doomed, weary quest is shared by the reader who shifts from story to story at the very moment when satisfactory closure is denied. Baited, the reader follows the narrator, from one gloomy place of horror to the next, trapped by the slippery, treacherous narrative pact. And yet the end tantalizingly escapes the reader's grasp, as Monçada and young Melmoth play detectives by the sea.

Because of its unusual structure and bitter darkness, *Melmoth the Wanderer* aroused a fascination which was to last for more than a

CATHERINE LANONE

century in France. Whereas Melmoth's son by Immalee dies mysteriously, perhaps strangled by his father, Melmoth's textual 'hideous
progeny' – to borrow Mary Shelley's expression – may well be found
across the Channel, especially among the poets of darkness. One
instantly thinks of Lautréamont or the Surrealists who redeemed the
Gothic in a new era of doubt and darkening political prospects, but the
most significant figure may well be Baudelaire – that advocate of modernity enamoured with satanic rebellion, who chose as poetical objects
skeletons, prostitutes and the depth of the abyss. Indeed, in his critical
writings Baudelaire repeatedly refers to Maturin as a key influence,
though he was no poet. He uses him to define his subversive aesthetic
perspective, claiming that the dominant mode of modern art must be
infernal: 'Je veux dire que l'art moderne a une tendance essentiellement
démoniaque'[2] (Baudelaire 1990: 770). Lumping together Beethoven,
Byron, Maturin and Poe, Baudelaire celebrates literary correspondences,
the deep dark unison illuminating the clouds lurking within the human
soul. We too may trace in his 'flowers of evil' the withered blossoms
plucked by the Wanderer, which mar the exotic purity of Immalee's
island. Balancing Christianity with erotic blasphemy, *Les Fleurs du mal*
(1861)[3] display dark beds as deep as tombs, perfume flasks containing the
decaying body of lost love, journeys beyond Eros towards Thanatos.
Indeed, the long poem entitled 'The Voyage' roams from place to place,
attempting to answer the haunting question, 'but what have you seen?',
yet the world shrinks, a mere oasis of horror in a wearisome desert.
In the end, the speaker yearns to dive into the unknown, no matter
whether it be heaven or hell, so long as he finds something new. Rather
than Baudelaire's beloved Poe, whom he translated,[4] the key influence
here is Maturin's Melmoth, hopelessly wandering on the margins of the
human world. Indeed, Baudelaire turned him into the epitome of the
romantic outcast:

> Let us remember Melmoth, this admirable emblem. His unbearable suf-
> fering comes from the disproportion between his marvellous skills, which
> he acquired instantly through the pact with the Devil, and the surround-
> ings where he is doomed to live as a creature of God. And none of those
> whom he wishes to seduce consents to buy back from him, at the same
> price, his own dreadful privileged condition ... The man who would be
> God has thus soon fallen, by virtue of an uncontrollable moral law, lower
> than his own real nature. This is a soul selling itself bit by bit. (Baudelaire
> 1976: 438)[5]

74

Presumably each narrative episode of *Melmoth* corresponds to the itemized decay of the unredeemed soul. Here the praise of Melmoth is connected with the 'sulphurous dawn' of drugs, as the modern way of selling one's soul to the devil, but elsewhere Baudelaire shows that he is not simply fascinated by doom and eternal wandering, by the quest for a victim, but by Melmoth's laughter, which he defines in his 'Essay on the essence of laughter'[6] as 'a laughter which never sleeps, like a sickness which goes its own way and obeys some providential order'. For him, Melmoth is a contradiction in terms, 'a living contradiction', whose icy laughter tears one's entrails: 'And thus Melmoth's laughter is the highest expression of pride, and perpetually fulfils its task, by tearing and burning the lips of the irremediably laughing man' (Baudelaire 1990: 250) (my translation). Laughter is the true sign of hubris, the true curse. Melmoth is of course in many ways a satirist, and Punter praises his 'supremely self-conscious wit' (Punter 1996: 126), while Lévy points out that such laughter comes from an inner split, as when Melmoth both seduces Immalee and wishes to protect her from himself; laughter becomes the seam between good and evil, self and other, at the very edge of pain, enjoyment and defiance. Such devilish laughter echoes in Baudelaire's prose poem 'The Flawed Glass Maker' (1862), in which the poet's persona, exhilarated by his own madness, drops a flowerpot on a maker of window glass – shattering all his panes – on the grounds that he should make magic glass, pink panes that prove that life is beautiful, rather than ordinary glass.

While Baudelaire's fascination with *Melmoth* is fairly obvious, it is perhaps more surprising to find Balzac among the early worshippers of the novel. While the Gothic implies darkness and mad desire, Balzac's fiction establishes the realm of realism and explores nineteenth-century society throughout the 'Human Comedy'. Though Hugo's romantic melodramatic tastes may be automatically deemed to descend from the Gothic, Balzac's achievement seems at first sight to have little, if anything, to do with the Gothic. Yet if Balzac set the bulk of his work within the boundaries of realism, his early writings show very different aspirations. Balzac chose as his early pen names the pompous British title 'Lord R'hoone' and then the more European-sounding 'Horace de St Aubin', which presumably echoes both Horace Walpole and Ann Radcliffe's *Mysteries of Udolpho*. In so doing, Balzac was obviously paying lip service to the tastes of fashionable friends such as Nodier. But there was more to this than a mere fad. For perhaps the

Gothic was the inevitable threshold of 'The Human Comedy': French realism was actually built on the very ruins of the Gothic, and Balzac had to exorcise the shadowy ghost of Melmoth before he could find his own voice.

Indeed, among what Balzac later called his literary 'rubbish',[7] the first significant text is unquestionably *Le Centenaire ou les deux Beringheld*, published in 1822, and re-issued in 1837 with little alteration under the title *Le Sorcier ou les deux Beringheld* (Balzac 1990). Clearly, though he openly criticized his early work, Balzac considered it worth publishing again. Unfortunately there is little magic in the Sorcerer's tale, and the frightful figure of the 'centenaire', the ageless old man who supposedly dominates the story, fails to arouse horror or even terror. The text is a clumsy attempt to rival the man he considered to be the greatest of English writers; indeed, Lévy points out that Balzac considered Maturin to be as important as Byron, Hoffmann or Goethe (Lévy 1995: 600). Certainly, *The Sorcerer* is so redolent of *Melmoth* that critics such as Breton and Barbéris (1965) dismiss the book as mere plagiarism. The text imitates the split between generations, and tries to spice it up by having the icy ancestor beget his own descendant, replacing an impotent father. Balzac also uses some of Immalee's love speeches (actually, he even drew upon them in writing his own love letters!). The Spanish Inquisition is replaced by Napoleon's campaign in Egypt. Balzac's wanderer retains Melmoth's fiery burning eyes, but he is extremely old throughout the novel, and he is preternaturally tall, clearly borrowing a few features from *Frankenstein*'s monster. Indeed, no longer content with attempting to steal souls, he abducts desperate maidens to steal the fluid of life so that he can regenerate himself. If Gothic castles bore Balzac and he considers their inhabitants degenerate, he nevertheless attempts tackling the subterranean maze at the end, only to complicate it with scientific apparatus (strangely enough, the wanderer has also proved to be a mysterious doctor who appears throughout the book). Misreading both *Melmoth* and *Frankenstein*, Balzac's work also botches the technique of embedded narrations, proudly announcing, for instance, Beringheld's memoirs, only to shift to a heterodiegetic flashback delivered by an intrusive if obsequious narrator who claims he is summing it all up for our own sake. Whilst we might retrospectively wish to dignify this work by describing it as pastiche, the book was probably meant to be taken seriously at the time of publication. It is Balzac's first piece of real writing, and might perhaps best lie forgotten, were it not for the fact that its very flaws suggest a desire to modernize the plot, and thus stage the action on the impossible boundary between a remote Gothic scenario and bourgeois society. The economy of restraint bars the powers of darkness, but they are not so easily subdued.

Melmoth réconcilié is Balzac's sequel to Maturin's novel, and it becomes extremely interesting as it attempts to lead us out of the Gothic into the world of proper bourgeois writing. But the parody seems to mock its own purpose. Perhaps Balzac was not simply yielding to fashion when he wrote *Le Centenaire*, since the fascination with *Melmoth* appears again in 1828, by which time Balzac had bought Cohen's 1821 translation, and was hoping to print a second edition. *Melmoth réconcilié* was first published in 1835, and Balzac gives as an afterthought a short summary of *Melmoth* in a postscript, for those who may not know the book and who thus cannot understand his own tale. Balzac adds that though it may have seemed reasonable to Maturin not to send his protagonist to Paris, the demon must needs have found on his own the path to a city where the odds for accepting the bargain must be about a thousand to one. Amusingly enough, as Le Yaouanc points out,[8] Balzac's Melmoth reaches Paris in 1821, precisely when the translation of the book appeared (Balzac 1979: 1400).

Melmoth réconcilié is usually seen as a metaphysical tale, in which Balzac asserts potential redemption.[9] Instead of vanishing near the home of his ancestors, Melmoth dies in peace; after having found a victim at last, he confesses his crimes and spreads the divine light of revelation among the people surrounding his death bed. In writing the novel, Balzac borrows a few features from the original *Melmoth*, such as the burning eyes, the grim laugh and the absolute knowledge of his victims' circumstances, as well as the heavenly music which is followed by a ghastly vision. A few new fantastic effects are introduced, as when Melmoth displays his power by replacing the rainy evening street by the spectacle of a bright summer's day, or creates double vision at the theatre where, instead of a comedy with a quick-change artist, the victim witnesses the comedy of his own life as his mistress cuckolds him, the very mistress who now sits and laughs beside him, and for whom he sells his soul. The process of wandering from place to place and story to story is condensed into a bifocal show.[10] What is shrinking here, however, is the very nature of the world beyond boundaries offered by the supernatural traveller and his Faustian pact. The abnormal rule which triggers an abnormal unquenchable thirst for rebellion is no longer cruel religion but money. Melmoth has fallen into a materialistic world: the cell is bound by the iron bars of a cashier's window, Paris becomes the hellish city of temptation: 'cette ville aux tentations, cette succursale de l'Enfer' (Balzac 1979: 346), and it is through mediocre orgies that the mediocre cashier learns to yearn for the divine, panting for the unknown with a soul parched by debauchery. For Castanier no longer attempts to spread evil, he is only a demon in the making, weak and mean, helpless and powerless. He ends up in the stock exchange, buying the soul of a bankrupt investor, and in a single evening the hellish alliance is exchanged so many times that it loses all value. Thus, the narrator cynically concludes, the enormous power unleashed by Maturin was lost.

Though fantastic, the story is neither a failure nor truly Gothic; instead, it is a Gothic recantation. What Balzac is staging is not so much devalued desire or the triumph of money, as the devaluation of Gothic clichés. It is no surprise that the story should focus on Castanier rather than Melmoth, and that he should be a mere cashier forging a letter to steal money from a London bank. Borrowing from England can only be a simulacrum. For the pact is the coin which shifts from hand to hand, losing its value. What Balzac is coming to terms with here, with savage irony, is his own failure to transpose the Gothic to modern Paris, and adapt it to modern society. In a society which has given up honour for money, or in Barthes's words a noble name for a financial figure, the wild darkness of absolute desire can only be commodified, and thus hollowed out. Gothic images shrink into worthless clichés, coins which are worn out as they slip from hand to hand. Hence the mirror image, when Melmoth's name first appears as he signs his name backwards, from right to left. Hence also the first portrait we have, which deliberately mingles myth and cliché, from the unbearable eyes to topical puritanical clothes, so that the apparition is simply cut out as an Englishman: '[everything], including the shape of his clothes, bespoke an Englishman. He reeked of Englishness' (Balzac 1979: 350) (my translation). The tale ends with the ludicrous babble of some German 'Demon-expert' and the jokes of 'a devil of' a clerk; but this is not a completely irrelevant ending. The repetition of '*fiat*' and '*fiat lux*' actually emphasizes the arbitrary nature of the dénouement, in which the writer's '*fiat*' dismisses the darkness of Gothic clichés.

Before discarding the circulation of Gothic clichés as sterile imitation, though, Balzac wrote a fascinating novel in which he seems to step beyond the boundaries of both realism and the Gothic and to reach a unique balance. In *The Wild Ass's Skin*, which was the literary event of 1831, Balzac does not seek to imitate *Melmoth*, but he does rediscover the pact with evil, and rewrites it as a metaphor for desire and the passing of time. We no longer have a tale spanning centuries to arouse despair but, by a metonymic inversion, a life which is reduced to a shrinking piece of shagreen. The echoing French title *La Peau de chagrin* refers to shagreen or leather, but also sounds like the skin of sorrow, stressing the horror of nightmarish imprisonment beyond the boundaries of ordinary human life. The protagonist, the fair angelic Raphaël, meets his tempter in the guise of an old antique dealer, a gaunt Mephistophelian seer. The antique shop mixes the realistic delight for lists of objects with the darker intricacies of the Gothic maze, in an 'ocean of furnishings, inventions, fashions, works of art and relics' (Balzac 1977: 37). In the gilded rooms packed with trinkets, the windows grow dark, the fantasmagoric portraits quiver and dance, objects shift shapes in a 'weird witches' sabbath worthy of the fantasies glimpsed by Dr Faust' (Balzac 1977: 42). As in *Melmoth the Wanderer*, a portrait appears, this time an icon of youth and beauty painted by Raphaël's namesake. Raphaël's Christ is the antithesis of the deadly talisman, the magic skin which materializes the paradoxical double find of transgression: it grants all wishes, thus allowing its owner to step beyond the bounds of human life, but it consumes itself, as each wish shrinks the limits of the owner's life. Like Melmoth, the owner can but wander through the liminal space of death-in-life. Granting utmost power and utter helplessness, the talisman with its uncanny shimmer and supple solidity glitters like a comet, an image which foreshadows the shortness of Raphaël's life. Once again, the comet suggests fire and ashes, endless wandering but also regular, inevitable repetition and return. When Raphaël cries out that he would like the skin to grant his wishes, the antique dealer quickly replies that he has signed the pact, though nothing has been written.

Dismissing conventions, Balzac then switches to the growing awareness and horror of the victim of the pact, a theme which is extremely similar in spirit, though not in detail, to the core of *Melmoth*. Satisfied boundless desire is contrasted with the obsessive mapping of the ever-shrinking boundary of the skin, the ever-dwindling red line signalling loss of life and energy. This time, Balzac gets all the uncanny effects right. Raphaël seeks a way out, not by looking for another victim but by begging science to save him, yet neither chemistry nor an hydraulic press can manage to stretch the skin. Science pales before uncanny reality; and the horrified Raphaël becomes a wanderer fleeing his beloved Pauline, for each desire burns away his life. Like Melmoth he is the shunned traveller whose presence is unbearable. When he attempts to take the waters, he is challenged to a duel as he refuses to leave, an episode which echoes the death of Immalee's brother. He then retreats to the middle of nowhere in the centre of France, Auvergne, a place which is clearly for Balzac beyond the boundaries of the civilized world, and which he describes fancifully, depicting sheer drops of lava. More than Balzac's unsteady geography, it is the abject appearance of Raphael's body which fascinates, the shrunken bloodless figure burnt by the hellish prospect of impending demise. Like Melmoth, Raphaël ultimately returns home, not to the place of his ancestors, but to his apartment in Paris where Pauline finds him. When she suddenly understands the situation and attempts to commit suicide to end all possibility of pleasure, Raphaël forgets all his resolutions to avoid desire and throws himself upon her. In this orgasmic 'embrace' he bites her breast, a dénouement which must be connected with the tale of the betrayed lovers who were starved below the convent in *Melmoth*.

The awkward epilogue gives us another key to Balzac's own version of the Gothic within this tale. While Pauline is turned into the spirit of Nature, and thus descends from Immalee's virgin island, Foedora, the other woman who first doomed Raphaël to attempt suicide, is suddenly identified as Society. The peremptory allegorical conclusion might puzzle the reader who remembers the vibrant erotic and voyeuristic scene in which Raphaël ventured into the countess's 'Gothic boudoir' and her bedroom to watch her go to bed. But it also adds a realistic element to the Gothic theme of a desire which burns unto death, for the pact with the Devil has been replaced by social hubris: one now loses one's soul by contracting debts and rashly adoring cold-hearted women, by following a new religion which obscures the pure Pauline. As such, *La Peau de chagrin* constitutes the true threshold of Balzac's 'Human Comedy'. Exposing in a nutshell the erotic economy of the modern world – and the modern text – the talisman creates a gloomy Gothic spell which is doomed to shrink and vanish, as dark textual enchantment yields to the cooler 'lost illusions' of the bulk of the work. Yet even in the ironic 'Human Comedy', some of the power of the dissections of the Parisian vanity fair may well come from unconscious Gothic reminiscences, as the arch deceiver and tempter Vautrin wanders from book to book, with the significant nickname of 'Trompe la Mort'...

Thus Maturin becomes a soothsayer, disseminating in France the ashes and sparks of his words, to use a Shelleyan image. Melmoth journeys to France not only to inform Baudelairian darkness or Surrealistic fantasies, but also to signify how a life can be corroded by barren capitalism as well as instinct and desire. Graham Robb considers that *The Wild Ass's Skin* is 'an astonishing exercise in psychic autobiography' (Robb 1995: 179), foreshadowing Balzac's theory of energy, abstinence and excess, which led to his own early death: 'The pattern of Balzac's life is laid out, as if in a premonitory dream' (Robb 1995: 179). The evil pact ultimately concerns writing itself, just as it did, perhaps, for Maturin. According to Michel Butor, the artist must choose to sacrifice his own share of heaven in order to bring revelation to men: 'such is the way Balzac interprets Faust and rewrites *Melmoth*' (Butor 1998: 123). As Sage points out, allusions to painting in *Melmoth the Wanderer* already question the mimetic connection between life and art, in 'that extraordinary anticipation of decadence which so attracts the French' (Sage 2000: xxiii). No wonder that Oscar Wilde, whose *Portrait of Dorian Gray* owes much to his great-uncle Maturin and Balzac's piece of shagreen, should have chosen to live in Paris under the fateful name of Sebastian Melmoth. Thus by crossing the Channel, *Melmoth* ceased to be a religious novel and turned into a metaphor for the curse of the artist. In Balzac's words, desire burns yet power destroys.

Notes

1   'In literary histories, *Melmoth the Wanderer* (1820) often marks the end of the Gothic romance proper, as a genre' (Sage 2000: vii).
2   This is taken from an essay on Théodore de Banville which was first published in 1861.
3   Though a first collection appeared in 1857, and poems were added in 1868, the 1861 edition is usually considered to be the most significant one.
4   In 1852, Baudelaire read Poe avidly, convinced he had found a kindred spirit; he felt tremendous admiration for his conception of poetry. He had already completed a short translation in 1848, and between 1852 and 1865 he translated Poe's major works, including among other things *The Raven*, *The Black Cat*, *The Murders in the Rue Morgue*, *The Narrative of Arthur Gordon Pym*, *Eureka*, *The Philosophy of Composition*, and *Tales of the Grotesque and the Arabesque*. One should pay particular attention to *Histoires extraordinaires*, which was published in 1856, and

Nouvelles histoires extraordinaires, which was published in 1857. The prefaces Baudelaire wrote show intellectual osmosis, to the point of sometimes plagiarizing Poe's *Poetic Principle*. Lemaître explains that towards the end of his life Baudelaire also wished to translate *Melmoth*, since he found the existing version deeply unsatisfactory (Baudelaire 1990: 249).

5 Translation mine. This appeared in 1860 as part of Baudelaire's preface to his long commentary (which included long extracts which he had translated) on De Quincey's *Confessions of an English Opium Eater*.

6 *De l'essence du rire* was first published in 1855 in *Le Portefeuille*.

7 The expression appears in a letter which Balzac addressed to his mother on 30 October 1835. When prefacing a recent edition of *The Sorcerer*, René Guise was so struck by the term that he checked the manuscript letter, assuming one should read 'oeuvres' (works) instead of 'ordures' (rubbish). But the hypothesis was proved wrong as the word 'ordures' appeared beyond all doubt.

8 Moïse Le Yaouanc is one of the editors of the famous 1979 'Pléiade edition', along with P.G. Castex, T. Bodin, P. Citron, M. Fargeaud, H. Gauthier and R. Guise.

9 The religious implications of Melmoth's failure to find a victim are discussed by Fowler; for her the righteous steadiness of the potential victims is crucial: 'Balzac's wry suggestion notwithstanding, it is not that Melmoth is remarkably stupid in selecting his targets … Like Satan, Melmoth fails to part his victims from God not because he is weak, but because they are strong' (Fowler 1986: 527–528). Balzac's deliberate shift is particularly revealing.

10 Interestingly enough, Sage draws attention to theatricality in *Melmoth*: 'For the Wanderer, moving across history and geography is like moving through the auditorium of a theatre' (Sage 2000: xx).

References

Baldick, C. (ed.) (1992) *The Oxford Book of Gothic Tales*, Oxford, Oxford University Press.
de Balzac, H. (1979) *La Comédie humaine*, coll. Pléiade, Paris, Gallimard.
—— (1990) *Le Sorcier ou les deux Beringheld* [1837], Preface by René Guise, Paris, José Corti.
—— (1977) *The Wild Ass's Skin*, trans. H.J. Hunt, Harmondsworth, Penguin.
Barbéris, P. (1965) *Aux sources de Balzac: les romans de jeunesse*, Paris, Les Bibliophiles de l'originale.
Baudelaire, C. (1976) *Oeuvres complètes*, ed. C. Pichois, coll. Pléiade, Paris, Gallimard.
—— (1990) *Curiosités esthétiques, L'Art romantique, et autres oeuvres critiques*, ed. H. Lemaître, Paris, Bordas.
Breton, A. (1996) *Preface*, in C.R. Maturin, *L'Homme errant*, Paris, Phébus [1965], pp. xi–xx.
Le Brun, A. (1982) *Les Châteaux de la subversion*, Paris, Jean-Jacques Pauvert.
Butor, M. (1990) *La Comédie humaine*, coll. Pléiade, Paris, Gallimard.
—— (1998) *Le Marchand et le génie*, Paris, Edition de la différence.
Fowler, K. (1986) 'Hieroglyphics in Fire: *Melmoth the Wanderer*', *Studies in Romanticism*, 25, pp. 133–147.
Jackson, R. (1988) *The Literature of Subversion*, London, Routledge [1981].
Lévy, M. (1995) *Le Roman gothique anglais 1764–1824*, Paris, Albin Michel [1967].
Maturin, C.R. (2000) *Melmoth the Wanderer*, ed. V. Sage, Harmondsworth, Penguin Classics [1820].
Punter, D. (1996) *The Literature of Terror*, Vol. 1, Harlow, Longman.

Robb, G. (1995) *Balzac*, London, Macmillan [1994].
Sage, V. (1988) *Horror Fiction in the Protestant Tradition*, London, Macmillan.
—— (2000) *Preface*, in C.R. Maturin, *Melmoth the Wanderer*, Harmondsworth, Penguin Classics.

5

Europhobia: the Catholic other in Horace Walpole and Charles Maturin

ROBERT MILES

In literature it is hard to avoid the 'other'. But in no genre is the other quite so unavoidable as in the Gothic. Indeed, through tales of doubles, hauntings and *Doppelgängers*, one may even say the Gothic raises the other to the status of a narrative principle. If this is a cliché, then so is the contention that, for the English Gothic, no other is quite so other as the European other. In the pages of the Gothic we seem to encounter the unfinished business of the Reformation, where the deformities of Catholicism are held up to the reader for the purposes of Protestant delectation. As an example, the opening scenes of Matthew Lewis's *The Monk* (1796) ring nearly every change in the repertoire of Protestant horror and disgust. The Church of the Capuchins is thronged with auditors:

> Do not encourage the idea that the crowd was assembled either for motives of piety or thirst of information. But very few were influenced by those reasons; and in a city where superstition reigns with such despotic sway as in Madrid, to seek for true devotion would be a fruitless attempt ... . The Women came to show themselves, the Men to see the women. (Lewis 1995: 7)

The Church is a site of magnificence rather than austerity, of display rather than of worship, and of sexual rather than religious pursuits. It is presided over by a power-mad monk, rather than an enlightened clergy; the society that clusters around to hear him is disfigured by the extremes of class; and given the absence of a deeper understanding, by irreligion on the part of the rich, and superstition on the part of the poor. In short, it is a society that is worldly where it ought to be religious, and religious where it ought to be worldly.

In this contrast between a pleasurably scandalized English reader, and a degenerate Catholic Continent, sunk back in priest-ridden Medievalism, we appear to have the makings of modern English Europhobia. As a fantasy genre, Gothic surely has something to tell us about the current horrid imaginings of British Eurosceptics, with their feverish denunciations of foreign plots hatched by the scarlet Europhiles of Brussels. If we are looking for cultural trajectories, what clearer example than the one that arcs between Europhobia and a genre drawing its life from the English fear of the European other?

Such trajectories may indeed exist, but not in the way either of the two clichés I have introduced would portend. We are not dealing with the simple detritus of the Reformation, with a vestigial Anti-Catholicism blending imperceptibly into Anti-Europeanism. The picture is far more mixed. For a start, nationalism has a history: the modern nationalism of contemporary Europhobia is linked to, but is not identical with, the 'proto-nationalism' of the eighteenth century. Nationalism is an ideological construct that emerges at a particular time, in a particular place, for particular reasons (Gellner 1998: 5–9; see also Gellner 1983). The question of where the boundaries fall between self and other in early Gothic writing is only initially answered by reference to what we now call Europhobia. In the Age of Revolution (to use Eric Hobsbawm's phrase) the boundaries are more to do with national politics for which anti-Catholicism is often a foil, albeit a complex one.

Moreover, as modern psychoanalytic theory has taught us to recognize, the other is never simply other. I refer to the psychic mechanism known as 'projection', and its consequence, 'abjection'. The great theoretician of abjection is of course Julia Kristeva, although her work in turn rests on foundations provided by Sigmund Freud and Jacques Lacan. For Kristeva, abjection does not belong to the economy of the ego; on the contrary, it arises with the subject surrendering to what Lacan refers to as 'jouissance', and what Freud denominates by the phrase 'beyond the pleasure principle'. Abjection arises when the subject's destructive slide into 'jouissance' is arrested by the super-ego; during this moment of arrest, the subject is flooded with feelings of nausea, disgust and horror, with a sense of the unclean and taboo. Given that Kristeva also glosses the 'super-ego as Other' as Lacan's Symbolic, there has been a strong tendency to interpolate abjection into the cultural dynamics of patriarchy (Butler 1990: 77–93, 133–134; 1993: 8). What has been less noticed is that Kristeva also invites us to read abjection historically: 'Abjection accompanies all religious structurings and reappears, to be worked out in a new guise, at the time of their collapse' (Kristeva 1982: 17). The process of secularization which typifies much of the eighteenth century, where religious paradigms are replaced with nationalist ones, may be characterized as just such a moment of 'collapse' and restructuring, a point one might take further by identifying the Gothic mode as the new 'guise' of abjection that emerged. Another point Kristeva insists upon is the ambiguity of the abject (Kristeva 1982: 9). This is partly because the abject is a 'border' between a prohibition and its transgression, between desire and law; but it is also because of the way in which the abject, as a literary mode, works. In the moment of abjection the individual may suffer in the frozen grip of the super-ego, but once translated into artistic form a new dynamic arises, one in which both sides of the border become manifest.

Although Kristeva does not mention projection, as such, the concept is actually crucial to her theory as a mode of cultural and aesthetic analysis. For instance, Western culture has an obsessive, 'abject' interest in body weight – so much so that, for some, 'fat' is the incarnation of the unclean. This obsessive interest tells us much about the current construction of the 'super-ego', or if you like, the 'Symbolic', within our culture. A subject so afflicted, who may herself be 'thin', will project her conflicted feelings, her sense of the abject, onto an other. We would, of course, be sadly mistaken if we took this representation of the other at face value; and just so the representation of the Catholic in Gothic writing. The hated figure of the Catholic other is a projection of a complex ambivalence, a process of abjection, arising out of the nationalist politics of the home culture.[1] Hence my earlier statement: literary otherness is not really about others; on the contrary, it signals something about ourselves, about the pressures involved in particular acts of identity formation. This results in a necessary adjustment to the claim that 'British' Gothic exhibits chronic anti-Catholicism. It does not. On the contrary, the Gothic cues us into some of the eighteenth-century sources of internal, Protestant, British unease.

David Hume's essay, 'Of Superstition and Enthusiasm', published in 1741, offers us a helpful way in. Hume begins his essay in language of immediate interest to us:'That *the corruption of the best things produces the worst*, is grown into a maxim, and is commonly proved, among other instances, by the pernicious effects of *superstition* and *enthusiasm*, the corruptions of true religion' (Hume 1963: 75). We begin with what appears to be a simple antithesis, with superstition and enthusiasm on one side, true religion on the other. The repeated use of the word 'corruption' ought to give us pause, as it suggests that we find ourselves within the terrain of the abject.

And so, I think, it proves: as Hume goes on, a clear hierarchical relation emerges between superstition and enthusiasm, one overturning his initial proposition that both are equal enemies of true religion. Hume tells us that his two species of 'false religion' are actually of a 'contrary nature'. Misfortune may lead us to believe that mysterious forces are leagued against us:

> As these enemies are entirely invisible and unknown, the methods taken to appease them are equally unaccountable, and consist in ceremonies, observances, mortifications, sacrifices, presents, or in any practice, however absurd or frivolous, which either folly or knavery recommends to a blind and terrified credulity. Weakness, fear, melancholy, together with ignorance, are, therefore, the true sources of Superstition. (Hume 1963: 76)

In misfortune, we abase ourselves, and seek to propitiate imaginary forces beyond our control. Hume's second form of false religion is contrary to the first in that its source is not abasement, but elevation:

> But the mind of man is also subject to an unaccountable elevation and presumption ... Hence arise raptures, transports, and surprising flights of fancy; and, confidence and presumption still increasing, these raptures, being altogether unaccountable, and seeming quite beyond the reach of our ordinary faculties, are attributed to the immediate inspiration of the Divine Being who is the object of devotion. In a little time, the inspired person comes to regard himself as a distinguished favourite of the Divinity ... Hope, pride, presumption, a warm imagination, together with ignorance, are therefore the true sources of Enthusiasm. (Hume 1963: 76)

In superstition, we throw ourselves into the dust and, through hocus pocus or mumbo jumbo, hope to propitiate forces 'mightier far than we'; whereas enthusiasm is something of a jumped-up phenomenon, whereby we give ourselves unearned spiritual airs and graces.

Hume goes on to consider how these contrary kinds of false religion influence government and society. His first reflection is that '*superstition is favourable to priestly power*' (Hume 1963: 76). Abashed by the sublimity of the invisible world, we look for a superior class of person to intercede on our behalf. 'Hence the origin of Priests, who may be regarded as the invention of a timorous and abject superstition ... '. The contrast with enthusiasm could not be starker: 'all enthusiasts have been free from the yoke of ecclesiastics ... ' (Hume 1963: 77). Indeed, the 'fanatic consecrates himself' (Hume 1963: 78), disputing the authority of anyone else to interpose between him and his divinity.

In his second reflection Hume contrasts the opposite progress of enthusiastical religions and Catholicism, for by this point in his argument superstition has become firmly associated with the 'Romish church' (Hume 1963: 79). Religions *which partake of enthusiasm, are, on their first rise, more furious and violent than those which partake of superstition; but in a little time become more gentle and moderate'* (Hume 1963: 78). Superstition 'on the contrary, steals in gradually and insensibly; renders men tame and submissive ... till at last the priest, having firmly established his authority, becomes the tyrant and disturber of human society' (Hume 1963: 79). Catholicism's insidious progress ends where enthusiasm begins, in religious strife and warfare.

Hume's third reflection completes the new hierarchy of values, which has surprisingly crept into his argument: *'superstition is an enemy to civil liberty, and enthusiasm a friend to it'* (Hume 1963: 79). Despite himself, Hume has turned Whig historian. The fierce 'sectaries' of the Civil War – the Quakers, Levellers, Presbyterians and Congregationalists – whatever their religious differences, leagued together in the patriotic defence of liberty, while, in the course of time, these once 'dangerous bigots, are now become very free reasoners' and, indeed (and what could be better for the establishment of civil society?), 'Deists' (Hume 1963: 79).

Hume concludes with a customary sneer across the channel. Jesuits, 'great friends to superstition', are unfavourably compared with the Janesinists, who are 'but half Catholics'; as such they 'preserve alive the small sparks of the love of liberty which are to be found in the French nation' (Hume 1963: 80). We appear to be back on familiar ground, with venerable Europhobia. For 'enthusiast' we are invited to substitute a Protestant, but particularly British, subject; for 'superstition' we are invited to read 'Catholicism' in general, and France in particular. Initially both enthusiasm and superstition are presented as equal corruptions of true religion, but in the course of the essay a stark antithesis emerges. The enthusiast becomes a token of the fierce, liberty-loving British subject, who, through necessity, arose in violence to assert his rights; but with the establishment of civil society, has become reasonable, and, indeed, 'civil'. Corruption has in fact become salubrious growth. Against the British enthusiast is set French Catholicism as the enthusiast's abject other: 'superstition ... renders men tame and abject, and fits them for slavery' (Hume 1963: 79).

Despite his famed independence of mind, Hume's essay clearly follows the contours of the supremacist Whig interpretation of the Glorious Revolution, in which a despotic and alien Catholicism was vanquished, and Britain's liberty permanently secured via the Bill of Rights. A Briton's natural tendency to elevate himself may initially result in civil disturbance, but in the long run it is part of liberty's progress, in the double sense of process and improvement. As such, enthusiasm's natural antithesis is abject superstition, with its psychology of abasement, inferiority and slavery. But behind the bland assumptions of Britain's glorious progress lie the violence and threat of the English Civil War. If we read the essay through Hume's own eyes, we clearly see that the threat posed to Britain lies in the Catholic armies then menacing its shores; but if we read it through Kristeva's, the ordering reverses itself. What comes to the fore is not the threat from without, but the threat from within, the fear that enthusiasm is 'corruption' indeed, a force equally compromised by a tendency to despotism, subjugation and religious war.

Turning to Horace Walpole's *The Castle of Otranto* (1765), the prototype of Gothic romance, is the quickest way of taking one's generic bearings when discussing early Gothic, which is what I wish now to do. After that I will briefly discuss Charles Maturin's *The Wild Irish Boy* (1808) and *The Milesian Chief* (1812). Maturin's *Melmoth the Wanderer* (1820), written by an author of Huguenot ancestry who was also an Anglican minister in Dublin and a fierce Protestant, appears to be the natural place to start exploring the Gothic representation of anti-Catholic sentiments. Portraying a continent disfigured by the Inquisition, Jesuitical conspiracy, and mob violence, Maturin's most famous novel has often been taken as the high-water mark of Gothic anti-Catholicism and Europhobia. However, we need to be careful. A brilliantly gloomy masterpiece of late Gothic, *Melmoth* has thrown his earlier work into shadow, so that the light falls with a deceptive clarity. Victor Sage rightly observes that Maturin's sensibility remained 'throughout his life that of an embattled and passionate Calvinist' (Sage 1988: 35). Maturin's religious views were 'embattled', and consequently eccentric. For example, Maturin's Bishop expressed the opinion that his views were such that he ought not 'in conscience, to seek employment' in the Church of England (Ratchford and McCarthy 1980: 17). Maturin explains his situation in a letter to Sir Walter Scott: 'I am a high Calvinist in my religious opinions, and therefore viewed with jealousy by Unitarian Brethren and Arminian Masters' (Ratchford and McCarthy 1980: 10). By 'Unitarian Brethren', Maturin means evangelical Methodists with bigoted, low-Calvinistic views on election and predestination — as depicted in *Women, or, Pour et Contre* (1818) — hence the 'high'; but against the Church establishment he asserts a Calvinism which is doctrinally closer to the 'Brethren' he affects to despise. One might characterize Maturin's difficult position by saying that he was politically, socially and religiously at odds with both the Catholic and Non-Conformist communities in Dublin, while being disaffected from the Anglo-Irish elite who, on the whole, supported the Act of Union of 1801, which he strongly opposed. Maturin's Calvinism is therefore a small part of a larger, more complicated, nationalist picture. In this respect Maturin presents the ultimate test case for my thesis that anti-Catholicism is frequently a screen for national concerns. I shall argue that Maturin's politics (and therefore his romances) are determined less by his Protestantism and his Calvinism (no more than the hinge of his difference) than by his Irish Nationalism. His two early tales are attempts at imagining an Irish romance of national becoming; his difficulty in so imagining is what I particularly want to focus on in this chapter.

The Castle of Otranto was written in 1764, in the peaceful interregnum between two violent events: the Jacobite uprising of 1745–46 and the Gordon riots of 1780. These events would seem to support Hume's view of the supremacy of the Catholic threat, given that the first involved a Catholic invasion, the second, riots sparked off by the Government's attempt to ease the restrictive acts designed to keep Catholicism in check. But as Ian McCalman has recently reminded us, the Gordon riots were not a simple case of surly, independent London Burghers gone berserk; it was a civil disorder with deep roots in Protestant enthusiasm. For instance, after the riots, Lord George Gordon drifted further into the lunatic fringes of enthusiasm, even converting to Judaism in accordance with extreme Protestant, millenarian prophecies. It seems that by his conversion, Gordon hoped to hurry on the anointed hour of the divine cataclysm (McCalman 1996: 358). During the 1790s there were fresh outbreaks of millenarian enthusiasm of an antinomian, Protestant kind (for example, see Mee 1992).

Although Richard Brothers was the most famous of these 'enthusiasts', he was not alone, nor was he an isolated eccentric. A vigorous pamphlet war erupted around his predictions and imprisonment (including, famously – and here we recall Hume's description of the enthusiast – Brothers' pretensions to be the nephew of the divinity (Miles 1995: 64–65)). There was also a matter of the Illuminati conspiracy, the clubs of Jacobinical, free-thinking, Aristocratic freemasons whom the paranoiac Abbé Barruel numbered in the hundreds of thousands, plus two million sympathizers, spread out across Europe (including England) plotting bloody revolution (Robison 1797; Barruel 1798: xiii). From where the Abbé Barruel stood, these were the very deists Hume earlier identified as 'true religionists'. From an English perspective, although primarily identified with Germany, the Illuminists were closely linked with the lunatic fringes of Protestant non-conformity (Schuchard 1995: 185).

In terms of Hume's 1741 essay on superstition and enthusiasm, all of this is a long time in the future, but when it comes to understanding the dynamics of early Gothic I think Hume has got it exactly, if unintentionally, right. Or rather he is right the first time, when he envisages a rational middle way between two extremes: of true religion flanked by superstition and enthusiasm, meaning, in terms of the Gothic, a literary form troubled by sectarian anxieties about both sides of the religious divide. As Hume's argument progresses, enthusiasm is transformed into a cypher for the liberty-loving British, a mark of national identity, set against the Catholic other. But as Hume's language abundantly indicates, this re-ordering of values signals a process of abjection, whereby the British enthusiast is embraced, the better to expel the foreign Catholic. Accordingly, we should be prepared to recognize how the abject Catholic body in the Gothic is often the shadow of enthusiastical Protestantism. The point is made by R.S. Esquire, in *The New Monk* (1798), an immediate, satiric riposte to Lewis's text, in which the Catholic zealot Ambrosia is transformed into a canting, enthusiastical, Jacobinical Methodist, a symbolic exchange governed by the logic of abjection. I am not suggesting that whenever we encounter a depiction of Catholic superstition we really need to see it as a disguised form of extreme Protestantism. Sometimes anti-Catholicism is simply anti-Catholicism. I am, however, claiming that in English Gothic the representation of the other is complicated by unresolved anxieties about both Catholicism and Protestantism (Tuite 1997: 1–2). If we keep Hume's essay firmly in mind we can see how the Gothic splits naturally into tales of 'enthusiasm' (James Hogg's *Confessions of a Justified Sinner*, Charles Brockden Brown's *Wieland*) and 'superstition' (such as *The Monk* or Radcliffe's *The Italian*).

However, the two have a shadow relationship with each other. This is partly a case of mirrored extremes, but more fundamentally Catholic abjection signals unresolved anxieties attendant upon the Reformation's fundamental challenge to authority. Once authority is placed in question, where does one draw the line? If authority is not lodged in genealogy – in immemorial continuity – where does it reside? This is precisely the question posed by radical Protestants, such as the antinomians. Just as, in Hume's essay, questions of an apparently religious nature (what is false religion?) inevitably lead to civil issues.

And so we find in Horace Walpole's *The Castle of Otranto*. *Otranto* is a curious and puzzling text, especially given its publishing history and the two prefaces Walpole attached to it. In the first, Walpole masquerades as William Marshal, gentleman, who claims to have found an Italian manuscript in the library of an ancient Catholic family from the North of England (where presumably they rode out the excesses of the Reformation). The reader is free to infer that William Marshal's family and the ancient Catholic family are one and the same. Marshal conjectures that although the events of the story are set around the time of the Crusades, the text was actually written shortly before its impression, in Naples, in 1529, to judge by its pure style. This leads Marshal to speculate that the text is the product of a crafty priest who aims to turn 'their own arms on the innovators', where by 'innovators' he means reforming clerics aiming to 'dispel the empire of superstition', and by 'arms' the art of writing clearly and rationally (Walpole 1996: 5).

The moral of the story is that the sins of the fathers are visited upon the sons to the third and fourth generations. *Otranto* is a ghost story in which the shade of the murdered Alfonso, somehow buried within the fabric of his ancestral house, revenges himself upon the grandson, and great-grandson and great-granddaughter, of his usurping murderer, irrespective of these individuals' personal guilt. The story is apparently designed to inculcate in the credulous reader the belief that God moves in utterly incomprehensible ways. In other words, it is meant as an engine of the Counter-Reformation designed to batter down reason while instilling a healthy, unquestioning, abject regard for God's mysteries.

When Walpole's imposture was discovered, there was outrage (Clery 1995: 64–65). In his second preface, Walpole points to, and occludes, the raw nerve. The book was, he says, 'an attempt to blend the two kinds of romance, the ancient and the modern. In the former all was imagination and improbability: in the latter, nature is always intended to be, and sometimes has been, copied with success' (Walpole 1996: 9). By 'ancient' romance Walpole means medieval verse epics of chivalry and enchantment, such as *Amadis of Gaul* or *Palmerin of England*, which were the sort of thing Don Quixote was hooked on. By 'modern' romance Walpole means what we would now call the novel; works which, by the 1760s, had come to be recognized as having succeeded in achieving probable depictions of contemporary manners, such as those by Fielding, Richardson or Smollet. A great deal of anxiety surrounded the invention of the modern novel, which was understood to have been revolutionized by print technology (making the circulating library possible) and by the new writing technology of 'realism'. Walpole's experiment provoked unease, partly because it wilfully interfered with the received Whig progress of literary history, from marvellous tales of adventure (fit for children, Catholics and other primitives) to probable representations of everyday life (fit for those living in a Protestant nation);[2] and partly because he was employing the arms of the novel-writing innovators in support of a tale whose sole aim appeared to be the undermining of the Protestant rationality of its readers. What was Walpole's game? One answer would be that there wasn't one. The imposture was meant to be transparent: as a pro-Catholic text *Otranto* is clearly self-subverting. Indulging in impostures and using the blessed invention of the novel to inculcate superstition is precisely the dastardly behaviour one would expect of Catholics, even those from ancient Northern English families.

However, such a reading gets us nowhere near the cultural dynamics that propel Walpole's literary experiment. These dynamics only become clear once we realize that *Otranto* is not about, is not a defence of, or an attack on, Catholicism. It is really about legitimacy, or rather the lack of it. The text may even be regarded as a verbal fugue on the term, as if its plot, and prefaces, were driven to include every possible construction of 'illegitimate'. The main plot line concerns Manfred, a usurper. In order to regenerate the family line, and so escape the doom that has come upon his illegitimate race, Manfred attempts legal incest by illegally divorcing his wife and forcing marriage upon Isabella, his son's intended spouse. There is a symbolic incest as well, insofar as Manfred 'accidentally' penetrates his daughter with his poniard. Theodore, the hero and legitimate heir of Otranto, is the son of a monk, although the suspicion of this illegitimacy is quickly cleared up. Walpole's literary experiment is the bastard progeny of generic miscegenation, while the first, framing preface raises the question of the Reformation; in other words secession, and the politically resonant senses of legitimacy secession raises.

Why this concern with legitimacy? I think we derive an answer when we look aside at Horace's relationship with his father, Sir Robert Walpole. By always insistently claiming that he was the 'the Only Unadulterated Whig' (Ford 1967: 24–43), Walpole was in a sense defending his father's reputation for political probity, something frequently questioned. Bolingbroke and Lord Cobham (via *The Craftsman*) in particular attacked Sir Robert Walpole in Gothic terms, as a vampyre (Clery and Miles 2000: 24–26) and Merlin (Colton 1976: 16), as a parasite on the body politic or an enchanter throwing the constitution into doubt via political hocus pocus. Given this highly factionalized politics, parties aimed to take the moral high ground by establishing their political lineages, presenting themselves as, say, the true defenders of the ancient constitution, or as the embodiment of the Saxon spirit which produced the constitution, or (in a different register) as the model of Republican virtue (see Kliger 1952; Pocock 1985; Smith 1987). In other words, the fight for political legitimacy was frequently fought out on the battleground of authenticating genealogies (as indeed Mark Madoff argues in his essay 'The Useful Myth of Gothic Ancestry', 1979).

In his public voice Horace Walpole appears unbothered by these accusations against his father, that Sir Robert was, in short, a usurper of the ancient constitution, a venerable fabric often figured as a 'Gothic castle' (Clery and Miles 2000: 60). But in his fiction Walpole shows himself to be very bothered indeed. In defining himself as the last true Whig, Walpole throws down, and abjects, the qualities of political illegitimacy hurled at his father, using them to fit out his anti-hero, Manfred, who is, indeed, the usurper of an ancient Gothic house. But behind these rhetorical puns (where Walpole literalizes the accusations against his father in the plot of his story) there lies, I suggest, a much deeper anxiety, one feeding the Gothic genre in general: the fear that the post-Glorious Revolution settlement is without legitimacy (Sage 1988: xiii; Lévy 1994: 2). Once one accepts that *Otranto* is grounded in the political controversy surrounding Walpole's father, it is difficult not to see the allusions to the Reformation in *Otranto*'s prefaces as code for the Glorious Revolution, the founding moment of contemporary Whiggism. Here, too, British liberties were preserved by the assertion of Protestantism against Catholic machinations. But this linking in turn raises the question of political legitimacy in a revolutionary age.

Otranto's concern with genealogy, with narratives of legitimating origin, is also manifest in Walpole's adaptation of Shakespearean romance. Shakespeare's late romances are filled with royal children who have been dispossessed, usually through an act of usurpation. By the time the play is through, the prince or princess hidden within the peasant has been revealed, families have been united, and the old order (and legitimacy) restored. When Walpole spoke of blending the ancient and modern romance, he may have meant poetic tales of chivalry; but hereafter, for the purposes of the Gothic, the conservative, Shakespearean romance plot becomes the dominant form. Contemporary critics were clear that Walpole's line of influence ran from Clara Reeve's *The Old English Baron* (1777) through Sophia Lee's *The Recess* (1783–85) through to Radcliffe's *The Castles of Athlin and Dunbayne* (1789), all texts built on the romance plot of royal foundlings (Miles 1995: 9–10). This narrative pattern achieved dominance because of the centrality of the genealogical issues the plot encodes, but with this difference: in the age of revolution, the Shakespeare romance plot is no longer sustainable because the very thing requisite for it – a transcendent conception of legitimacy – is no longer available. The tendency of the Shakespearian romance plot to come unstuck in the Gothic is attributable to the cultural ambivalence generated by the Glorious Revolution, whose settlement left Englishmen imaginatively suspended between Divine Right and the ancient constitution, or monarchy and abstract rights. Or rather, the romance plot is sustainable, but only if the symbolic links between familial and national legitimacy are obfuscated.

And so it is with Maturin's two Irish tales, both romances: one ends in marriage, and is therefore 'comic'; the other ends in death and disaster, and is therefore, obviously, tragic. The comic romance is indirectly about the resurrection of the Irish nation, the tragic romance directly about it. These relationships are not accidental. The romance directly addressing Irish nationhood ends tragically, because, for Maturin, happy nationhood is finally unimaginable. *The Wild Irish Boy* is the comic romance, and was the first to be published (in 1808). Both texts are allegories in that the marriage plots feature the coming together of the Irish and English in a mutual process of national self-definition. Another dominant feature of both texts is their theatricality. Maturin's central characters suffer an authenticity deficit. Without strong national roots, without a settled identity, the world is a stage. Maturin's protagonists are marked out by their awareness of their postmodern condition (conversely, his villains are unaware of the performative nature of their selfhood). This leads to the strange situation whereby Maturin's most sensitive characters reveal the trueness of their feelings through self-dramatization, a paradox of inauthenticity, where for the sophisticated, only acting permits 'truth'. The exceptions to this are the indigenous Irish (as opposed to the Anglo-Irish) who are, by and large, uncomplicated primitives.

The wild Irish boy is Ormsby Bethel, who is neither very Irish nor very wild. Ormsby's father was one of four penniless Milesian brothers named Delacy, who, in the manner of down-at-heel aristocracy, have become professional soldiers free-booting across Europe. A maternal uncle unexpectedly leaves the Delacys a fortune, under the condition that they take his name of Bethel. The others, beginning with the eldest, proudly refuse to sell their Milesian heritage in this way, except for Ormsby's father, a luxury-loving libertine, who lives abroad with his mistress and Ormsby's mother, Miss Percival, a promiscuous Godwinian bluestocking. Ormsby's parents are at first sight an odd couple: he loves claret and a good dinner, she is infatuated with radical Enlightenment philosophy; he is a ruined dandy, while she dresses in the austere fashion of a Voltairean free thinker. But in fact their relationship is allegorical in that they represent the two main branches of libertinism, the moral and philosophical. As committed libertines, they naturally do not marry, leaving Ormsby to cope with his illegitimacy as best he can. With his health and fortune broken, Bethel retires to Ireland, to be near the Milesian Chief, his older brother, whose fortunes have now been repaired, in the hopes of making Ormsby the heir. While in Ireland Ormsby falls in love with Lady Montrevor, who has followed her English husband to his Irish estates subsequent to the shameful revelation of his having usurped his English title and property for some 30 years. The brilliant socialite Lady Montrevor is closely modelled on Maria Edgeworth's Lady Delacour, from *Belinda* (1801), an example of Irish literary success much admired and envied by Maturin. Lady Montrevor has several daughters, married to the great and good of English society, including the British Prime Minister. Although a matron, she becomes Ormsby's passionate, and secret, love object. She naturally has her own private sorrow, which is that in her youth she quarrelled with her true love, marrying (out of spite) Lord Montrevor, a cold, vain, punctilious English fop.

Ormsby is brought up abroad, first in France, and then England. He has a favourite daydream born out of his deracinated existence:

> I have imagined some fortunate spot, some abode peopled by fair forms, human in their affections, their habits, in everything but vice and weakness; to these I have imagined myself giving laws, and becoming their sovereign. I therefore imagined them possessed of the most shining qualities that can enter into the human character, glowing with untaught affections, and luxuriant with uncultivated virtue; but proud, irritable, impetuous, insolent, and superstitious. (Maturin 1808: I 102)

The subject of his dreams is of course Ireland. It is, self-evidently, a dream of national becoming. The longed-for event is implicitly linked to the advent of a Washington, or father/Moses figure. Although it is not stated, this is what, implicitly, Ormsby is, or hopes to be.

As the putative, future father of the country, Ormsby draws his authority from his genealogical links with the past, here embodied by the Milesian chief: 'They who speak of a Milesian Chief describe him as a being, obsolete as Brien Born, or Fingal; as a being, who talks the language of Ossian, and wears the robes of a bard' (Maturin 1808: I 181). But the myth is real, for this is exactly the character of the elder Delacy: 'His demeanour was marked with dignity, but it was a wild and original dignity; that of a chief of a warlike country, lofty with unborrowed grandeur and habitual command; amid the polished forms of modern life, he looked the oak, amid the poplar and the willow' (Maturin 1808: I, 182). The Milesian chief himself makes the case for the antiquity of the Irish. Here he explains why there are no physical remnants of past Irish greatness: 'Because the monuments of recent greatness are more easily preserved than those of remote; the structures of Irish greatness, were perhaps falling into ruins before those of Rome were erected. The great enemy to the existence of our ancient monuments was Christianity' (Maturin 1808: I 194). Maturin's strategy is to adopt a time frame that renders the Reformation insignificant. Maturin's Irish nationalism is not an internecine question of Protestant versus Catholic vying for supremacy. For Maturin, such a division is itself a product of Ireland's modern history of fragmented statehood.[3] Thus there is no contradiction, or tension, in the mysteriously Protestant Ormsby Bethel becoming the adamantly Catholic Delacy's heir.

Ormsby marries Lady Montrevor's daughter by mistake, after Delacy privately arranges the marriage assuming that the daughter, not the mother, is Ormsby's secret love. In many respects the rest of the complicated story is about how Ormsby learns to prefer his wife to his mother-in-law. Ormsby's progress is counterpointed by the Gothic subplot. A spectral figure haunts a ruined tower next to the property of the Milesian chief. He is, above all else, a figure of Irish dispossession. He is also, as it turns out, in true Shakespearean fashion, Lady Montrevor's first lover, Delacy's brother, Ormsby's father, and an Irish aristocrat. It seems that the promiscuous Miss Percival had, as a Godwinian proponent of free love, taken both brothers as lovers in quick succession. Having been impregnated by the elder brother, she blames it on the younger. A series of providential deaths clears the way for the marriage of Ormsby's father and Lady Montrevor, the new Milesian chief and the brilliant Anglo-Irish woman. The marriage symbolizes the unification of Ireland, and the restoration of the ancient line of Irish self-rule. Ormsby's infatuation with Lady Montrevor was in fact a symptom of his national alienation, his un-rootedness; with order restored, his desire naturally re-focuses on his wife, child and Irish futurity.

The indirectness of the text as an expression of Irish national aspirations is owing to the allegorical nature of the tale and to the obfuscations of the property plot, which deals with usurpation obliquely by displacing the act onto Lord Montrevor. Although he holds his Irish lands by just title, he comes to Ireland tainted with the scandal of his English usurpation. Although Montrevor is an English usurper living in Ireland, he is not, legally, a usurper of Ireland. Maturin's next romance, *The Milesian Chief* (1812), tackles the property issue head on. Thirty years previous to the time of the story, the English Lord Montclare had bought an estate from a ruined Milesian family, the O'Morvens. Scandalously to both sides of the family, Montclare's sister married 'the son of the ancient proprietor' (Maturin 1812: I 48), bearing him two children, Connal and Desmond. The elder child is raised by his grandfather in an ancient tower, the last remnant of the O'Morven property. As far as the grandfather is concerned, Montclare's possession of the O'Morven estate is a simple case of usurpation, brought on by English policies since the time of Elizabeth, when the last expression of

Gaelic nationhood, the uprising of Hugh O'Neill, the 'Irish Prince', was crushed in 1601 (Foster 1989: 3–4). Interestingly, the heroine of the tale, Armida, Montclare's daughter, a women of extraordinary talents and learning, employs the plot of *Otranto* to imagine the plight of the young O'Morvens: she thinks of the state of mind

> that comforts itself in being compelled to inhabit ruins by tracing among them the remains of ancient palaces; that like the spirit in Otranto stalks amid its ancient seat till it swells beyond it, and stands forth amid the fragments dilated and revealed, terrifying the intrusion of modern usurpers. (Maturin 1808: I 52)

The Montclares are, indeed, the legal usurpers of Irish territory. A clause in the contract stipulates that the estate shall revert to the O'Morvens in the event of no male heir. Nor is there one, for the apparent son, Endymion, is really a girl in disguise. In order to retain a hold over Lord Montclare, and then the property itself, Lady Montclare raises her daughter, Inez, as a boy. Somewhat improbably, Inez is unaware of the true nature of her sexuality until her love for Desmond brings about a crisis of disclosure. Although both Desmond and Connal discover the imposture, their extreme pride prevents them from profiting from the knowledge, until too late in the day. Connal O'Morven is the very image of a Celtic chief, by way of Ossian: of gigantic stature, proud, warlike, chivalrous, with an exquisite sensibility. Hence his squeamishness in pursuing his own self-interests, in complete contrast to Armida's betrothed, the wicked Colonel Wandesford. Once again a vivacious Anglo-Irish heroine is inappropriately linked to a shallow, vain, ill-educated Englishman, although in Wandesford's case one has to add a streak of vicious misogyny ('The hearts of your whole sex ... are not worth the earth I tread' (Maturin 1808: II 165) is a fairly typical example). He is also the apparent villain of the piece. Despite herself, Armida falls in love with Connal, who is driven into a rebellion through Wandesford's double dealing. It is, it appears, 1798 all over again, or, perhaps more topically, a reference to Robert Emmet's uprising of 1803 (Henderson 1980: 86). Armida elopes with Connal to his rebel camp, where they marry. When we first encounter Armida, in Naples, she, too, suffers the paradox of inauthenticity. Caught up in the luxury of artistic refinements, she is only able to be herself when placed on show. But with Connal she recovers her authenticity and, with it, a womanly simplicity.

The rebellion is doomed, and with it, owing to Wandesford's machinations, Connal, who dies before a firing squad. Armida perishes shortly after, through suicide. But Wandesford is not the ultimate antagonist. The person pulling the strings, including Wandesford's, is Lady Montclare, an Italian Catholic who selfishly manipulates her family through her agent, the priest Morosoni. Wandesford is, I think, Maturin's English abject. Maturin clearly internalizes the chivalric values of sensibility, which, through Macpherson, are the medium of his nationalist, Gaelic, aspirations: Maturin's English gentlemen are almost always brutal, but Wandesford's vicious misogyny holds a particular disgust for Maturin. However, in the end, Maturin can no more let the buck stop with a member of the English ascendancy than he can imagine a happy outcome for Connal and Armida, for their plot is unambiguously the Otranto-like one of national resurrection. The Catholic-Italian Lady Montclare is in fact an abject *deus ex machina* brought in to get Maturin off the hook of his own nationalist plot.

I was initially led to choosing Maturin's texts because I wanted to refute the general and widely held view (frequently attributed to Maturin in particular) that the Gothic is motivated by anti-Catholicism. As I trust I have shown, it is not; or at least, not in any way susceptible to being described by such a bald statement. The logic of national romance, of self and other, project and abject, is in fact a far stronger generic determinant. In the figure of the scheming, conspiratorial, priest-beset Lady Montclare, Maturin may be reverting to conventional Europhobia; but as a scapegoat she also has projected onto her the racial stereotypes of which the younger O'Morvens are carefully cleansed. Maturin's plot at once confronts these anti-Catholic stereotypes, and succumbs to them; but the energy that propels it is not anti-Catholicism *per se*, but Irish nationalism. If we think back to Walpole (as Maturin invites us to do, through his references to *Otranto*) we also begin to see how the figure of the Catholic is inextricably linked to questions of authority, authenticity and, finally, legitimacy, all of which were intensified by the emergence of nationalism as an ideological force in the eighteenth century. In order for the newly forged stories of national becoming to maintain their integrity (as, in Kristeva's terms, a restructured 'super-ego'), abject material (concerning the illegitimate) had to be expelled onto a convenient other. Given that Catholicism constituted the former paradigm by which present illegitimacies were measured, the figure of the Catholic held a special relevance as the projective object; but the secret of that object's meaning is to be found in the nationalist energies that focused upon it.

Maturin's *Melmoth* may present us with what seems to be a familiar, Protestant, rogue's gallery of Catholic chicanery, but to understand it fully one has to place it within a wider context. Part of that context is Maturin's other work, and here, as we have seen, a significant projective object is the figure of the English officer or landowner onto whom abject material is loaded. In these works Maturin's Catholics stand out as bold, forthright and open Ossianic enthusiasts, while his English subalterns adopt the cowardly, underhand, scheming ways identified by Hume as the trademark of an abased, Catholic mentality. This moment of Irish, ideological resistance is subsequently obscured by the importation of a stock, Catholic malefactor: Lady Montclare and her henchman, Morosoni. Nevertheless, such a vacillation reveals a nationalist, rather than purely secular, agon. The opposition between British subject and European other breaks apart into regional nationalisms where the invisible subject, the norm of Englishness, comes suddenly into view as an abject of the margins. The representation of the European other in early Gothic, then, is not part of a single binary of Protestant/Catholic, Briton/European, but is constitutive of a complex fabric 'haunted' (to use the figure of the unresolved) by the issue of legitimacy inevitably provoked by the task of forging nations.

Notes

1   For a more developed treatment of these themes, see my 'Abjection, Nationalism and the Gothic' (Miles 2001).
2   The best example of such a Whiggish progress is James Beattie's 'On Fable and Romance' of 1783 (Beattie 1974). Richard Hurd, *Letters on Chivalry and Romance* (1762) and Thomas Warton, *The History of English Poetry* (1778) are more ambivalent, but finally concur with the standard, progressive view.
3   Maturin's nationalism bears some affinity with that of the United Irishmen; see Thuente 1992.

References

Barruel, A. (1798) *Memoirs, Illustrating the History of Jacobinism*, trans. Robert Clifford, London, n.p.

Beattie, J. (1974) *Dissertations Moral and Critical, The Philosophical and Critical Works of James Beattie*, Vol. II, Hildesheim and New York [1783].

Butler, J. (1990) *Gender Trouble: Feminism and the Subversion of Identity*, New York and London, Routledge.

—— (1993) *Bodies That Matter: On the Discursive Limits of 'Sex'*, New York and London, Routledge.

Colton, J. (1976) 'Merlin's Cave and Queen Caroline: Garden Art as Political Propaganda', *Eighteenth Century Studies*, 10, 1–20.

Clery, E.J. (1995) *The Rise of Supernatural Fiction*, Cambridge, Cambridge University Press.

Clery, E.J. and Miles, R. (eds) (2000) *Gothic Documents*, Manchester, Manchester University Press.

Ford, A.S. (1967) 'The Only Unadulterated Whig', in W.H. Smith (ed.), *Horace Walpole: Writer, Politician, and Connoisseur*, New Haven and London, Yale University Press.

Foster, R.F. (1989) *Modern Ireland: 1600–1972*, Harmondsworth, Penguin.

Gellner, E. (1983) *Nations and Nationalism*, Oxford, Blackwell.

—— (1998) *Nationalism*, London, Phoenix.

Henderson, P.M. (1980) *A Nut Between Two Blades: The Novels of Charles Robert Maturin*, New York, Arno Press.

Hobsbawm, E. (1977) *The Age of Revolution*, London, Abacus.

Hume, D. (1963) *Essays Moral, Political and Literary*, Oxford, Oxford University Press.

Hurd, R. (1762) *Letters on Chivalry and Romance*, London, T. Burton.

Kliger, S. (1952) *The Goths in England: A Study in Seventeenth and Eighteenth Century Thought*, Cambridge MA, Harvard University Press.

Kristeva, J. (1982) *Powers of Horror: An Essay on Abjection*, New York, Columbia University Press.

Lévy, M. (1994) '"Gothic" and the Critical Idiom', in A.L. Smith and V. Sage (eds) *Gothick Origins and Innovations*, Amsterdam, Rodopi, pp. 1–15.

Lewis, M. (1995) *The Monk*, ed. Emma McEvoy, Oxford and New York, Oxford University Press.

McCalman, I. (1996) 'Mad Lord George and Madame La Motte: Riot and Sexuality in the Genesis of Burke's *Reflections on the Revolution in France*', *Journal of British Studies*, 35, 343–367.

Madoff, M. (1979) 'The Useful Myth of Gothic Ancestry', *Studies in Eighteenth-Century Culture*, 9, 337–350.

Maturin, C. (1808) *The Wild Irish Boy*, 4 vols, London, Longman, Hurst, Rees, and Orme.

—— (1812) *The Milesian Chief, A Romance*, 4 vols, London, Henry Colburn.

—— (1818) *Women, or, Pour et contre*, Edinburgh, Constable.

Mee, J. (1992) *Dangerous Enthusiasm: William Blake and the Culture of Radicalism in the 1790s*, Oxford, Oxford University Press.

Miles, R. (1995) *Ann Radcliffe: The Great Enchantress*, Manchester, Manchester University Press.

—— (2001) 'Abjection, Nationalism and the Gothic', in F. Botting (ed.), *Essays and Studies*, Cambridge, D.S. Brewer, pp. 47–70.

Pocock, J.G.A. (1985) 'Varieties of Whiggism from Exclusion to Reform: A History of Ideology and Discourse', in *Virtue, Commerce and History*, Cambridge, Cambridge University Press, pp. 215–310.

Ratchford, F.E. and McCarthy, Jr., W.H. (eds) (1980) *The Correspondence of Sir Walter Scott and Charles Robert Maturin*, New York and London, Garland Publishing.

Robison, J. (1797) *Proofs of a Conspiracy Against all the Governments of Europe, Carried on in Secret Meetings of Freemasons, Illuminati, and Reading Societies*, Edinburgh, George Forman.

Sage, V. (1988) *Horror Fiction in the Protestant Tradition*, Basingstoke, Macmillan.

Schuchard, M.K. (1995) 'William Blake and the Promiscuous Baboons: A Cagliostroan

Seance Gone Awry', *British Journal for Eighteenth-Century Studies*, 18 (Autumn), 185–200.

Smith, R.J. (1987) *The Gothic Bequest: Medieval Institutions in British Thought, 1688–1863*, Cambridge, Cambridge University Press.

Thuente, M.H. (1992) 'The Literary Significance of the United Irishmen', in M. Kenneally (ed.), *Irish Literature and Culture*, Irish Literary Studies 35, Gerrards Cross, Colin Smythe, pp. 35–54.

Tuite, C. (1997) 'Cloistered Closets: Enlightenment Pornography, The Confessional State, Homosexual Persecution and *The Monk*', *Romanticism on the Net*, 8 (November), 1–10.

Walpole, H. (1996) *The Castle of Otranto*, ed. E.J. Clery, Oxford and New York, Oxford University Press.

Warton, T. (1778) *The History of English Poetry from the Close of the Eleventh to the Commencement of the Eighteenth Century*, 2 vols, London, J. Dodsley.

6

European Gothic and nineteenth-century Russian literature[1]

NEIL CORNWELL

'Russian Gothic' as a term has only recently begun to enjoy any real currency in critical studies of Russian literature. The word 'Gothic' is commonly used in connection with, for instance, certain early works by Dostoevsky or, to a lesser extent, his later and more famous novels, which may be recognized as including Gothic elements or traces. Otherwise, what might have been termed 'the Gothic in Russian literature' has tended, with rare exceptions, to be submerged under the blanket heading of 'Russian romanticism' or 'the fantastic' (as noted in various of the essays included in Cornwell 1999). This situation may be partly explicable in terms of the vicissitudes of Soviet literary criticism, during the more depressing stretches of which even 'romanticism' and 'Dostoevsky' were dirty words and 'socialist realist' critical energies were certainly not to be expended on such areas as the Gothic, the fantastic or the supernatural. As one recent surveyor of the Gothic field in general has expressed it, in any event: 'all goth writers worth any attention are forever returning to that immorality which defies or subverts ruling authority, and thus provides power systems' necessary dark antithesis' (Davenport-Hines 1998: 3). Furthermore, the burgeoning of interest in Gothic as a literary style, even in the West, is still comparatively recent. Gothic novels did occasionally achieve publication in Russian translation in the later part of the Soviet era and there is now, in post-Soviet Russia, a 'Gothic novel' series emanating from the Moscow publisher 'Terra'.

Even the anthology entitled *Russian 19th-century Gothic Tales*, compiled by Valentin Korovin and published in Moscow in 1984, however, seems to have acquired that title for its English-language edition by chance (the Russian title being given as *Fantasticheskii mir russkoi povesti* – 'The Fantastic World of the Russian Novella'). The range of stories included extends from Antonii Pogorelsky and Orest Somov, in the 1820s, to Vladimir Odoevsky's *The Living Corpse* (*Zhivoi mertvets*: published 1844, but dated 1838) and A.K. Tolstoy's early story *Vampire* (*Upyr'*, 1841, and appearing at the time of 'the sunset of [Russian] romanticism' — Markovich 1990: 36). Pushkin, Lermontov and Gogol are represented therein, as well as a number of the more minor figures of Russian prose (Mikhail Zagoskin, Osip Senkovsky and the poet Evgenii Baratynsky). The blurb to this collection, which has no general introduction, refers to 'enchanting flights of the imagination, vivid imagery borrowed from folk tale and legend, grotesque fantasy and utopian dreams of a distant, happy future'.[2]

While all this might (just about) have something in common with western perceptions of the Gothic, we may well prefer to stress alternative features – old castles, hapless maidens, wicked and grasping relatives, and mysterious revenants – as more characteristic of the genre. Another Russian literary historian lists the following as Gothic motifs: 'a curse hanging over a whole family, a secret of evil doing that has brought on this curse, the selling of human souls to the devil, ancient villas populated by ghosts, etc.' (Markovich 1990: 37). V.E. Vatsuro, undoubtedly the leading Russian commentator on the Gothic in recent decades, nominates '"gothic" heroes, conflict, and the basic motifs and technique of "mystery"' as fundamental props of the Gothic narrative whole, with the castle and incest, for instance, as important subsidiary motifs (Vatsuro 1995: 208–209).[3]

A certain input from folklore, and other such further native medieval ingredients as chronicles and saints' lives apart, Russian Gothic can be said to derive principally from an amalgam of European influences: the English Gothic novel, the tales of Hoffmann, the French *fantastique* and *frénétique* traditions, and the various schools of European idealist and esoteric thought.[4]

The English and European background

'Gothic', as an ethnic and a cultural concept, it may scarcely need here be said, originates in Europe, and the manuals of European history tell us that Gothic settlement developed from the east to the south and west. If anything, however, it remains more popularly associated with the north. Detailed considerations of the exact pre-medieval, medieval and architectural connotations of 'Gothic' aside, the cultural revival of the term, particularly in a literary sense, is generally viewed as developing in a reverse direction: from west to east.[5] Certainly, what is now regarded as the Gothic novel, together with the allied, or anticipatory, phenomenon of 'graveyard poetry', stems from eighteenth-century England. The eastward spread, however, soon mingled with kindred local currents and a process of cross-fertilization ensued, embracing structure, style, setting, themes and common sources. A reverse wind quickly wafted the fashion back to England – and beyond, to Ireland and America – as well as returning it again to eastern Europe, from where some of its themes at least, such as that of the 'undead', appear to have originated.

'Vampirisation' has been seen as *reverse* colonisation', and a Slavic counterpart to Christianity's the Devil (Gelder 1994: 12, 40), although even dead alcoholics could commonly be vampire suspects in Russia (Rickels 1999: 2). The west–east and east–west movements (with an original pre-history in the east) in the plotting of Bram Stoker's *Dracula* serve as an effective emblem of the whole process (counting, for this purpose, Transylvania, Hungary, Greece and other East European lands as falling within the domain of 'eastern', or Slavic, folk belief).[6] Jan L. Perkowski classifies vampires under four headings: the folkloric, the psychotic, the psychic and the literary (the first being mythological and the fourth fictional, the middle two are 'actual').[7] The 'Slavic folkloric vampire' may be understood as 'an anthropomorphized symbol for mysterious illness and death' (Perkowski 1989: 145). Furthermore:

> it is reasonably safe to conclude that Slavic vampirism, in the form in which it penetrated to the West early in the XVIIIth century, evolved in the Balkans, starting in the IXth century, as the result of the confrontation of Slavic paganism, Bogomilism, and Orthodox Christianity. The conflict culminated in the eventual victory of Orthodoxy and the subsequent relegation of pagan and Bogomil beliefs to demonology. (Perkowski 1989: 32)

In other senses too, of course, the political, social, cultural and religious anxieties of the eighteenth century were felt throughout Europe-wide (indeed, throughout the northern hemisphere) and paraded themselves across the entire continent. Consequently, in the view of the Marquis de Sade (in his essay 'Idée sur les romans'):

It was therefore necessary [for writers] to call upon hell for aid in the creation of titles that could arouse interest, and to situate in the land of fantasies what was common knowledge, from mere observation of the history
of man in this iron age; ... [the Gothic genre was] the inevitable product of
the revolutionary shocks with which the whole of Europe resounded.
(quoted in Mulvey-Roberts 1998: 204)

The craze for Gothic dates, of course, from Horace Walpole's classic
formulation of the genre in *The Castle of Otranto* (1765), with its
combination of economic and sexual intrigue, based on an accursed
dynastic succession (and, at the same time, 'an extended camp joke'
(Davenport-Hines 1998: 9)), to the accompaniment of supernatural
manifestations in a southern European medieval Gothic-castle setting.
Near-contemporaneous European works – and their successors (east
and west) – may repeat, vary, extend or develop alternative emphases
upon these – soon enough to be noted as stereotyped – ingredients. It
has frequently been observed that Gothic fiction extended to, or shaded
into, psychological analysis, the uncanny (in the senses outlined by
Freud and reapplied by Todorov), horror (and/or 'terror' in some differ-
entiations), the fantastic (Todorov again), and the marvellous (see
Todorov 1973; Freud 1990).

A number of extra-literary cultural models were internationally
shared, in addition to a primal Gothic or medievalist nostalgia. Pan-
European literary images derived from the engravings of Piranesi (particularly the *Carceri d'invenzione*); his impenetrable imaginary prisons
and impossible blueprints, affecting Gothic writers from Walpole in
England to Odoevsky in Russia (see Odoevsky 1997), paralleled in their
labyrinthine mental processes the most complex features of Gothic
architecture. Images of tyranny or incarceration – within ruins, castle,
prison, asylum or monastery – had their objective correlatives in the
architectural monuments of real institutional power (which in turn
took on a literary significance): Versailles, the Bastille, Charenton and
Notre Dame within France; the Castel Sant'Angelo in Rome; the
Piombi in Venice; Metternich's Spielberg; and the Peter and Paul
Fortress in St Petersburg are prominent examples. Mental and structural landscape juxtaposed with the natural, as observed alpine scenery
vied as a source of inspiration with the rugged vistas of Salvator Rosa
and the symbolized depictions of Caspar David Friedrich. Various
strands of idealist philosophy (including Jena Romanticism and Neoplatonism) joined with the hermetic and esoteric traditions, plus an

input from Jewish and eastern influences, to furnish Gothic writers with some sort of an ideological platform of the mystical, in addition to the Enlightenment-inspired social.

Just as feudalism, or the *ancien régime*, was threatened and finally confronted by revolution, so did constitutionalism subsequently do battle across Europe with reaction. Gothic fiction, as one of the facets of Romanticism, duly reflected this binary conflict. Traditional dynastic requirements opposed new value systems, as the past met the present and the autocratic status quo was challenged by rebellion, legitimacy by usurpation. From this, within the Gothic idiom, followed a whole series of dualistic clashes. At a spiritual level the supernatural vied with the natural, as mysticism challenged, and was again challenged by, materialism; or religion by science (and cult by pseudo-science). On all planes death would contend with life. On a socio-political and an individual level, tyrant would rage against victim and victimization would engender vengeance; incarceration would oppose freedom and hierarchy would strive to control individuality. Heritage or inheritance would be threatened by subversion, actual or potential, and authoritarianism by permissiveness, while, on a sexual level in particular, repression would tilt against desire.

A historical period setting would often give way to the more recent past, or even contemporary surroundings, just as exotic locations would be replaceable by a more local topography, and the classic chronotope of the historic Gothic castle (castles being 'places for intrigues, pathos, lunacy, ignominy and illusory security' (Davenport-Hines 1998: 102)) could be succeeded by a rural mansion or an atmospheric townhouse. Gothic in the novel, or tale, could extend to, or incorporate, poem or drama. Nevertheless – typically – Gothic writing would take the form of prose fiction; writers from northern (and mainly Protestant) Europe would set their main (or most Gothic) works in the (largely Catholic) south; east Europeans would frequently prefer a western (or at least partly western) setting; imposing edifice (whether menacingly metropolitan or forlornly remote) may well alternate with an awe-inspiring nature.

What we may now see as 'classical Gothic', then, will normally involve dynastic disorders, set at some temporal and spatial distance and in a castle or manorial locale; defence, or usurpation, of an inheritance will threaten (and not infrequently inflict) violence upon hapless (usually female) victims amid a supernatural ambiance. What, amounting to much the same thing, Davenport-Hines (1998: 6) calls 'revival gothic' is preoccupied with 'power, excess and inversion', enlisting '[melo]drama and artifice'. Often (but not always) the heroine will be saved, the villain unmasked and the supernatural phenomena dispersed (explained or confirmed, as the case may be). Variations on such a classic Gothic masterplot allow the genre to overlap with, or merge into, the fictional modes of psychological realism, the uncanny, the fantastic or the marvellous (in which, in Todorov's terms, the supernatural may be resolved by realistic explanation, never resolved, or found, within the terms of the fiction, to exist). An emphasis on hesitation over the supernatural may result in what we might call 'fantastic Gothic'; the establishing of a philosophical, occult or religious system of dualism (involving perhaps the 'existence' of demonic emissaries, revenants, demon lovers, sylphs or salamanders, and confirmed contact or 'correspondences' between the two worlds) will push a work into the realm of what might be termed 'Romantic Gothic' (largely Germanic in origin, and termed *dvoemirie* in its Russian utilization: to be revived and developed later in the nineteenth century as Symbolism). Further impetus in that direction would result in the Todorovian marvellous: a fictional world akin to that of Hoffmann's *The Golden Pot*, the 'distant lands' of the German Romantics, or pure fairy tale.

The 'occult' (a term often interchanged with 'esoteric'), according to Bernice Rosenthal, may be said to encompass: the 'occult sciences' (alchemy, astrology and magic); the Kabbala (Jewish and Christian); and 'the post-Renaissance doctrines of Rosicrucianism, Spiritualism, Theosophy and Anthroposophy', incorporating, in their turn, elements from the more ancient teachings of hermetism, Gnosticism, Neoplatonism and early Christianity (Rosenthal 1997: 2). One offshoot of this was Freemasonry. Another important aspect was the concept of a 'living nature', which may be related to *Naturphilosophie* and the 'cosmic pantheism' of Schelling. There was a considerable vogue for the occult in late nineteenth-century Russia, but the eighteenth-century influx of Freemasonry and esoteric elements within the Romantic movement were also important. In addition to the (two-world) concept of *dvoemirie*, Russia had the phenomenon of *dvoeverie* (dual faiths), the coexistence, or blending, of paganism with Orthodox Christianity. However, it is primarily what Rosenthal calls the 'practical side' of the occult – the 'attempt to enlist invisible or supernatural forces, divine or diabolic, to attain health, wealth, love, and other personal goals' – that really brings it into convergence with the Gothic (Rosenthal 1997: 5).

On the psychological side, the accentuation may fall on character analysis (most commonly of villainy) or on a crisis of identity, often introducing the *Doppelgänger* theme (which, in its turn, may resolve itself into a supernaturally or a psychically induced 'double'). Moreover, as Renate Lachmann puts it:

> Rampantly proliferating reinterpretations of archaic narratives of creation, heretical readings of the Book of Genesis, and systematizing amalgamations from Gnosis, Cabbalah, and alchemy find their way into the literature of doubling, even as the religious function is replaced by a psychologically or socially descriptive one. (Lachmann 1997: 299)

Strong psychological elements of dream and fantasy are contained within the style of 'fantastic realism', a term particularly associated with the mature work of Dostoevsky.[8] Greater concentration on setting may define 'historical Gothic' or, if contemporaneous, 'society (or social) Gothic'; other emphases again may lead to 'horror' or 'criminal' Gothic; the idea of 'the carnival world of the gothic' prompts consideration of Gothic in terms of the theories of Mikhail Bakhtin.[9] A yet further sub-division is identifiable as 'artistic Gothic', in which Gothic elements are involved with, or subordinated to, themes from art or music, bringing into play artistic works or figures (painters or paintings, musical composers or works, the fate of the artist, the animation of images or statues). In all such cases, some elements at least of the basic, or classic, Gothic ingredients need to be present for the term 'Gothic' to remain justifiable. Beyond these widely attested categories of the European Gothic tale, vestigial Gothic traces are to be found throughout what is considered mainstream realist European fiction over the whole of the nineteenth century, leading towards a subsequent Neo-Gothic revival, in the main coincidental with Symbolism and *fin de siècle* decadence.

European elements were, then, an important factor throughout the evolution of English Gothic (and the reverse could also be the case). Not only were the settings of the most prominent examples of the English Gothic novel (by Walpole, Radcliffe, Lewis and others) European, but Beckford's *Vathek* (1786), like Wilde's Gothic-decadent play *Salome* a century later, was actually written in French. French, too, was the language of composition of *The Manuscript Found in Saragossa*

(*Manuscrit trouvé à Saragosse*), an extraordinary framed novel-compilation of stories reflecting the darker side of a burgeoning European Romanticism. This work was written between about 1797 and 1815 by the polymath Polish nobleman, Jan Potocki (who is alleged to have committed suicide in 1815 with a home-made silver bullet). European, as well as English, influences and themes were also important in works by Charles Brockden Brown and Washington Irving, the first exponents of American Gothic; an Anglo-European element remained vital to this style of American fiction through successive works by Poe, Hawthorne and Melville, and on to Henry James.

In France itself, in the decade after Walpole had launched the Gothic novel in English, Jacques Cazotte published his short novel *The Devil in Love* (*Le Diable amoureux*, 1772). A work much later to catch Todorov's attention, *The Devil in Love* was promoted in the late 1820s as the main instigator of the prose tradition of *le fantastique*, then approaching the height of its popularity in France. Cazotte's emphasis is on erotic temptation and demonology, but the psychological dimension and underlying dynastic concerns place *The Devil in Love* at the very least on the edge of the Gothic. Also on the French Gothic margins lurks the Marquis de Sade, who, perhaps not surprisingly, included a baroque farrago of Gothic elements in his works, while 'sadism', in the modern sense of the word (and it has been observed that sado-masochism emerged simultaneously with Gothic literature), is a phenomenon widely to be found in Gothic fiction – if seldom employed on quite the elaborate scale favoured by the 'divine Marquis'. De Sade's overall impact on the wider development of Gothic, fantastic, Romantic and decadent fiction, as on psychoanalysis, would be hard to underestimate (as elaborated in Mario Praz's seminal study, *The Romantic Agony*, first published in English in 1933). For instance, Charlotte Dacre's novel *Zofloya, or The Moor* (1806) – which appeared chronologically mid-way between the Gothic romances of Radcliffe and Mary Shelley's *Frankenstein* – in addition to drawing on elements from both Radcliffe and Lewis, is at least equally close to de Sade in its depiction of a heroine with a fully conscious commitment to vice and in its weighing, albeit at a less sophisticated level, of the attractions of criminality and the insidious progression of depravity.

Much of what might be called French Gothic fiction can be seen to stem from these prototypes, together with the impact of English Gothic and the German Romantics (in particular, from the cult status acquired by Hoffmann in the late 1820s). Such cultural cross-fertilization is exemplified by the publication, in the *Revue de Paris* in 1829, of Scott's critical essay on Hoffmann (and, for that matter, his 'Introduction' to Mrs Radcliffe was translated into Russian, via French, in 1826). The revived vogue for *le fantastique* and *l'école frénétique* can be seen as Gothic offshoots. Crime, horror and incarceration loom large in the writings of Pétrus Borel. Crime and psychological intrigue underpin a number of works by Balzac, while a little earlier the psychological frontiers of nightmare had been tested by Charles Nodier. Gothic, or near-Gothic, works of one tendency or another emerged too in this period from such prominent writers as Victor Hugo, Jules Janin, Théophile Gautier, Alexandre Dumas *père*, Prosper Mérimée and Gérard de Nerval (the last-named left the second part of his main contribution to the genre, *Aurélia, or Dream and Life*, in unrevised form when he hanged himself in 1855). Later additions to such a list would include Villiers de l'Isle-Adam and Guy de Maupassant.

From Germany, Gottfried Bürger's ballad *Lenore* (1773) provided his European and American successors with one of Gothic's archetypal figures: that of the revenant-bridegroom; the poem was translated into English by Walter Scott and into Russian by Zhukovsky (with versions and adaptations by others). Such an apparition manifests itself too at the climax of Schiller's influential and popular early story *The Ghost-Seer* (1784), itself influenced by Cazotte. This story, which – like *Lenore* – achieved multiple early translations into English, contains many of the ingredients of classic Gothic and the fantastic. Coleridge was a great admirer of Schiller, Byron was inspired by *The Ghost-Seer*, and it would be difficult to doubt that Maturin's *Melmoth the Wanderer* was influenced by it. Schiller's broader impact on Europe and Russia is, of course, well attested.

There also developed in Germany a genre of popular literature known as the *Trivialromane*, analogous to and influential upon English Gothic fiction (see the famous listing in Jane Austen's *Northanger Abbey*). At the turn of the century, the remarkable stories of Heinrich von Kleist (1777–1811) and the extraordinary anonymously published *The Nightwatches of Bonaventura* (1804) are not without their Gothic qualities. Kleist's *The Beggarwoman of Locarno*, for instance, qualifies as a supreme example of a Gothic miniature (of just three pages), while his *The Marquise of O—* has been considered, by Ernest Jones among others, an archetypal vampire story (Frayling 1992: 144–145). In his *The Foundling*, an historical Italian setting provides the backdrop for an uncanny doubling (of the foundling Nicolo and the dead Colino) in a series of confusions: of a portrait and its real life resemblances, and of the living and the dead, in sharp relief against polarities of good and evil. Not in entirely dissimilar vein, 'Bonaventura', in his sectionalized 'Night Watches', furnishes the reader with a unique admixture of apocalyptic vision along with the grotesque and the gruesome, underpinned with a substratum of cemetery nihilism.

Arguably, however, the most influential figure of German Romantic prose, in its Gothic-fantastic and *Märchen* modes at least, was E.T.A. Hoffmann (1776–1822). Several of his works can be identified as particularly Gothic in form, or as massively influential upon the later development of European Gothic-type fiction. *The Entail* (1817) is perhaps his most classically Gothic story, set in a sinister Castle R., in which the narrator's sensitivities are heightened by reading Schiller's *The Ghost-Seer*, and by the presence in the castle of 'an evil family secret' and 'a dreadful ghost' (see Hoffmann 1982); dynastic inheritance is the issue; buried treasure and murder unfold; the ghost of the murderer still wails from the ruins. More significantly, the by now already traditional figure of the manic monk is developed by Hoffmann in his own redoubtable contribution to the Gothic novel, *The Devil's Elixirs* (1816: a fundamental work of the European Gothic style, long overdue a reprint in its English translation (Hoffmann 1963)). Focusing on the dual concepts of the divided self and the vicissitudes (and the metaphysics) of coincidence, and presented through the time-honoured Gothic-romantic device of the 'manuscript', Hoffmann's novel deals with the expiation of the sins of a degenerate line, by means of conflict between forces of the divine and the demonic and redemption through love. Skilful exploitation of the multidudinous familiar trappings of Gothic horror build this work into a thrilling novel of suspense; and yet the darkness of Brother Medardus's life achieves its ultimate redemption, just as the manifold enigmas of interwoven plot and subplot are granted demystification. The main impact of this novel, however, arose from Hoffmann's treatment, in this most complex of his works, of crises of identity, bizarre and terrifying mental experiences arising under extreme duress, and the theme of doubles. Many subsequent works in the Gothic mode (by Nerval or Gogol, Poe or Dostoevsky, and indeed many others) would seem inconceivable without Hoffmann.

NEIL CORNWELL

Russia

The involvement of a classical Pantheon of deities (demons, or diabolism) – even in Russian affairs – can be found in certain eighteenth-
century texts, and has been traced (from a work of 1769 by Vasilii Maikov
onward) in a recent essay by Richard Peace (Peace 1999). The first Russian Gothic story proper, however, appears to be *The Island of Bornholm*
(*Ostrov Borngol'm*, 1794), by Nikolai Karamzin (see Offord 1999). A
sentimentalist author of stories, poetry, essays and travelogues,
Karamzin (1760–1826) subsequently turned himself into Russia's first
major historian. Under the influence of English and European Pre-
romanticism, Karamzin's stories emphasize sentimentalist and historical themes, with a tinge of graveyard Gothic (as in his most famous tale,
Poor Liza, of 1792). In just one instance, *The Island of Bornholm*, this
formula is reversed, to result in a predominantly Gothic tale with the
trappings of sentimentalism (for these stories, see Karamzin 1969).

Gothic works in Russia remained few and far between before the
1820s, although one little-known novel of this period, *Don Corrado de
G[u]errera, or the Spirit of Vengeance and the Barbarity of the
Spaniards* (1803), by Nikolai Gnedich (1784–1833: better known as
the translator into Russian of *The Iliad*), has recently been exhumed
for examination (Tosi 1999). The romantic poet Vasilii Zhukovsky
(1783–1852) twice reworked Bürger's *Lenore* into Russian versions:
Svetlana (1808–12 – an English version is in Rydel 1984: 111–113); and
Liudmila (1808), and much later produced a translation (*Lenora*, 1831:
on these works see Pursglove 1999). Clara Reeve's *The Old English Baron*
had been translated into Russian as early as 1792. French translations of
English Gothic fiction were commonly known in Russia (where the educated elite were far more accustomed to reading in French than in Russian), and translations of English fiction into Russian were frequently
made from the French (as were many of the early translations into English of Russian works). Ann Radcliffe's novels appeared in Russian in the
early 1800s, leading a wave of Gothic translations, along with certain
works of others falsely attributed to her (a not uncommon 'convention'
of the time). These included Matthew Lewis's *The Monk* (no less!), and
The Romance of the Pyrenees, by a certain Catherine Cuthbertson.
Obscure English authors of popular Gothic to achieve appearances in
Russian in this period include Anna Maria McKenzie, George Walker and
W.H. Ireland (see Vatsuro 1996; 2000, on 'pseudo-Radcliffiana'[10]).

114

Vatsuro's work on the Gothic in Russia and Todorov's theory of the fantastic apart, the Soviet critic N.V. Izmailov had traced a tradition of the fantastic in Russia (Izmailov, 1973). This had been a somewhat negative category to the radical critic Vissarion Belinsky (involving the far-fetched, the supernatural and the otherworldly), but had been rather more frivolously approached by Osip Senkovsky (1800–58), who had written tales of his own of this stamp under the name of 'Baron Brambeus'. Eastern influences (Senkovsky was himself an orientalist), folkloric motifs and the fairy tale all fed into the Russian fantastic, along with the idealist philosophy of Schelling and the impact of the Gothic and the ballad (identified by Izmailov as subgenres of pre-Romanticism); fate, revenge and the intervention of otherworldly powers (often resulting in gloom, tragedy, moralizing and mysticism) lead this version of the fantastic to merge with Vatsuro's ideas of a Russian Gothic. Izmailov (1973: 141–145) dates the beginning of this tradition proper to the stories of the somewhat Hoffmannian cycle by Pogorelsky (1787–1836) entitled *The Double, or My Evenings in Little Russia* (*Dvoinik, ili moi vechera v Malorossii*, collected 1828: English translation Pogorelsky 1988); he then traces it in some detail up to 1844, the year of publication of Odoevsky's in effect valedictory *Collected Works* (*Sochineniia*). Similarly, V.M. Markovich (1990: 6) dates the beginning of the 'fantastic novella' tradition in Russia to stories by Pogorelsky and Bestuzhev-Marlinsky of 1825. It should be added that, in Russia by the 1840s, 'there were already sixty translations of Hoffmann's stories and fourteen articles about him' (Downes 1999: 55 n. 7).

'Are there really such things? ... [as Russian novels]', the aged Countess of Pushkin's *The Queen of Spades* (*Pikovaia dama*, 1834) asks her nephew; 'I want the sort where the hero doesn't strangle either his father or mother, and there are no drowned bodies' (Pushkin 1997: 76). Russian prose fiction indeed matured slowly over the first quarter of the nineteenth century and, if there was a heyday of Russian Gothic fiction, it certainly fell in the second quarter. Aleksandr Bestuzhev (1797–1837), later known under the pen-name 'Marlinsky' after being imprisoned and exiled for his role in the Decembrist uprising against the accession of Nicholas II of 1825 (and subsequently disappearing in action in the Caucasian colonial wars) published, under the impact of Radcliffe, Scott and Irving (plus touches of Shakespeare and Schiller), a number of Gothic tales in the 1820s and early 30s, mostly still untranslated into English.[11] These comprise, by general consensus, *The*

Traitor (*Izmennik*) and *Castle Eisen* (*Zamok Eizen*, both of 1825); and a trio of 'mature' stories from the turn of the 1830s: *An Evening at a Caucasian Spa in 1824* (*Vecher na Kavkazskikh vodakh v 1824 godu*), *The Terrible Fortune-Telling* (*Strashnoe gadan'e*), and *The Cuirassier* (*Latnik*). Marlinsky combines strong Gothic elements with historical settings and folkloric motifs.[12] *The Cuirassier*, however, progresses to near-contemporaneity (an established trend in Russian fantastic tales by the 1830s (Markovich 1990: 12)), a more sophisticated narrative technique, and the fullest range of Gothic motifs.

Another writer to pour Romantic-Gothic motifs into popular fiction in this period was the historian, dramatist and journalist Nikolai Polevoy (1796–1846). In particular, his tale *The Bliss of Madness* (*Blazhenstvo bezumiia*, 1833) is a potboiler of overt Hoffmannism (complete even with a framing device of a group of friends reading a Hoffmann tale). An obsession with a woman he believes to comprise half his soul leads the protagonist to his doom in a madhouse, in a narrative bestrewn with trappings of the occult, conjuring an Italian atmosphere in St Petersburg, and motivated on a more realistic plane through card-sharping and fortune hunting. The main trio of characters in the embedded tale (sensitive artistic man, mysterious young woman, and demonic father-figure) are to be found too in Gogol's *Terrible Vengeance* (*Strashnaia mest'*) and recur later in Dostoevsky's *The Landlady* (*Khoziaika*). A not entirely dissimilar triangle occurs in Elena Gan's *Society's Judgement* (*Sud sveta*), of 1840 (English version in Andrew 1996); the proposition that the works of Gan (1814–42) include at least an element of 'Female Gothic' (a concept all but unrecognized in commentaries on Russian literature of the period hitherto) has now been examined in a recent essay (Ayers 1999).

Mikhail Lermontov (1814–41), by the end of a brief and stormy literary career, had left two unfinished works of Gothic fiction, *Vadim* and *Shtoss*. The latter is a tale of mystery and demonic card-playing, begun only months before Lermontov's fatal duel (English versions in Korovin 1984; Rydel 1984). *Vadim* (written 1832–34, published 1873), the principal product of Lermontov's prose juvenilia, comprises a little over a hundred pages of a historical novel of the eighteenth-century Pugachev rebellion, apparently influenced by Scott and Hugo. The eponymous protagonist is a demonically depicted hunchback, whose mission of righteous revenge in a family feud (against a tyrannical landowner, somewhat in the mode of Walpole's Manfred) turns, entangled in the mayhem of a Cossack uprising and fuelled by an unbridled jealousy inspired by designs of incest, into pure malevalence. A slightly grotesque concentration on beggars and mutilation gells with motifs of the monastery, confinement, torture and a labyrinthine cave, described in detail suggestive of both Gothic architecture and fiction.[13] This place, named Devil's Lair (*Chortova logovishcha*), where unclean spirits are thought to hold sway, is clearly destined to be the *locus* of a melodramatic climax – were the novel to have been completed.

The other major figure of Russian prose in this period, Nikolai Gogol (1809–52), incorporated Gothic settings or features into a number of his Ukrainian and Petersburg tales. An important example of the artistic Gothic is his Hoffmannian *The Portrait* (*Portret*, 1835; somewhat toned down Gothicwise in the revision of 1842), which projects a Gothic struggle of good and evil into the creative process itself, highlighting the eponymous evil-eyed and cursed painting.[14] The demonic Ukrainian story *Vii* and the Petersburg extravaganza *The Nose* (*Nos*) have been treated as a Gothic pair, or 'double', in themselves (see Meyer 1999: English versions are in Gogol 1994 and 1995 respectively). For that matter, Lachmann prefers to see Gogol's *The Nose* and Dostoevsky's *The Double* (*Dvoinik*, 1846) as 'a process of textual doubling' (Lachmann 1997: 303).

However, it might be argued, the most impressive body of fiction at least approximating to a genuine form of Russian Gothic writing belongs to Vladimir Odoevsky (1804–69). This would include several of the stories contained within his philosophical frame-tale *Russian Nights* (*Russkie nochi*: first integral publication 1844), along with a number of independent tales or novellas. Most notable of these are his 'dilogy' *The Salamander* (*Salamandra*, 1841) and *The Cosmorama* (*Kosmorama*, 1839).[15] In addition, Odoevsky wrote shorter Gothic stories, such as *The Ghost* (*Prividenie*: English versions in Korovin 1984; Minto 1994), which could almost be taken as a whimsical reworking of Hoffmann's *The Entail*. Two of his stories, 'The Improvisor' (*Improvizator*, from *Russian Nights*: see Odoevsky 1997) – word for word – and, to a lesser degree, *The Sylph* (*Sil'fida*, 1837: in Odoevsky 1992), it has now come to light, were plagiarized – via a French translation of the 1850s – by the Irish-American fantastic-Gothic writer Fitz-James O'Brien (1828–62).[16] Frequently dubbed, though not of course entirely accurately, 'the Russian Hoffmann', Odoevsky includes a full gamut of occult and Gothic paraphernalia scattered through his collective tales: magical and alchemical effects, the suspension of time and place in an ultra-Gothic-Romantic extension – indeed the dissolution – of what is now seen as the Bakhtinian chronotope, supernatural arson and spontaneous human combustion, through to the walking dead. He also specialized in proto-science fiction and anti-Utopia, as well as artistic delirium, or a kind of manic *Künstlernovellen*, in tales based on Piranesi, Beethoven and J.S. Bach (in addition to his literary and governmental service careers, Odoevsky was, among yet other things, a musicologist and an amateur alchemist).[17] Odoevsky's use of (German) romantic and esoteric-inspired 'poetical mysticism', however, is not to be confused with 'religious mysticism' (Markovich 1990: 34).

Like Lermontov (but four years earlier), Aleksandr Pushkin (1799–1837) cut short his literary career through a fatal duel. No text can rival Pushkin's *The Queen of Spades* for the position of undisputed masterpiece of Russian Gothic. Neither has any comparable short Russian text (given its mere 30 pages in length) been accorded such massive critical attention. *The Queen of Spades* can be read as a Gothic tale *par excellence*, as Gothic parody, or – given that it is a prime example of the pure fantastic (and recognized as such by commentators stretching from Dostoevsky to Todorov) – in almost any number of yet further ways: from society tale, to psychological study, to numerological puzzle.[18] Among the many possible sources tapped by Pushkin can be numbered *The Devil's Elixirs* and another Hoffmann story, *Gambler's Luck* – both of which feature hallucinations or obsessions with cards. The epitome of the 'Petersburg tale' in Russian literature, *The Queen of Spades* extends from its near contemporary metropolitan Russian setting back in time to the 1770s and geographically west, to the Paris of the *ancien régime* and the pseudo-occultism of the Count Saint-Germain. Economic drive, sexual exploitation, *idée fixe*, the clash of two eras and the judgment of fate all engage in what is a virtuoso performance of condensed prose. One recent commentator, Andrew Kahn, concludes that: 'Like all works of the supernatural and of the Gothic, *The Queen of Spades* tantalizes by a potential naturalistic explanation of the fantastic, and winks now and then at the pseudo-scientific' (Pushkin 1997: xxvi).

In the following decade of the 1840s, Dostoevsky (1821–81), who claimed to have read Radcliffe's novels while still a child, opened his career with a strong Gothic flourish, offering such works as *The Double* and *The Landlady* (1847).[19] It has been claimed that the narrative logic of *The Double* itself pursues a double strategy, provoking indecision as to 'whether the "substance" of the story is a fantastic reality or a narrated phantasm' (Lachmann 1997: 305). However, Dostoevsky's own near encounter with a Tsarist executioner and an ensuing decade of Siberian exile turned him more toward the directions of political conservatism and psychological realism; nevertheless, residual Gothic elements are apparent throughout his *oeuvre* and made something of a comeback in his later period, both in his short stories of the 1870s and in his final novel, *The Karamazov Brothers* (*Brat'ia Karamazovy*: see Miller 1983; Avsey 1999). Moreover, he was given to an elaborate form of Gothic sketching in his working notebooks.[20]

Another acknowledged master of Russian realism to have begun his career in the 1840s, Ivan Turgenev (1818–83), included amidst his largely realist works a sprinkling of Gothic-fantastic tales, including *Faust* (1856: see Burnett 1999), *Phantoms* (*Prizraki*, 1864) and the late story *Clara Milich* (1883). Still in the early 1840s, however, A.K. (or Aleksei) Tolstoy (1817–75: a distant cousin of the famous Lev Tolstoy and nephew of Pogorelsky) had published vampire tales – partly, at least, under the impact of John Polidori's *Vampyre* (1819: a Russian translation of which, attributed as usual to Byron, had been published in Moscow in 1828).[21]

Tolstoy's *The Family of the Vourdalak*, rated 'one of the most impressive vampire stories ever written' (Frayling 1992: 254), was penned in French by a Russian Count and set in eighteenth-century Serbia. His novella-length tale *Vampire* follows Polidori in positing the operation of vampires within high society – in this case in a largely Russian setting, though with pre-histories (recent and distant) removed to Italy, medieval Hungary and (by vision) mythological Greece. Polidori apart, it is claimed (see Karpov 1990: 662) for the tradition of Hoffmann, Gogol, de la Motte Fouqué, Goethe (*The Bride of Corinth*) and Mérimée (*La Guzla*). Echoes of works by Schiller and Odoevsky may also be detected, while the levels of embedded narration, together with the featuring of brigands, doubles, visions, drugged punch, and other forms of explained (or partly explained) mystification are reminiscent of Potocki. The final existence of vampires within this plausibly parodic imbroglio remains in some doubt (as does precise identification of the eponymous revenant), while the revelation of an underlying family curse brings the tale closer both to what we have termed classical and society Gothic.

Madness, of one type or another, was a frequent ingredient of Russian fiction, from Pushkin through to Vsevolod Garshin's *The Red Flower*

(*Krasnyi tsvetok*, 1883) and Anton Chekhov's *Ward No. 6* (*Palata No. 6*, 1892). Other writers to essay something resembling a Gothic style include Nikolai Leskov and Aleksei Apukhtin (see their stories in Minto 1994). In the main, however, a relatively straight realism seemed to be the dominant force in Russian literature until the Symbolist movement emerged towards the end of the century, when Romantic and Gothic dualities returned with something of a vengeance. In that *fin de siècle* ambiance, even the medical realist Chekhov (1860–1904) turned his hand to Gothic phantasmagoria – in one tale at least: *The Black Monk* (1894: on which see Komaromi 1999).

The demonic (or forms of diabolism, or the satanic), witchcraft and other Gothic appurtenances continued to resurface in Russian litera-ture, even into the Soviet period (see the collection of essays in David-son 2000), most notably in the writings of Mikhail Bulgakov (see Menhennet 1983, on Hoffmann and Bulgakov), while the city of St Petersburg (renamed Petrograd, Leningrad, and finally St Petersburg again) has continued to exercise its own Gothic-type mystique. Indeed, the St Petersburg theme (or 'text') in Russian literature (from Pushkin, Gogol and Dostoevsky, on to Andrei Bely and beyond) could even be said to contribute a sub-category of its own: 'St Petersburg Gothic'.

We have already seen a number of instances of cross-fertilization at play in the literary developments outlined above. In recent times, Carlos Fuentes, writing of the literary origins of his novella *Aura*, traced its basic plot (through *The Queen of Spades*, its reworking in *The Aspern Papers* by Henry James, and analogously with the figure of Miss Havisham in *Great Expectations*) back to a Chinese tale, deriving in its turn from 'the traditions of the oldest Chinese literature, that tide of narrative centuries that hardly begins to murmur the vastness of its constant themes: the supernatural virgin, the fatal woman, the spectral bride, the couple reunited' (Fuentes 1988: 38). Such is the process by which literature evolves.

Cazotte's pioneering *The Devil in Love* made its impact on Schiller, Matthew Lewis and subsequently Hoffmann. We have already com-mented, in this respect, also on Schiller's *The Ghost-Seer* and Bürger's ballad *Lenore*. Mary Shelley's *Frankenstein* had its Russian connec-tions[22] (not least in the final chase over the northern ice); moreover, Odoevsky reviewed her later novel *The Last Man*, the theme of which he later sketched in a powerful short work called 'The Last Suicide' (form-ing a part of *Russian Nights*). Poe's celebrated 'double' tale *William*

Wilson derived from a Spanish sketch by Washington Irving, in its turn
based on an abandoned project of Byron's drawn from Spanish literature
and suggested to him by Percy Shelley: and there is no saying where its
influence stopped (it continued and evolved, at least as far as Vladimir
Nabokov). As for the Germanic influences on Poe, which were common
also to Odoevsky (and Poe was admired by both Odoevsky and Dostoevsky, as well as, subsequently, by the French and Russian Symbolists)
... ; again, we cannot begin here to take such things further.

Among the direct influences on Odoevsky were Saint-Martin and
Schelling. Odoevsky apart, Cazotte and Balzac were fascinated by the
occult tradition and the *Illuminati* (see Balzac's novella *Séraphita*).
Hoffmann, Gautier and Odoevsky, to name but three, were exercised by
divided-self mental states. Cazotte, Bürger and Gautier portrayed diabolical lovers; vampirism featured in works by Hoffmann, Nodier, Gautier and A.K. Tolstoy. Schiller, Hoffmann and Odoevsky exploited the
theme of the ghostly curse. Hoffmann, Balzac, Odoevsky and Gogol
combined Gothic trappings with art or music. Pushkin, Eichendorff
and Mérimée employed animated statues. Balzac even composed a
sequel to Maturin's *Melmoth the Wanderer* (entitled *Melmoth reconcilié*); *Melmoth* had its impact on both Gogol and Dostoevsky. A
number of writers of Gothic-type fiction (and Russians not least) lived
– or died, or nearly died – somewhat Gothic lives: by duelling, suicide
or even execution; Gogol may have realized one of his long-standing
anxieties by actually suffering premature burial (see Karlinsky 1992,
313–314, n. 54).[23] And so we could continue. And thus, moreover, were
assembled throughout European Gothic literature of the first half of
the nineteenth century more than sufficient ingredients to fuel and
fuel again – across Europe and into Russia – subsequent Gothic revivals
and Neo-Gothic movements.

One final vampirical footnote. It was apparently reported in
Weekly World News (15 August 1989) that, according to a certain
Professor W.H. van der Moer, the AIDS epidemic had 'wiped out almost
all the vampires in Europe!'. Less than a few dozen were thought to
have survived and most of those had fled to the Soviet Union (as was),
which (at that time still) had a lesser incidence of AIDS than western
Europe: 'A spokesman in the Soviet Embassy in Washington, D.C.,
declined to comment on the vampire population of Russia' (Rickels
1999: 106–107).

NEIL CORNWELL

Notes

1 The present essay is a revised and expanded version of my 'Russian Gothic: An Introduction' (published in Cornwell 1999: 3–21). I am grateful to the series editors of
Rodopi's 'Studies in Slavic Literature and Poetics' for approving my reworking of
this previously published material for the present volume. A briefer version, but
with greater emphasis on the European side, appeared as 'European Gothic' in
Punter (2000: 27–38).

2 Blurb to Korovin (1984); for further collections of such Russian material in English
translation, see Proffer 1979; Rydel 1984; Minto 1994.

3 See also Vatsuro (1996); and Vatsuro (2000), the latter comprising extracts from his
book on the subject being prepared for posthumous publication (Vatsuro died in
Januar 2000: see his essays and the tributes to him in *Novoe literaturnoe obozrenie*, 42, 2000). An invaluable general source on Anglo-Russian links over the period
in question is Alekseev (1982). An attempt to survey the impact of English Gothic
on Russian literature has also been made by Simpson (1986).

4 For an account of this topic and its impact on Russia (though concentrated on
the Symbolist period and since), see Bernice Glatzer Rosenthal's 'Introduction'
(Rosenthal 1997: 1–32). For a full historical account of this area of thought, see
Faivre 1994. For general collections of essays on this area in Russian literature,
see Mandelker and Reeder 1988; Cornwell 1999; Davidson 2000. On Hoffmann
in Russia, see: Passage 1963; Ingham 1974; Botnikova 1977; Menhennet 1983;
Downes 1999.

5 For a discussion of the pre-history of Gothic, see Samuel Kliger, 'The "Goths" in
England (1945)', reprinted in Sage (1990, 115–30); Botting 2000; Sowerby 2000.

6 On East European vampires, see Frayling 1992, *passim*; Gelder 1994: 38–41; Rickels 1999: 1–14. For more specialist studies, see Perkowski 1976; 1989, especially
18–34 on Slavic (Balkan and ultimately perhaps Iranian) origins, and 32–34 on the
etymology (almost certainly Slavc – Bulgarian, Macedonian, South Serbian) of
vampir; and Bogatyrev, 1998. For a succinct general vampire summary, though, see
Hughes 1998.

7 Frayling (1992: 62) identifies 'four archetypal vampires in nineteenth-century
fiction': the Satanic Lord; the Fatal Woman; the Unseen Force; and the Folkloric
Vampire.

8 See in particular: Burnett 1981; Jones 1990; 1997.

9 Jones suggests the term 'social gothic' (1990: 120) and employs the phrase 'carnival world of the Gothic' (1990: 125) in his discussion of *The Idiot*. For an attempt
at elucidating the English Gothic novel in terms of Bakhtinian dialogism and
heteroglossia, see Howard 1994.

10 The most bizarre example of this phenomenon was a supposed French translation
of a (spurious) 'posthumous' Radcliffe work: (*Le Tombeau*, ouvrage posthume
d'Anne Radcliffe, traduit par H. Chaussier et Bizet, Paris, 1799) which found its way
into a Russian version (*Grobnitsa*, Moscow, 1802: Vatsuro 2000: 125); on this work
see Lévy 1968: 224–225, 492n.

11 See, however, 'The Terrible Fortune-Telling', trans. K.M. Cook, in Korovin (1984:
133–166).

12 See Vatsuro (1995), who concentrates on *Castle Eisen* and *The Cuirassier*; on the
former see also Bagby 1995: 128–133; and, on *The Traitor*, Leighton 1975: 78–82
and (on 'the tales of horror') 98–106.

13 See Chapter 18 of *Vadim*: Lermontov 1937: 65–71. The entrances to the cave system
are through burial mounds, each of which 'serves as though as a vault for the dark

underground gallery' (67); also within is 'a wide round hall ... paved with stones [which] has four cavities in the shape of niches' and 'a four-cornered pillar [which] supports its clay vault, rather expertly formed' (68) [my translations]. At one point (the end of Chapter 20 and the beginning of Chapter 21), the words 'fantastically' (*fantasticheski*) and 'Gothic hall' (*kak boi chasov v syroi goticheskoi zale*) appear within a dozen lines of each other (84). For an English translation (unavailable to me), see Lermontov 1984; on *Vadim* and the Gothic tradition, see Vatsuro 2000: 143–145.

14   The more usually published second version is included in Gogol 1995; the first version is to be found in English in Rydel 1984.

15   On these two stories, see Cockrell 1999; Ramsey 1999. English versions of both are in Odoevsky 1992.

16   See Cornwell 1998: 157–167.

17   For a full account of Odoevsky's career, see Cornwell 1986; on Odoevsky and the philosophical tradition (esoteric and Romantic), see pp. 91–114.

18   See Whitehead 1999. For a variety of readings, see Cornwell 1993. For a numerological analysis, see Leighton 1994: 131–152; on Hoffmannian parody, see Reeder 1982.

19   Critical literature on *The Double* is widespread. For a recent attempt to rehabilitate the much-denigrated *The Landlady*, see Gaustad 1997.

20   This has recently been examined in some detail by Konstantin Barsht (1999).

21   See Karpov 1990: 662. 'Vampire', is to be found in Korovin 1984: 525–595; also available as 'The Vampire', (Tolstoy 1969). See also Alexis Tolstoy, 'The Family of the Vourdalak', translated by Christopher Frayling (Frayling 1992: 254–279).

22   For an exploration of this theme, see Freeborn 1985; and Alekseev's research on Claire Clairmont and Russia: 'Moskovskie dnevniki i pis'ma Kler Klermont' (Alekseev 1982: 469–573).

23   See, for instance, Karlinsky 1992: 313–314, n. 54: 'The legend that Gogol was not dead, but in a cataleptic trance, at the time of his burial has cropped up persistently in the twentieth century, most recently in a poem by Andrei Voznesensky and in Andrei Sinyavsky's book [published under the name of Abram Terts: *V teni Gogolia*, Overseas Publications Interchange, London, 1975] ... The various versions claim that when Gogol's grave was opened [for the purposes of reburial], his skeleton was found (1) lying face down, (2) on its side, or (3) on its hands and knees. There seems to be no factual confirmation for these stories. Their source is probably the passage in the "Testament" section of *Selected Passages* where Gogol voices his fear of being buried alive and awaking in his coffin and asks that he not be buried until decomposition sets in.' The theme is similarly broached by Gogol in a letter of December 1844 (cited in Fanger1979: 294, n. 37).

References

Alekseev, M.P. (1982) *Russko-angliiskie literaturnye sviazi (XVIII vek – pervaia polovina XIX veka), Literaturnoe nasledstvo*, vol. 91, Moscow, Nauka.

Andrew, J. (trans.) (1996) *Russian Women's Shorter Fiction: An Anthology 1835–1860*, Oxford, Clarendon Press.

Avsey, I. (1999) 'The Gothic in Gogol and Dostoevskii', in N. Cornwell (ed.), *The Gothic-Fantastic in Nineteenth-Century Russian Literature*, Amsterdam and Atlanta GA, Rodopi, pp. 211–234.

Ayers, C.J. (1999) 'Elena Gan and the Female Gothic in Russia', in N. Cornwell (ed.), *The*

Gothic-Fantastic in Nineteenth-Century Russian Literature, Amsterdam and Atlanta GA, Rodopi, pp. 171–187.

Bagby, L. (1995) *Alexander Bestuzhev-Marlinsky and Russian Byronism*, University Park, The Pennsylvania State University Press.

Barsht, K. (1999) 'Goticheskii ieroglif Dostoevskogo', *Novoe literaturnoe obozrenie*, 39:5, 59–84.

Bogatyrev, P. (1998) *Vampires in the Carpathians: Magical Acts, Rites, and Beliefs in Subcarpathian Rus'*, trans. S. Reynolds and P.A. Krafcik, New York, East European Monographs.

Botnikova, A.B. (1977) *E.T.A. Gofman i russkaia literatura*, Voronezh, Izd. Voronezhskogo universiteta.

Botting, F. (2000) 'In Gothic Darkly: Heterotopia, History, Culture', in D. Punter (ed.) *A Companion to the Gothic*, Oxford, Blackwell, pp. 3–14.

Burnett, L. (1981) 'Dostoevsky, Poe and the Discovery of Fantastic Realism', in L. Burnett (ed.), *F.M. Dostoevsky (1821–1881): A Centenary Collection*, Colchester, University of Essex, pp. 58–86.

—— (1999) 'The Echoing eart: Fantasies of the Female in Dostoevskii and Turgenev', in N. Cornwell (ed.), *The Gothic-Fantastic in Nineteenth-Century Russian Literature*, Amsterdam and Atlanta GA, Rodopi, pp. 235–255.

Cockrell, R. (1999) 'Philosophical Tale or Gothic Horror Story? The Strange Case of V.F. Odoevskii's *The Cosmorama*', in N. Cornwell (ed.), *The Gothic-Fantastic in Nineteenth-Century Russian Literature*, Amsterdam and Atlanta GA, Rodopi, pp. 127–143.

Cornwell, N. (1986) *The Life, Times and Milieu of V.F. Odoyevsky*, London, Athlone and Athens, Ohio University Press.

—— (1993) *Pushkin's 'The Queen of Spades'*, London, Bristol Classical Press.

—— (1998) *Vladimir Odoevsky and Romantic Poetics*, Oxford, Berghahn Books.

—— (ed.) (1999) *The Gothic-Fantastic in Nineteenth-Century Russian Literature*, Amsterdam and Atlanta GA, Rodopi.

Davenport-Hines, R. (1998) *Gothic: 400 years of Excess, Horror, Evil and Ruin*, London, Fourth Estate.

Davidson, P. (ed.) (2000) *Russian Literature and its Demons*, New York and Oxford, Berghahn Books.

Downes, S. (1999) 'E.T.A. Hoffmann and the Establishment of Russian Prose Writing in the 1830s', *Essays in Poetics*, 24, 32–57.

Faivre, A. (1994) *Access to Western Esotericism*, Albany, State University of New York Press.

Fanger, D. (1979) *The Creation of Nikolai Gogol*, Cambridge MA and London, The Belknap Press of Harvard University Press.

Frayling, C. (1992) *Vampyres: Lord Byron to Count Dracula*, London, Faber.

Freeborn, R. (1985) 'Frankenstein's Last Journey', *Oxford Slavonic Papers*, New Series, 18, 102–119.

Freud, S. (1990) 'The "Uncanny" (1919)', in *Art and Literature*, Harmondsworth, Penguin, pp. 335–376.

Fuentes, C. (1988) 'How I Wrote One of My Books', in *Myself with Others: Selected Essays*, London, Andre Deutsch, pp. 28–45.

Gaustad, R. (1997) 'Rebuilding Gothic on Russian Soil: The Roles of Religion and Intertwining of Minds in Dostoevskii's *The Landlady*', in K.A. Grimstad and I. Lunde (eds), *Celebrating Creativity: Essays in Honour of Jostein Børtnes*, Bergen, University of Bergen, pp. 205–215.

Gelder, K. (1994) *Reading the Vampire*, London, Routledge.

Gogol, N. (1994) *Village Evenings Near Dikanka and Mirgorod*, trans. C. English, intro. R. Peace, Oxford, Oxford University Press.

—— (1995) *Plays and Petersburg Tales*, trans. C. English, intro. R. Peace, Oxford, Oxford University Press.

Hoffmann, E.T.A. (1963) *The Devil's Elixirs*, trans. R. Taylor, London, John Calder.

—— (1982) *Tales of Hoffmann*, trans. R.J. Hollingdale, Harmondsworth, Penguin.

Howard, J. (1994) *Reading Gothic Fiction: A Bakhtinian Approach*, Oxford, Clarendon Press.

Hughes, W. (1998) 'Vampire', in M. Mulvey-Roberts (ed.), *A Handbook to Gothic Literature*, Basingstoke and London, Macmillan, pp. 240–245.

Ingham, N.W. (1974) *E.T.A. Hoffmann's Reception in Russia*, Würzburg, jal-verlag.

Izmailov, N.V. (1973) 'Fantasticheskaia povest'', in B.S. Meilakh (ed.), *Russkaia povest' XIX veka: Istoriia i problematika zhanra*, Leningrad, Nauka, pp. 134–169.

Jones, M.V. (1990) *Dostoyevsky After Bakhtin: Readings in Dostoyevsky's Fantastic Realism*, Cambridge, Cambridge University Press.

—— (1997) 'The Evoltion of Fantastic Realism in Russian Literature: Gogol, Dostoevskii and Bulgakov', in K.A. Grimstad and I. Lunde (eds), *Celebrating Creativity: Essays in Honour of Jostein Børtnes*, Bergen, University of Bergen, pp. 58–69.

Karamzin, N.M. (1969) *Selected Prose of N.M. Karamzin*, trans. H.M. Nebel Jr, Evanston, Northwestern University Press.

Karlinsky, S. (1992) *The Sexual Labyrinth of Nikolai Gogol*, Chicago and London, The University of Chicago Press.

Karpov, A.A. (ed.) (1990) *Russkaia fantasticheskaia proza epokhi romantizma (1820–1840 gg.)*, Leningrad, Izd. Leningradskogo universiteta.

Komaromi, A. (1999) 'Unknown Force: Gothic Realism in Chekhov's *The Black Monk*', in N. Cornwell (ed.), *The Gothic-Fantastic in Nineteenth-Century Russian Literature*, Amsterdam and Atlanta GA, Rodopi, pp. 257–275.

Korovin, V. (ed.) (1984) *Russian 19th-century Gothic Tales*, Moscow, Raduga.

Lachmann, R. (1997) *Memory and Literature: Intertextuality in Russian Modernism*, trans. R. Sellars and A. Wall, intro. W. Iser, Minneapolis and London, University of Minnesota Press (first published in German in 1990).

Leighton, L.G. (1975) *Alexander Bestuzhev-Marlinsky*, Boston, Twayne.

—— (1994) *The Esoteric Tradition in Russian Romantic Literature*, University Park, The Pennsylvania State University Press.

Lermontov, M.I. (1937) *Polnoe sobranie sochinenii v piati tomakh*, Moscow-Leningrad, Academia.

—— (1984) *Vadim*, trans. H. Goscilo, Ann Arbor, Ardis.

Lévy, M. (1968) *Le Roman 'gothique' anglais 1764–1824*, Toulouse, Association des Publications de la Faculté des Lettres et Sciences Humaines de Toulouse.

Mandelker, A. and Reeder, R. (eds) (1988) *The Supernatural in Slavic and Baltic Literature: Essays in Honor of Victor Terras*, Columbus, Slavica.

Markovich, V.M. (1990) 'Dykhanie fantazii', in A.A. Karpov (ed.) *Russkaia fantasticheskaia proza epokhi romantizma (1820–1840 gg.)*, Leningrad, Izd. Leningradskogo universiteta, pp. 5–47.

Menhennet, A. (1983) 'Hoffmann, Bulgakov and the "Fantastic Tradition"', *Strathclyde Modern Language Studies*, III, 3–20.

Meyer, P. (1999) 'Supernatural Doubles: *Vii* and *The Nose*', in N. Cornwell (ed.), *The Gothic-Fantastic in Nineteenth-Century Russian Literature*, Amsterdam and Atlanta GA, Rodopi, pp. 189–209.

Miller, R.F. (1983) 'Dostoevsky and the Tale of Terror', in J. Garrard (ed.), *The Russian Novel from Pushkin to Pasternak*, New Haven, Yale University Press, pp. 103–121.

Minto, M. (ed. and trans.) (1994) *Russian Tales of the Fantastic*, London, Bristol Classical Press.

Mulvey-Roberts, M. (ed.) (1998) *A Handbook to Gothic Literature*, Basingstoke and London, Macmillan.

Odoevsky, V.F. (1992) *The Salamander and Other Gothic Tales*, trans. N. Cornwell, London, Bristol Classical Press; Evanston, Northwestern University Press.

—— (1997) *Russian Nights*, trans. O. Koshansky-Olienikov and R.E. Matlaw, Evanston, Northwestern University Press [1965].

Offord, D. (1999) 'Karamzin's Gothic Tale: *The Island of Bornholm*', in N. Cornwell (ed.), *The Gothic-Fantastic in Nineteenth-Century Russian Literature*, Amsterdam and Atlanta GA, Rodopi, pp. 37–58.

Passage, C.E. (1963) *The Russian Hoffmannists*, The Hague, Mouton.

Peace, R. (1999) 'From Pantheon to Pandemonium', in N. Cornwell (ed.), *The Gothic-Fantastic n Nineteenth-Century Russian Literature*, Amsterdam and Atlanta GA, Rodopi, pp. 23–35.

Perkowski, J.L. (ed.) (1976) *Vampires of the Slavs*, Cambridge MA, Slavica.

—— (1989) *The Darkling: A Treatise on Slavic Vampirism*, Columbus, Slavica.

Pogorelsky, A. (1988) *The Double, or My Evenings in Little Russia*, trans. R. Sobel, Ann Arbor, Ardis.

Proffer, C.R. (ed.) (1979) *Russian Romantic Prose*, Ann Arbor, Translation Press.

Punter, D. (ed.) (2000) *A Companion to the Gothic*, Oxford, Blackwell.

Pursglove, M. (1999) 'Does Russian Gothic Verse Exist? The Case of Vasilii Zhukovskii', in N. Cornwell (ed.), *The Gothic-Fantastic in Nineteenth-Century Russian Literature*, Amsterdam and Atlanta GA, Rodopi, pp. 83–101.

Pushkin, A. (1997) *The Queen of Spades and Other Stories*, trans. A. Myers, ed. A. Kahn, Oxford, Oxford University Press.

Ramsey, C.C. (1999) 'Gothic Treatment of the Crisis of Engendering in Odoevskii's *The Salamander*', in N. Cornwell (ed.), *The Gothic-Fantastic in Nineteenth-Century Russian Literature*, Amsterdam and Atlanta GA, Rodopi, pp. 145–169.

Reeder, R. (1982) 'The Queen of Spades: A Parody of the Hoffmannian Tale', in G.J. Gutsche and L.G. Leighton (eds), *New Perspectives on Nineteenth-Century Russian Prose*, Columbus, Slavica, pp. 73–98.

Rickels, L.A. (1999) *The Vampire Lectures*, Minneapolis and London, University of Minnesota Press.

Rosenthal, B.G. (ed.) (1997), *The Occult in Russian and Soviet Culture*, Ithaca and London, Cornell University Press.

Rydel, C. (ed.) (1984), *The Ardis Anthology of Russian Romanticism*, Ann Arbor, Ardis.

Sage, V. (ed.) (1990) *The Gothick Novel*, Basingstoke and London, Macmillan.

Simpson, M.S. (1986) *The Russian Gothic Novel and its British Antecedents*, Columbus, Slavica.

Sowerby, R. (2000) 'The Goths in History and pre-Gothic Gothic', in D. Punter (ed.), *A Companion to the Gothic*, Oxford, Blackwell, pp. 15–26.

Todorov, T. (1973) *The Fantastic: A Structural Approach to a Literary Genre*, trans. R. Howard, Cleveland and London, The Press of Case Western Reserve University (first published in French in 1970).

Tolstoy, A. (1969) *Vampires: Stories of the Supernatural*, trans. F. Nikanov, ed. L. Kuehl, New York, Hawthorn Books.

Tosi, A. (1999) 'At the Origins of the Russian Gothic Novel: Nikolai Gnedich's *Don Corrado de Gerrera*', in N. Cornwell (ed.), *The Gothic-Fantastic in Nineteenth-Century Russian Literature*, Amsterdam and Atlanta GA, Rodopi, pp. 59–82.

Vatsuro, V.E. (1995) 'Iz istorii "Goticheskogo Romana" v Rossii (A.A. Bestuzhev-Marlinskii)', *Russian Literature*, 38, 207–226.

—— (1996) 'A. Radklif, ee pervye russkie chitateli i perevodchiki', *Novoe literaturnoe obozrenie*, 22, 202–225.

—— (2000) 'Goticheskii roman v Rossii (1790–1840): Fragmenty iz knigi', *Novoe literaturnoe obozrenie*, 42, 125–145.

Whitehead, C. (1999) 'The Fantastic in Russian Romantic Prose: Pushkin's *The Queen of Spades*', in N. Cornwell (ed.), *The Gothic-Fantastic in Nineteenth-Century Russian Literature*, Amsterdam and Atlanta GA, Rodopi, pp. 103–125.

7

The robbers and the police: British romantic drama and the Gothic treacheries of Coleridge's *Remorse*

PETER MORTENSEN

Over the last decade or so, British Romantic drama has undergone what Greg Kucich accurately calls 'an important revaluation ... with numbers of critics (Donohue, Otten, Gottlieb, Cox, Richardson) showing that the dismissal of Romantic drama has arisen from conventional and mistaken assumptions about its strategies and principles' (1992: 464). No longer are plays such as Wordsworth's *The Borderers* (1796) Shelley's *The Cenci* (1819) or Byron's *Sardanapalus* (1821) routinely dismissed as so many dull exercises in static closet drama and pseudo-Elizabethan blank verse. And yet, at the same time, revisionist criticism of Romantic drama has often proceeded in ignorance of, or even indifference towards, the perhaps most intriguing context for the creation of a substantial and noteworthy body of Romantic drama in Britain: the large-scale invasion of closets and stages, both in London and in the provinces, by European Gothic spectacles and bourgeois tragedies. The 1790s and early 1800s, as Allardyce Nicoll has shown, were the heyday of translation-drama in British theatrical history (1927: 56–73). Not only did both Drury Lane Theatre and Covent Garden Theatre rely on foreign sensational matter to fill their vast galleries. Some of the period's most spectacularly popular plays, such as James Boaden's *Fountainville Forest* (1794), J.C. Cross's *Julia of Louvain; or, Monkish Cruelty* (1797) and Thomas Holcroft's *The Child of Mystery: A Melo-drame* (1801), were based on recent French plays, and around 1800, as Timothy Grieder observes, at a time when 'the main current of Romanticism began to flow in full force', the 'vogue for German drama in England was sufficiently great to be referred to as "the rage"' (1964: 39). Nevertheless, the very same critics whom Kucich cites have for the most part studiously ignored, if they have not actively opposed, any suggestion that the influx of popular French or German plays might have had an impact upon the theatrical climate in late eighteenth- and early nineteenth-century Britain, or that the foreign theatre might even have influenced the tradition of British Romantic drama that they seek to recuperate and re-evaluate.

Romantic-period writers, though, were painfully aware that the nation's theatres were, in the words of one commentator, being 'inundated' by 'Gothic barbarism', 'translated trash' and 'foreign novelty', completing 'the conquest of haste and incorrectness over the English stage' (Preston 1802: 80, 93). Already at the beginning of the 1790s, conservative commentators beginning with Edmund Burke had established the theatre as an unstable and volatile site, vulnerable to subversion and contamination (Burke 1969). By the late 1790s, complaints about foreign dominance of English theatres, accompanied by warnings about the outlandish drama's invasive ability to mislead the *ingénue* devotees of playhouse and circulating library, became almost inescapable. Cultural critics and historians have taken stock of the many predicaments plaguing Britain both at home (starvation, bread riots, fiscal crisis, Luddism, a series of highly publicized sedition and treason trials) and abroad (escalating war, naval mutinies at Spithead and the Nore, Irish rebellion) during the 1790s and 1800s (Hobsbawm 1962; Thompson 1968; Emsley 1979; Colley 1992). These events serve equally well, no doubt, to contextualize the surge of nationalist sentiment that one detects in British theatrical discourse and periodical reviewing towards the turn of the century. British writers, in short, were gripped by an intense cultural xenophobia (Simpson 1993). In attacking European Gothic and sentimental drama, they began with ready-made arguments going back at least as far as Pope's and Swift's attack on the Grub Street hacks in the 1720s, impugning lowbrow romance and spectacle as unfit reading-material for women and the non-leisured classes. But as the soaring number of translation-plays was joined by rumours of secret societies intent on world revolution, and as the spectre of cultural invasion was linked up with very real fears of French invasion throughout 1797–98, the tone and terms of the Romantic reviewers' abuse of Continental texts changed, moving from detached scepticism to controlled condescension and finally to exaggerated condemnation of a seductive form apparently without redeeming social value. The critic John Wilson Croker, for example, constructs a Gothic scenario, maintaining that English stages, in being taken over by foreigners and foreign agents, have been exposed to no less than a 'revolution':

> For I would seek the wond'rous cause,
> That abrogates our ancient laws,
> And like the Gallic revolution,
> Subverts old Crow-street's constitution;
> Thus Shakespeare, Monarch of the realm
> Of plays, his subjects overwhelm,
> And mad with rebel fury grown,
> Insult, and sentence, and dethrone;
> Thus Fletcher, Jonson, Otway, Rowe,
> The nobles of the stage, are low,
> Or else dispers'd by barbarous arts,
> Are *émigrés* in foreign parts;
> Whilst in their places rise and sit,
> The very *tiers-etat* of wit
> (Croker 1804: 27, ll. 21–34)

These are strong words indeed, but Croker was not alone in using the loaded language of invasion, encroachment and usurpation to characterize developments in the theatrical world, and he was far from the only writer who suspected that the British reading and viewing publics needed protection from impious and un-English forms of entertainment. An anonymous writer for the *Anti-Jacobin Review* perhaps most concisely captured these feelings of entrenched hostility and defensiveness when, in surveying the current pitiful situation of Britain's patent theatres, he discerns 'a kind of systematic plan for corrupting the public taste and national morality of Englishmen by the undistinguishing praise and introduction of foreign trash' (Anon. 1800: 568).

The British Romantic writers were influenced by, and participated in, the anti-Jacobin cultural establishment's revulsion against European drama and its shocking popularity on the stage and in the closet. Several of Romanticism's best-known literary manifestos and programmatic declarations, including Wordsworth's 'Preface' to *Lyrical Ballads* (1800) and Coleridge's *Biographia Literaria* (1817), contain paradigmatic passages in which the poets anathematize the flood of dramatic translations that they believed jeopardized the nation's moral and intellectual health (Wordsworth 1974: i, 128–130; Coleridge 1983: ii, 184–185). But the Romantics also developed a different, more diplomatic and ultimately more powerful method for countering the untoward popularity of

Continental Gothicism. Each of the Romantic writers criticized foreign sensationalism and emotionalism as corrupting and contaminating influences, yet each attempted to manipulate these genres' mechanisms, re-deploying them as the focal symbolic ingredients of his or her own writing. With the possible exception of Blake, in fact, all the six 'Great Romantics', at various points in their careers and with varying degrees of success, chose to include the generic resources of Gothic spectacle within their own publications, capitalizing on this genre's success even while harnessing it to their own aesthetically and ideologically revisionist programme. This critical re-deployment of cultural power resembles the process that Walter Benjamin, following Bertolt Brecht, called 're-functioning' (*Umfunktionierung*) (Benjamin 1977: 46–78). Even so, it must also be acknowledged from the outset that the form of Romantic revisionism that concerns me here most often involves a shift of political allegiances very different from, if not antithetical to, the one that these two twentieth-century Marxists envisioned.

This essay dwells on Samuel Taylor Coleridge's *Remorse* (1813), and I explore this play by focusing on Coleridge's response to, and assimilation of, the best-known and most controversial foreign text that ever found its way into Romantic England: Friedrich Schiller's early *Sturm und Drang* masterpiece *Die Räuber* (1780). In so doing, I wish to speculate on the significance which European pre-revolutionary and revolutionary drama acquired during the restive years of British war-time censorship and xenophobia, and to illuminate the ideological and national implications of the embedding, harnessing and denaturing of Continental, extravagant and outlandish discourse which is carried out by Coleridge's legitimate stage-tragedy. I wish to speculate, in other words, on the ways in which literary appropriation could be used and was used, during the Romantic period, to 'inoculate' illicit and pernicious texts, by suppressing their dangerous tendencies and replacing them with more wholesome fare (Barrell 1991: 16).

I

At the beginning of *Die Räuber*, the honourable and talented Karl Moor has been unfairly dispossessed of the title and the property that is rightfully his by his evil brother Franz, who takes advantage of his father's feebleness. In response to being ostracized, Karl pledges his life to the protection of those who have been unjustly trampled upon by the powers that be, and he directs his titanic anger not just against the aristocratic tyrant directly responsible for his own disinheritance, but against all of respectable society. In swiftly changing scenes alternating between Franconia and Bohemia, Schiller then pits the egalitarian camaraderie and bonhomie of Karl's robber-band against the decadent absolutism of Franz. After a series of heroic acts, involving the sacking of a town and the conquest of an entire imperial army, Karl and his rebels return to his native region. Here Karl exposes the tangled plot that his brother has contrived and releases his father, who has been left to die in a dungeon. Finally, the two brothers confront each other, and Franz is vanquished in a violent showdown singled out by the critic Henry Mackenzie for its 'barbarous heroism' (Mackenzie 1790: 190).

Whatever else the plot might have meant in its original, pre-revolutionary context, turn-of-the-century British reviewers were almost bound to consider it a thinly veiled endorsement of Jacobinical ideas and beliefs: a piece of radical propaganda intended to foment destructive desires and encourage anti-social forms of behaviour, by presenting outlawry and brigandage in an ethically understandable and even attractive light. Tytler's English rendition of *Die Räuber*, consequently, was received and excoriated as a malicious and incendiary play, advocating violent retaliation as the only proper reaction to social suppression and economic inequality. Already Mackenzie, in his otherwise positive discussion of *Die Räuber* in 'Account of the German Theatre', alerts his readers to the moral and political malignancy implicit in Schiller's alluring representation of Moor. To point his audience to the potentially baleful effects that Schiller's play and protagonist may have, 'especially on young minds', Mackenzie narrates an anecdote concerning a group of Freiburg university students, who, having read *Die Räuber* and having been 'struck and captivated with the grandeur of the character of its hero Moor', formed their own gang of cut-throats in the forests of Bohemia. 'Hence', Mackenzie further argues, 'the danger of a drama such as this. It covers the natural deformity of criminal actions with the veil of high sentiment and virtuous feeling, and thus separates (if I may be pardoned the expression) the *moral sense* from that morality which it ought to produce' (Mackenzie 1790: 191–192). With his manifest anxiety about Schiller's spellbinding play's socio-political influence, and with his remarks about Moor's power to incite lax morality and bewitch readers into civic insubordination, Mackenzie anticipated later critics' fascinated yet overwhelmingly negative reception of *Die Räuber*.

So universal and so vociferous was the critical condemnation of *Die Räuber* that even A.F. Tytler himself, in the postscript to the second edition of his version (1795), somewhat disingenuously declares that the translator wishes 'earnestly ... that he had *left undone* what he *has done*' (Schiller 1795: v). And so powerful were the objections mounted against Schiller's tragedy that even the Scottish hero-worshipper Carlyle, writing more than 30 years after the publication of *Die Räuber* in *The Life of Friedrich Schiller* (1825), evidently still feels that he has to mention the story of the misled Freiburg scholars. In his portrait of Moor, Carlyle cautiously adds, Schiller may well be accused 'of having set up to the impetuous and fiery temperament of youth a model of imitation, which the young were too likely to pursue with eagerness, and which could only lead them from the safe and beaten tracks of duty into error and destruction' (Carlyle 1896–99: xxv, 2).

II

An enthusiastic letter from Coleridge to Robert Southey, written in November 1794, shows that he had already become fascinated by Schiller and *Die Räuber*. In it he praises the German 'Convulser of the Heart' in extravagant terms (Coleridge 1956–71: i, 122). Most students of Coleridge's career, however, also agree that the author's poetic priorities and political views underwent a drastic sea-change during the years around 1800, when he suddenly began to publicly distance himself from 'Jacobinism' of every sort (cf. Woodring 1961; Thompson 1969; Watson 1976; Roe 1988). Having finished an early version of *Remorse* (*Osorio*) in 1797, it was not until 1813 that Coleridge, perhaps nettled by the 'unwonted popularity' of Schiller's play (which he then described as 'a monster not less offensive to good taste, than to sound morals'), decided to wager his literary fortunes on an anti-Jacobin rewriting of *Die Räuber* (Coleridge 1983: ii, 210, 212).

Comparing *Die Räuber* and *Remorse*, one is immediately struck by a series of almost remarkable resemblances, not only between individual characters, but also between the series of events which bring these characters together. The plays' aristocratic fathers, Count Moor and Lord Valdez, are flawed patriarchs who, since they are no longer masters in their own houses, cannot see the evil that is being perpetrated before their very eyes. The younger brothers Franz and Ordonio, in turn, are stock Gothic misanthropes, who justify their scheming with

quasi-nihilistic reasoning. In Schiller's play, the physically and emotionally crippled Franz has, by an intricate ruse involving purloined
and forged letters, sent his older brother Karl into exile, thus dislodg-
ing him from his proper position as heir to the Moor estate. In
Coleridge's tragedy, similarly, Ordonio – with 'his proud forbidding eye,
and his dark brow' – has displaced his older brother Alvar from his
legitimate position as his father's chief counsel and companion
(Coleridge 1813: 1.2.81). In both plays, then, the central plot-develop-
ment concerns the older brother's attempts to re-establish himself in
the bosom of his family and regain his father's trust, while also exposing the younger brother's treachery to the world. In both plays additional interest attaches to this narrative insofar as Franz/Ordonio have
not only financial but also erotic motives for their sinister machinations: these younger brothers have designs not only on Karl's/Alvar's
title and inheritance, but also on their betrothed Amalia/Teresa.

Virtually all aspects of *Remorse* (the title, the overriding theme of
fraternal betrayal, the medieval and Mediterranean setting, the emphasis on secret conspiratorial societies) recapitulate the effects of German
and Anglo-German robber and revenge drama. The erotic triangula-
tions and interfamilial entanglements in *The Robbers* and *Remorse*
seem so closely akin that they almost lend credibility to some of the
harsh accusations – of lacking originality, unscrupulous composition-
methods and downright intellectual fraudulence – so often brought
against Coleridge over the years (McFarland 1969). With this knowledge in mind, one may find it tempting to agree with Carl Woodring,
who finds the difference between *Die Räuber* and *Remorse* to be on the
whole 'not very great'; with John David Moore, who considers it 'odd'
to 'find a man who had, since 1802, been exerting his talents to dissociate himself from past Jacobinism ... suddenly reviving a play that, ...
could easily have directed the public's attention to the very Jacobinical
ideals that its author had disavowed'; or even with Norman Fruman,
who holds that in Coleridge's tragedy 'all seems echo, imitation, patch-
work' (Woodring 1961: 201; Moore 1982: 455–456; Fruman 1971: 254).
But if *Remorse* seems at first sight only to bear straightforward testimony to Schiller's power and prominence within the cultural marketplace, Coleridge's play upon closer scrutiny breaks down into a complex
mixture of generic conventions, driven by interlocking national, political and literary aspirations. Seeing *Remorse* as one of the 'countless
imitations' that were the 'spawn' of *Die Räuber* does not automatically

make Coleridge, as so many critics have suspected, a plagiarist (Coleridge 1983: ii, 210). If *Remorse* is far from adverse to popular dramatic fashions, the play is also by no means merely another piece of warmed-over imitation-drama. In rewriting *Die Räuber* for post- and counter-revolutionary audiences, Coleridge in fact does considerably more than simply reconstruct the terms and elements of Schiller's tragedy: he skilfully redirects the dangerously exciting lines of recent literary tradition.

Coleridge, most importantly, complicates Schiller's tragedy by introducing a third party in the conflict: the Arab woman Alhadra, who leads the Moorish insurgents. Coleridge, one might argue, splits Schiller's protagonist in two, which allows him to highlight a new thematic and foreground a new message. Alvar's exchanges with Alhadra lie at the heart of *Remorse*; indeed they provide a theoretical framework for understanding the play's fundamental problem: the distinction between revenge and improvement (cf. Carlson 1994: 100–105). Like Alvar, Alhadra has been victimized, several times over, by Ordonio and the corrupt regime that he represents, and understandably enough this has filled her with rage. There is 'no room' in her heart, she says, 'for puling love-tales' (Coleridge 1813: 1.2.322). Instead she is driven by a 'deep contempt for all things' not immediately connected with her thirst for 'revenge' (Coleridge 1813: 4.3.12–13). Upon her first entry, the dagger-clutching Alhadra relates her mistreatment at the hand of the Christians, and she instructs Teresa in the logic of violent retaliation: 'Know you not, / What nature makes you mourn, she bids you heal? / Great evils ask great passions to redress them, / And whirlwinds fitliest scatter pestilence' (Coleridge 1813: 1.1.228–231). The last time we encounter Alhadra, she fulfils her dramatic role by burying her dagger in the chest of the man who has imprisoned her, and who has also meanwhile murdered her husband, Isidore:

> ALHADRA. Why did'st thou leave his children?
> Demon, thou should'st have sent thy dogs of hell
> To lap their blood. …
>   …
> The time is not yet come for woman's anguish,
> I have not seen his blood – Within an hour
> Those little ones will crowd around and ask me,
> Where is our father? I shall curse thee then!
> Wert thou in heaven, my curse should pluck thee thence!

TERESA. He doth repent! See, see, I kneel to thee!
  O let him live! That agéd man, his father.
ALHADRA. Why had he such a son?
*(Shouts from the distance of Rescue! Rescue! Alvar! Alvar! and the voice
of VALDEZ heard.)*
  Rescue? and Isidore's spirit unavenged? –
  The deed be mine!
(Suddenly stabs ORDONIO)

(Coleridge 1813: 5.1.237–254)

Before this climax, Alhadra makes several appearances, in which she reprimands Alvar for his dishonourable timidity in relation to those who torment him. When Alvar relates that he has often 'prayed to the great Spirit that made me, / Prayed, that Remorse might fasten on their hearts, / And cling with poisonous tooth, inextricable / As the gored lion's bite!' Alhadra asks: 'But dreamt you not that you returned and killed them? / Dreamt you of no revenge?' (Coleridge 1813: 1.2.309–314). Misled by Alvar's Oriental disguise, but also shrewdly recognizing his obvious charisma, Alhadra later calls upon him to become a masterful and combative presence on the military and political scene: 'If what thou seem'st thou art, / The oppressed brethren of thy blood have need / Of such a leader' (Coleridge 1813: 2.2.3–4). In response, however, Alvar rebukes Alhadra for her impatience and lack of self-command, and he tells her to put her faith in Providence and the civilizing powers of time:

Of this be certain;
Time, as he courses onward, still unrolls
The volume of concealment
...
I sought the guilty
And what I sought I found: but ere the spear
Flew from my hand, there rose an angel form
Betwixt me and my aim. With baffled purpose
To the Avenger I leave vengeance, and depart!
(Coleridge 1813: 2.2.5–19)

As the widow of a murdered husband and the member of a relentlessly persecuted race, Alhadra appears to have been conceived to exhibit, even to the verge of caricature, the avenging position that Alvar might have chosen. Yet Alvar resists Alhadra's arguments. All change for the better, according to Alvar, takes time. Rather than actively reforming the world, Alvar will give the world a chance of reforming itself. Rather than countering evil with good, he will set up a structure in which evil can convert itself to good.

Alvar's behaviour throughout the play constitutes a serious and thoughtful rebuttal of Alhadra's and Schiller's 'Moorish' call for 'revenge'. Like Moor, Alvar returns, sword in hand, to his native country, where he hopes to right the wrong that has made his existence a death-in-life. Like Moor, Alvar has, in his own words, been 'Injured indeed! O deeply injured' by the very man whom he was most likely to trust (Coleridge 1813: 1.1.115). Coleridge, one may speculate, even hints at this intimate connection between the two characters, when he has Alvar dress up as a Moorish chieftain throughout the entire play. Alvar, though, arrives alone, accompanied by no band of lawless horsemen, and he does not immediately thrust himself upon Ordonio to make him stand trial for his crimes. Unlike Alhadra and unlike his prototypes in European Gothic drama, most significantly, Alvar also arrives already determined to administer justice by pursuing a course of peaceful reform, rather than violent vengeance. Alvar wants to make Ordonio see, and regret, the evil of his ways: hence the title of the play, and hence Alvar's long opening and closing speeches on 'REMORSE'. In his initial conversation with his Arab factotum Zulimez, Alvar first formulates his plan. The mistreatment that he has received at his brother's hands, Alvar explains, is no reason for him to seek a bloody confrontation with the usurper. On the contrary, he says, 'the more behoves it I should rouse within him / Remorse! that I should save him from himself' (Coleridge 1813: 1.1.18–19). Later Alvar reiterates this intention and specifies his project in somewhat greater detail:

> Let me recall him to his nobler nature,
> That he may wake as from murder!
> O let me reconcile him to himself,
> Open the sacred source of penitent tears,
> And be once more his own beloved Alvar.
> (Coleridge 1813: 5.1.94–98)

When landing in Spain, Alvar clings to the hope that Teresa's honour, at least, is not as stained as circumstances make it appear: 'Yes,' he says, 'still as in contempt of proof and reason, / I cherish the fond faith that she is guiltless' (Coleridge 1813: 1.1.86–87). Alvar's faith in Teresa's innocence is quickly vindicated, as it becomes clear that she had no part in the malicious cabal that led to his banishment. Conversely, of course, this realization only casts an even darker shadow of guilt on Ordonio, and it only deepens the schism and exacerbates the conflict between the two brothers. Yet even when he possesses 'damning proof' of Ordonio's patent 'perfidy', Alvar assumes the therapeutic rather than the avenging role, insisting that his is a mission of pacific redemption rather than punitive reprisal (Coleridge 1813: 1.1.71, 38). Alvar has a right to everything that Ordonio owns and is; nevertheless, Alvar insists on dealing leniently with his would-be murderer. Ordonio, Alvar insists, must voluntarily recant his misdeeds; otherwise nothing positive will have come of the entire affair. The moral regeneration of individual or society, to be truly efficient and truly moral, must come from within, develop by its own dynamic and in its own time. It cannot be imposed by force, but can only be helped along by ingenuous devices and artful contrivances. Throughout *Remorse*, Ordonio gives Alvar no indication that the 'pangs of conscience' are about to dispel his villainy and call forth his 'nobler nature' (Coleridge 1813: 1.1.41–44). On the contrary, Ordonio continues to slaughter his one-time accomplice Isidore, beguile his father Lord Valdez, plan the seduction of Teresa, and plot the poisoning of Alvar. And yet, throughout the play Alvar, inveterate Christian humanist that he is, continues to hold out the hand of salvation towards his brother, hoping against all evidence to the contrary that Ordonio will finally bear out his enduring trust in human nature.

Readers have often been struck and mystified by the fact that very little happens in *Remorse*. Henry Crabb Robinson, one of Coleridge's earliest critics, saw that the tragedy's 'poetical merit' was superior to its 'dramatic value' (Robinson 1938: i, 117). The perversely undramatic quality of *Remorse*, however, has less to do with Coleridge's general dramaturgical principles (say, his privileging of character over incident) than it does with his decision to focus the play on a male protagonist who has a seemingly limitless patience for deferral, and who adamantly (and perhaps perversely) opposes bellicosity of any kind. At various times in *Remorse*, other characters confront Alvar to make him give up his 'all too gentle purpose' and assume a more commanding stance towards his oppressor (Coleridge 1813: 1.1.11). For instance Zulimez, whose opinion Alvar respects, opposes his master's disguise-stratagem from the beginning. 'Claim you rights', he beckons his master: '[your project] is too hazardous! reveal yourself, / And let the guilty meet the doom of guilt!' (Coleridge 1813: 1.1.10–12). Zulimez's cautious rejoinder, which he repeats when Alvar embarks upon the wizard-scheme that occupies the middle part of the play, reminds us of the risks which Alvar is willing to take in his effort to 'uncover all concealed guilt' (Coleridge 1813: 3.1.34).

Alvar's reason for repudiating revenge, significantly, is not the simple one of cowardice or womanliness. At one point, he tells Zulimez that 'Manhood has swoln my chest, and taught my voice / A hoarser note' (Coleridge 1813: 1.1.106–107). Alvar also claims that he is in fact a seasoned warrior who, after the attempted assassination three years before, involved himself in religious warfare in 'the Belgic stages', where he 'joined the better cause; / And there too fought as one that courted death!' (Coleridge 1813: 1.1.175–176). 'Long time against oppression have I fought', he later tells Alhadra, 'And for the native liberty of faith / Have bled and suffered bonds' (Coleridge 1813: 2.2.6–8). When Teresa remembers Alvar's looks, she recalls above all 'his commanding eye – his mien heroic, / Virtue's own native heraldry!' (Coleridge 1813: 4.2.55–56). Yet Lord Valdez insists that Alvar, unlike Ordonio, 'ne'er fought against the Moors, – say rather / He was their advocate' (3.3.151–152). Coleridge is eager to make it clear to the reader that Alvar shares Alhadra's zeal for restitution, that he even has the potential for martial and manly self-assertion, but that he consciously chooses to avoid trading blows or crossing swords with his brother. Therefore, the references to Alvar's experiences during his militant captainship remain vague and indeterminate. (What, for example, has happened in 'the Belgic states'? And what is 'the better cause'?) Schiller's Karl Moor, characteristically, makes himself jury, judge and executioner in the condemnation of his own brother and the corrupt social order which he represents. But when it comes to confronting Ordonio, Alvar hesitates, foregoes active campaigning and stubbornly refuses to take justice into his own hands.

III

One of the many features that link *Remorse* with the Gothic heritage in fiction and drama is Coleridge's play's obvious fascination with techniques of supervision, penalization and imprisonment (cf. Byrd 1977; Bernstein 1991). The most obvious evidence for this is, of course, Alhadra's long soliloquy about her incarceration by the Inquisition, when she was cast, 'a young and nursing mother, / Into a dungeon of their prison house' (Coleridge 1813: 1.2.206–207). This speech was singled out for special attention by Coleridge and Wordsworth, who published it as a separate dramatic monologue (entitled 'The Dungeon') in the 1800 and 1802 *Lyrical Ballads*. Besides 'The Dungeon', *Remorse* contains a remarkable number of scenes set in or around prisons, crypts and subterraneous caverns. Hence it is only fitting that the culminating scene of a play so obsessed with techniques of control and correction should be played out in 'A Dungeon', with an imprisoned Alvar confronting his brother Ordonio, who has by now also become his jailer.

More specifically, *Remorse* condemns coercive power, by identifying it with Montviedro, the brutal Catholic Inquisitor. Montviedro directly enters the action of *Remorse* only twice. In the beginning of the play, he accosts Ordonio to retrieve information about Isidore, whom he holds in 'strong suspicion of relapse / To his false creed, so recently abjured', and whom he wants to bring before the 'supreme tribunal' of the Inquisition (Coleridge 1813: 1.2.111–112, 115). In the third act, following Alvar's make-believe summoning of ghosts, Montviedro once again bursts upon the stage, accompanied by armed officials, to take the accused sorcerer to 'a dungeon underneath this castle' (Coleridge 1813: 3.1.141). But even if Montviedro makes few direct intrusions into Coleridge's tragedy, he nevertheless weighs heavily on the other characters' thoughts, discourse and experience. Teresa, for example, bursts out in anger when she discovers Montviedro following a 'new scent of blood', while Lord Valdez warns her not to underestimate the 'stern Dominicans' and 'the horror of their ghastly punishments' (Coleridge 1813: 1.2.105, 4.2.105–106). Alhadra likewise swears vengeance on 'these fell inquisitors! these sons of blood!' (Coleridge 1813: 1.2.182). And Alvar, too, is conscious of the Inquisition's all-encompassing authority: immediately after arriving in Spain he is 'stopped' and 'question'd' by its commissars (Coleridge 1813: 1.2.157, 160).

Remorse is set in a sixteenth-century Spain which is clearly a police state, not unlike the Regency Britain of Coleridge's own experience. Devoid of what he calls 'merely human pity', and operating through a network of 'spies', 'familiars' and 'secret servants', the 'stern Dominican' Montviedro holds the country in an iron grip (Coleridge 1813: 1.3.165, 2.1.154, 1.2.193, 1.2.113). Ordonio, the hereditary prince of the realm, has wisely chosen to enter a strategic alliance with the 'Holy Church' (Coleridge 1813: 1.2.122). Not surprisingly, we are informed that Ordonio 'fought ... bravely / Some four years since to quell these rebel

Moors', and he respectfully addresses the Inquisitor as 'reverend father' (Coleridge 1813: 1.2.124, 130–131). Yet Coleridge's demonization of the Inquisition and its repressive state apparatus is misleading, for this invective conceals the fact that Alvar also represents, and deploys, a form of hegemonic power, especially in relation to the Moors, who are also the objects of inquisitorial violence. Alvar rather finesses the power of the Inquisition, translating it into a different, moral and psychological register. Reeve Parker has patiently teased out the subtle slippages that occur in the relationship between the two brothers, often making it difficult to tell where Alvar's identity ends and where Ordonio's identity begins. Both Alvar and Ordonio have a gloomy and priestly demeanour, and both are associated with religious warfare. Both, moreover, 'are tale-tellers and dissemblers' who possess a 'power to dominate and seduce others to their will'. And at certain strategic moments, such as the conjuring scene of the third act, the play's referential system almost appears to break down, as Alvar and Ordonio become 'demonic versions of each other', and as their 'twin plots collapse into one endlessly proliferating villainy' (Parker 1994: 125, 138). Far from being coincidental, I believe, such obscurities and discontinuities make clear that Alvar and Ordonio cannot be placed in the absolutely antithetical positions that they might have occupied in a more traditional revenge-tragedy. Above and beyond what such a superficial reading would suggest, these overlappings reveal a deeper continuity in what Alvar and Ordonio are, and what they seek to achieve.

The difference that separates Ordonio's, Montviedro's and Alvar's perspectives on the world, ultimately, is not the distinction between tyranny and freedom, villainy and heroism. Instead, one might argue, the fraternal conflict allegorizes the transition from a pre-modern, overt form of discipline, which operates from without on the body of the condemned person, to a modern, discrete form of discipline, which is all the more pervasive and efficient in that it enlists the subject in the project of his or her own domination (Foucault 1977). In teaching the Moors to let bygones be bygones, Alvar seeks to constitute them as modern disciplinary subjects, capable of self-policing and self-improvement. Preaching remorse and forbearance represents a new and more streamlined technology of power, but a technology of power none the less. Hence, a subtle realignment or displacement takes place within the pages of *Remorse*. Like *Die Räuber*, *Remorse* is a play about the conflict between two morally opposed brothers, but *Remorse* is not the libertarian play that it may seem to be, and which Coleridge may have intended it to be when he set out to write *Osorio* in 1797. Coleridge's finished tragedy, finally, is less concerned with the danger posed by Montviedro's and Ordonio's authoritarian brand of power, and more concerned with finding new, more poignant and economical methods for confronting and containing the more immediate danger represented by the Moresco insurgency. Alvar, to judge by his reactions, is more upset by Alhadra's proto-Jacobinical speeches than he is distraught at having been robbed of his fiancée and his possessions. Similarly, it is striking that Alvar spends fully as much time in the play convincing Alhadra about the evils of revolution as he does concocting schemes to improve Ordonio, supposedly the real culprit of the piece. Alvar certainly misses no opportunity to lecture the other characters, especially the truant and rebellious Moors, on the value of Christian forgiveness and individual self-restraint; he constantly urges them to follow his own stoic example, by checking their own unlawful impulses and controlling their powerful cravings. From this perspective, then, it almost begins to seem as though Alvar and Ordonio are associates rather than enemies, and at times it almost becomes impossible to tell them apart. *Remorse*, in other words, repudiates one mode of repressive authority only to install another in its place. Within the play, alliances are subtly reimagined in such a way as to pit the two brothers not so much against each other, but rather against the common foes currently threatening the stability of the realm.

IV

The British Romantic writers' intertextual transactions with European Gothic plays must be viewed as a subtle and carefully calculated bid to incorporate and co-opt Continental tales of wonder and excess, capitalizing on their sensational popularity while also using them to convey very different political messages. Linda Colley, in her book *Britons: Forging the Nation 1707–1837*, has argued that British national identity was an invention constructed during the series of Continental wars in the eighteenth and early nineteenth centuries. The confrontation with the obviously hostile European 'Other' encouraged the British to define themselves against it (Colley 1992). The foreign Gothic drama functioned exactly as such 'an-Other', an alien and hostile presence which could be rhetorically conquered through opposition or appropriation, thus enhancing the power of British literature and nationhood. The Romantic solution to Britain's post-revolutionary crisis, then, involves the strategic reinvigoration of popular romance-fictions, to combat those of German, French and English radicals. Considered in their own right, it is true, foreign plays such as Schiller's *Die Räuber* or Goethe's *Götz von Berlichingen* may, as Coleridge writes, result in 'a moral and intellectual *Jacobinism* of the most dangerous kind ... [namely] the confusion and subversion of the natural order of things' (Coleridge 1983: ii, 190). Yet by rewriting foreign writers' transgressive plots, the British Romantic poets, novelists and playwrights could still exploit the success of this dangerously un-English genre, even while using it to solidify a national culture and buttress a national identity in the period of the Revolutionary and Napoleonic wars.

Schiller's *Die Räuber* is a tragedy about disenfranchisement and revenge, but Coleridge's *Remorse* is a revenge-tragedy shrewdly written as a moral critique of revenge. Reacting against Schiller's 'material sublime', and registering his own increasing reservations about all forms of reformist violence and public activism, Coleridge allies his protagonist Alvar with those thoughtful men (poets, priests and philosophers, primarily) who possess 'absolute' genius, and who 'rest content between thought and reality, as it were in an intermundium' (Coleridge 1983: i, 32). Coleridge's adaptation of *The Robbers* made the proto-revolutionary motif of the wronged but virtuous son palatable, enjoyable and even commercially profitable for British theatrical culture during the years of the counter-revolutionary consolidation. The first Romantic play to succeed or even triumph on the London stage, *Remorse* ran for twenty nights at Drury Lane, appeared simultaneously and subsequently in the provinces and America, went through three printed editions before the year was over, and earned the impecunious Coleridge a much-needed profit of '£400: including the Copy-Right' (Coleridge 1956–71: iii, 437).

Interestingly, the ideological function of *Remorse* – the fact that it works as an august corrective to the pre-Romantic cult of the wilful ego – was explicitly recognized in the reviews. *Remorse*'s reception-history indicates that many critics lauded the play as an antidote to corrupt dramatic practices, and as proof of an imminent theatrical revival in Britain: in short, as a welcome example of the kind of writing which would contribute to the moral, political, and aesthetic education of the volatile, newly literate masses. Critics for the *Morning Post* and the *Literary Panorama* commend *Remorse* for its moral tendency, which they declare 'perfect' and 'honourable' (Jackson 1970: 118, 136). A writer for *La Belle Assemblée* tellingly writes that 'this Tragedy ... holds out a promise that the Muse of Tragedy has not quite deserted the English stage' (Jackson 1970: 137). In contrast to the language of seduction, irresponsibility and excess, which dominated discussions of contemporary French, German or Franco-German plays, *Remorse* was consistently constructed in the critical vocabulary of enclosure and decorum. Most remarkably, in an essay that must surely have inspired Coleridge and the other romantic stage-reformers with a sense of triumph, an exuberant critic for the *Christian Observer* points out that *Remorse*, while 'rivalling some of the best of the German plays',

> has no resemblance to them in their affection of strained and extravagant sentiment, and still less in the sublime inversions and suspensions of the ordinary rules of morality. ... Its general design is to exhibit the moral dangers of pride; the proneness of the descent from imaginary perfection to the lowest depths of depravity; the miseries attendant upon conscious guilt; the consolations and the rewards of virtue. It has, besides, the rare recommendation of being totally free from every stain of indelicacy, and the praise, among all other plays, peculiar (we believe) to this, of enforcing the Christian duty of the forgiveness of injuries. On this last ground it is not easy to applaud Mr. Coleridge too highly. We hail with delight every attempt to infuse genuine principle into a class of composition which, of all others perhaps the most effective in the formation of character, has hitherto been exclusively employed either in cherishing the bad passions, or, at best, in inculcating the heathen virtues. (Jackson 1970: 147)

The *Christian Observer* makes no secret of its intense and usually inflexible anti-theatricalism. It asks:

> What Christian has not lamented that the fascinations of the stage, the mingled attractions of shew, and song, and dance, of graceful gesture and impressive intonation, should be so inseparably in league with a pernicious or defective moral, lending their whole influence in opposition to that sacred cause which they might be applied with irresistible effect to promote? (Jackson 1970: 148)

In Coleridge's case, however, the journal is willing to make an exception, for Coleridge has made an important intervention in the ongoing cultural warfare; he has contributed to the hegemonic project of re-colonizing the stalls of Britain's circulating libraries, and of re-conquering the stages

THE ROBBERS AND THE POLICE

of the nation's Theatres Royal for Christian civilization. Confronted with world imperialist crisis, severe economic hardship and intensifying working-class militancy, the *Christian Observer* argues, Britain stands in need of just the kind of strategic compromise which Coleridge has to offer. Classed with tragedies by Shakespeare, Corneille, and Otway, *Remorse* represents that rare thing, a playable and viewable yet ethically impeccable play, written not to excite but to 'controul and purify' the passions, 'by the inculcation of a genuine and Christian morality' (Jackson 1970: 148). Coleridge has taken important steps towards redeeming the British stage. Most recently a site of social subversion, the theatre has now once again become what it (presumably) was in Shakespeare's day: a forum of national subject-formation. Where the foreign drama sprawls, exhilarates and proliferates, *Remorse* regulates, constrains and contracts. It rectifies the errors of the past, replacing vice with virtue. 'It is, indeed, a work of highly moral, and, we may almost say, of religious tendency' (Jackson 1970: 147).

References

Anon. (1800) 'The Literati and Literature of Germany', *The Anti-Jacobin Review and Magazine*, 5, 568–580.
Barrell, J. (1991) *The Infection of Thomas De Quincey: A Psychopathology of Imperialism*, New Haven, Yale University Press.
Benjamin, W. (1977) *Understanding Brecht*, trans. A. Bostock, London, New Left Books.
Bernstein, S. (1991) 'Form and Ideology in the Gothic Novel', *Essays in Literature*, 18, 151–165.
Burke, E. (1969) *Reflections on the Revolution in France*, ed. C.C. O'Brien, Harmondsworth, Penguin.
Byrd, M. (1977) 'The Madhouse, the Whorehouse, and the Convent', *Partisan Review*, 44, 268–278.
Carlson, J.A. (1994). *In the Theatre of Romanticism: Coleridge, Nationalism, Women*, Cambridge, Cambridge University Press.
Carlyle, T. (1896–99) *The Works of Thomas Carlyle*, 30 vols, London, Chapman.
Coleridge, S.T. (1813) *Remorse. A Tragedy, in Five Acts*, London, W. Pople.
—— (1956–71) *Collected Letters of Samuel Taylor Coleridge*, ed. E.L. Griggs, 6 vols, Oxford, Oxford University Press.
—— (1983) *Biographia Literaria*, eds W.J. Bate and J. Engell, 2 vols, Princeton, Princeton University Press.
Colley, L. (1992) *Britons: Forging the Nation 1707–1837*, New Haven, Yale University Press.
Croker, J.W. (1804) *Familiar Epistles*, Dublin, John Barlow.
Emsley, C. (1979) *British Society and the French Wars 1793–1815*, London, Macmillan.
Foucault, M. (1977) *Discipline and Punish*, trans. A. Sheridan, New York, Pantheon.
Fruman, N. (1971) *Coleridge: The Damaged Archangel*, New York, George Braziller.
Grieder, T. (1964) 'The German Drama in England, 1790–1800', *Restoration and 18th-Century Theatre Research*, 3, 39–50.

Hobsbawm, E.J. (1962) *The Age of Revolution 1789–1848*, London, Weidenfeld and Nicholson.

Jackson, J.R. de J. (ed.) (1970) *Coleridge: The Critical Heritage*, New York, Barnes and Noble.

Kucich, G. (1992) '"A Haunted Ruin": Romantic Drama, Renaissance Tradition, and the Critical Establishment', *The Wordsworth Circle*, 23, 64–75.

McFarland, T. (1969) *Coleridge and the Pantheist Tradition*, Oxford, Clarendon.

Mackenzie, H. (1790) 'Account of the German Theatre', *Transactions of the Royal Society of Edinburgh*, 2, 154–192.

Moore, J.D. (1982) 'Coleridge and the "Modern Jacobinical Drama": *Osorio, Remorse*, and the Development of Coleridge's Critique of the Stage, 1797–1816', *Bulletin of Research in the Humanities*, 84, 443–464.

Nicoll, A. (1927) *A History of Late Eighteenth Century Drama 1750–1800*, Cambridge, Cambridge University Press.

Parker, R. (1994) 'Osorio's Dark Employments: Tricking Out Coleridgean Tragedy', *Studies in Romanticism*, 33, 119–160.

Preston, W. (1802) 'Reflections on the Peculiarities of Style and Manner in the late German Writers, whose Works have appeared in English; and on the Tendency of their Productions', *Edinburgh Magazine*, 20, 353–361, 406–408; 21, 9–18, 89–96.

Robinson, H.C. (1938) *Henry Crabb Robinson on Books and their Writers*, ed. E.J. Morley, 3 vols, London, J.M. Dent.

Roe, N. (1988) *Wordsworth and Coleridge: The Radical Years*, Oxford, Clarendon.

Schiller, F. (1795) *The Robbers*, trans. A.F. Tytler, second edn, London, G.G.J. and J. Robinson.

Simpson, D. (1993) *Romanticism, Nationalism, and the Revolt Against Theory*, Chicago, University of Chicago Press.

Thompson, E.P. (1968) *The Making of the English Working Class*, New York, Vintage.

—— (1969) 'Disenchantment or Default? A Lay Sermon', in C.C. O'Brien and William Dean Vanech (eds), *Power and Consciousness*, London, University of London Press, pp. 149–181.

Watson, G. (1976) 'The Revolutionary Youth of Wordsworth and Coleridge', *Critical Quarterly*, 18, 49–66.

Woodring, C.R. (1961) *Politics in the Poetry of Coleridge*, Madison, University of Wisconsin Press.

Wordsworth, W. (1974) *The Prose Works of William Wordsworth*, eds W.J.B. Owen and J.W. Smyser, 3 vols, Oxford, Clarendon Press.

8

Translating Mary Shelley's *Valperga* into English: historical romance, biography or Gothic fiction?

JOHN WILLIAMS

Valperga was Mary Shelley's second published novel. Though the idea for it took root while the Shelleys were living at Marlow in 1817, it was not published until February 1823, seven months after Percy Shelley's death. It by no means took that long to write, however. Having found the subject of Castruccio, the Tuscan warrior politician who became embroiled in the struggles for liberty in fourteenth-century Italy, Mary Shelley's opportunity to work on it was disrupted by the decision to return to Italy in March 1818. A series of traumatic events then channelled Shelley's creative drive into writing a novel of desertion and suicidal despair, *Matilda*. She resumed work on *Valperga* when the couple moved into the Casa Frasi in Pisa in January 1820. Read biographically, the progression from *Matilda* to *Valperga* describes a woman coming to terms with the deaths of her three children (her first child died in 1815, Clara and William in 1818 and 1819 respectively), and with her husband's continued infatuations with other women. For *Valperga* she read her way into the history of medieval Italy and (with marketability in mind) undertook a serious study of Scott's technique in blending historical fact with fiction for his Waverley novels.

In *Valperga* Shelley set out to explore a number of different boundaries, and for the most part she did so in a highly self-conscious, deliberate way. There were pressing economic motives for producing a safe novel that would sell well, but Shelley was her father's daughter, and *Valperga* aimed also to educate and improve its readers. The historical novel format ought to have ensured commercial success; Shelley's interest and facility in historical research and biography confirmed it as a wise choice. *Frankenstein* may have brought her to public notice as an author despite its anonymity, but the Shelley circle (including Godwin) was of the opinion that it was too difficult and controversial a novel ever to find a mass readership. Scott had mastered the craft of negotiating the boundary between history and fiction, and between antiquarian interest and current affairs in a format that the public clearly relished. Shelley was more than adequately in command of her historical material; she needed to study Scott's technique in blending his ingredients to produce interesting characters and a compelling story-line.

Given the Italian setting of the novel, relating the past to the present did not, on the face of it, appear likely to create problems for a politically nervous publishing industry in England. A part of the increasingly independent life Shelley began to build for herself at Pisa was the interest she took in the chaotic political situation that existed in Italy after the Napoleonic wars. Metternich's partitioning of Italy at the Congress of Vienna in 1818 had, of course, been quite literally all about establishing boundaries between the victors and the vanquished, both on the map and in the mind. Castruccio's story, set in a politically divided land rife with political intrigue, could be made to act as a commentary on the divided state of modern Italy with little difficulty.

Indeed, this was what one of her major historical sources had been concerned to do. J.C.L. Sismonde de Sismondi's *Histoire des républiques italiennes du moyen âge* (1809–18) celebrated the virtues of the medieval Italian Republics in a manner that left little doubt as to his abhorrence of the way autocratic rule was sweeping across Europe in the wake of the Napoleonic wars. Besides Sismondi, Shelley's sources included Machiavelli's and Tegrimi's biographies of Castruccio, and Villani's *Florentine Annals*; but it was no doubt Sismondi (whose book was as yet unavailable to English readers) who provided a model for translating the historical record of Italy in the middle ages into a novel that might offer powerful support to the aspirations for political liberty that were stirring in contemporary Europe, and Italy in particular.

Recent research has highlighted Mary Shelley's enduring sense of engagement with the cause of Italian unity, along with her conviction that writing fiction was a powerful means of disseminating the issues and encouraging a response. For instance, Nora Crook has now confirmed Emily Sunstein's earlier tentative attribution of the essay 'Modern Italian Romances' to Mary Shelley (Crook 1999). The essay was written in 1838 for Dionysius Lardner's *Monthly Chronicle*, and recommends the novels of Guerrazzi and D'Azeglio to its readers. Like her own

Valperga (and later, *The Fortunes of Perkin Warbeck* 1830), these are novels which engage with current political issues through fictions woven into narratives of the historical past. The attribution of 'Modern Italian Romances' to Shelley prompts further speculation as to the extent of Shelley's awareness of Italian revolutionaries in exile in London during the 1830s. At the time she was writing *Valperga*, however, this still lay in the future. In the early 1820s, already a committed scholar of Italian history, she would have been studying also the extent to which Sismondi was prepared to massage the historical record to present republicanism in as favourable a light as possible. If she had misgivings in this respect as an historian, as a novelist she was prepared to follow Scott's example and make adjustments where appropriate. Most notably in this case, she altered the dates of Castruccio's life.

However, the insinuation that this blend of past and present might also be read as a critique of contemporary British political life was seen as unavoidably problematic. Where Scott was concerned, history invariably taught the need for pragmatism and reconciliation. Shelley, as might be expected, intended to offer her readership a somewhat less compromising lecture at a time when hopes of genuine political reform seemed to be receding in the face of continued complacency and hypocrisy on the part of the political establishment. Writing to Maria Gisborne in July 1820 of the impending coronation of George IV, she revelled in the news of the scandal surrounding Caroline of Brunswick:

> The Queen! The Queen! The Queen! Does it not rain Queens in England, or at least orations sent post from Heaven with pleadings in favour of our heroic – magnanimous – innocent – virtuous – illustrious and lion-hearted British one ... Tantini said he saw her at the Campo Santo – She had on a black pelisse, tucked up to her knees, and exhibiting a pair of men's boots. A fur tippet that seemed as if it would cover ten such – a white cap, and a man's hat set on sideways. – to be sure, she is injured, but it is too great a stretch of imagination to make a God of a *Beef-eater*, or a heroine of Queen Caroline. – but I wish with all my heart downfall to her enemies, and that is no great stretch of compassion. Besides her, you have the coronation to carry joy to the hearts of H.M.'s subjects. Oh! they are a pretty set! Castlereagh's impudence and Brougham's speechifying – I believe the latter to be a good man at bottom, but he is naturally cautious, *canny*, as they say in his Country. (Bennett 1980–88: 1, 156)

Translating Sismondi into English through the pages of *Valperga* would carry the message of political justice from Europe into the heart of a nation still in thrall to a reactionary government, a nation where even men like Brougham who were to be looked to for enlightened and humanitarian views could not wholly be trusted, a nation ruled over by a disreputable monarchy that now appeared to be in a state of total disarray.

Castruccio, born a Ghibelline, gravitated towards the Guelph faction, the party of absolutism for whom any notion of rule by popular consent was anathema. His mentor in *real politik* is Alberto Scoto, who explains to him that:

> A chief in Italy ought to pay strict attention to the discipline and equipment of his followers, and to the spreading the terror of his name among his enemies. This must be his first step; and without that the foundations of his power are as sand; for to have many cities subject to his command is as nothing in the hour of danger, since if he control them not with iron, gold will ever find its way into the councils of citizens; and woe and defeat are to that chief, who reigns only by the choice of the people; a choice more fickle and deceitful than the famed faithlessness of woman. (Shelley 1997: 57)

Motivated by personal greed and love of power, Castruccio typified for Shelley the forces of repression that continued to oppose the champions of Italian nationalism in her own time. Representative of the liberal, democratic tendency is Euthanasia Adimari, whose family home is the castle of Valperga, where Castruccio receives his education as a child. As Johanna M. Smith has observed, Euthanasia's father and his friend Francesco de Guinigi are made to preach the equivalent of French Enlightenment physiocracy (Smith 1996: 70). Castruccio soon rejects their pacifist ideals and egalitarian dreams.

Valperga provided Shelley with a scenario that enabled her to show just how thoroughly she had learnt from Scott's use of the sense of place in his novels, where certain values and ideals become associated with specific locations as the story unfolds. Castruccio and Euthanasia are childhood lovers; politically they subsequently drift poles apart. Their differences become encapsulated in Castruccio's restless, wandering life, which contrasts with Euthanasia's settled, idyllic household at Valperga. Unlike Scott, however, Shelley was not prepared to write towards an ending that promised a resolution of differences; she chose tragedy. And in the process, writing about Valperga itself, she also chose to distance herself from the way in which not only Scott, but many other contemporary writers would have depicted the castle stronghold.

The popularity of Gothic romances had designated castles (or their equivalents) as the seat of tyrannical male authority; we do not have to read far into the story of *Ivanhoe* (1820) before being reminded of this:

> The kings of the Norman race, and the independent nobles, who followed their example in all acts of tyranny, maintained against this devoted people a persecution of a more regular, calculated, and self-interested kind. It is a well-known story of King John, that he confined a wealthy Jew in one of his royal castles, and daily caused one of his teeth to be torn out, until, when the jaw of the unhappy Israelite was half disfurnished, he consented to pay a large sum, which it was the tyrant's object to extort from him. (Scott 1996: 81)

By Chapter 24 of this novel Scott has arranged for most of his worthy characters to be incarcerated within the 'grey and moss-grown battlements' of the fortress of Torquilstone:

> It was a fortress of no great size, consisting of a donjon, a large and high square tower, surrounded by buildings of inferior height, which were encircled by an inner court-yard. Around the exterior wall was a deep moat, supplied with water from a neighbouring rivulet. Front-de-Bœuf, whose character placed him often at feud with his enemies, had made considerable additions to the strength of his castle, by building towers upon the outward wall, so as to flank it at every angle. The access, as usual in castles of the period, lay through an arched barbican, or outwork, which was terminated and defended by a small turret at each corner. (Scott 1996: 223–224)

Within the forbidding building, Scott's heroes and heroines are to face an assortment of horrors worthy of the genre. In so doing, however, he was not writing a 'Gothic novel' so much as importing elements of Gothic into his story to aid and abet what is best categorized as an historical novel; by the same token Shelley was by no means slavishly prepared to follow the Gothic formulae, and here she reassembled a Gothic set piece in a particularly interesting light. Our first sight of the castle seems to establish a familiarly Gothic context:

The road that led from Lucca to Valperga struck directly across the plain to the foot of the rock on which the castle was built. This rock overhung the road, casting a deep shade; and projected, forming a precipice on three sides; the northern side, at the foot of which the Serchio flowed, was disjoined from the mountain by a ravine, and a torrent struggled in the depth, among loose stones, and the gnarled and naked roots of trees that shaded the side of the cleft. Castruccio began to ascend the path which led to the portal of the castle, that was cut in the precipitous side of this recess, and was bordered by chesnut trees; the foliage of these had fallen; and their spoils, yellow, and brown, and red, were strewed on the shining leaves of the myrtle underwood. (Shelley 1997: 101)

Johanna Smith and others have recently drawn attention to the way in which the castle of Valperga, 'Gothic' though its appearance might be from without, is in fact an oasis of domestic felicity ruled over by Euthanasia who represents 'a maternal legacy of political liberty and public virtue' (Smith 1996: 73). Here certainly is one explanation why the novel was destined never to become the bestseller it was hoped it might be. Unlike Montoni's mouldering castle in Ann Radcliffe's *The Mysteries of Udolpho* (1794), Valperga is a comfortable home; unlike the forbidding monastery of San Stefano in which Ellena is incarcerated in *The Italian* (1797), Valperga is light and airy. Euthanasia's room in particular symbolizes civilized living:

A small tripod of white marble curiously carved, stood in the middle of the room, supporting a bronze censer in which the incense was burning; several antique vases and tripods adorned the room; the tables were of the finest stones, or of glass mosaic; and the seats or couches were covered with scarlet cloth inwoven with gold. Within this was Euthanasia's own apartment; it was hung with blue silk, and the pavement was of mosaic; the couches were richly embroidered, and a small table of *verde antique* stood in the middle of the room. In the recesses were several stands for books, writing materials, &c.; and in the embrasures of the widows were bronze stands, on which were placed finely embossed gold vases, filled with such flowers as the season afforded. But, amidst all this luxury, the richest ornament of the room was the lovely possessor herself. (Shelley 1997: 102–103)

Valperga challenged the politics of the Treaty of Vienna, and in particular it challenged the political Establishment inhabited by its British supporters. As she wove these themes into the historical narrative of Castruccio's career, Shelley also found herself engaging critically and subversively with her literary models; with Scott in particular, but more generally with the popular taste for Gothic romance, and the way in which its progeny tended to reinforce Europhobia among its English readers. Jane Austen's experience of reading Radcliffe had, of course, left her with quite the opposite anxiety as to the effects of Gothic, and in *Northanger Abbey* (published 1818) she managed to encapsulate the complacent frame of mind that Shelley most detested:

Charming as were all Mrs. Radcliffe's works, and charming even as were the works of all her imitators, it was not in them perhaps that human nature, at least in the midland counties of England, was to be looked for. Of the Alps and Pyrenees, with their pine forests and their vices, they might give a faithful delineation; and Italy, Switzerland, and the South of France, might be as fruitful in horrors as they were represented. Catherine dared not doubt beyond her own country, and even of that, if hard pressed, would have yielded the northern and western extremities. But in the central part of England there was surely some security for the existence even of a wife not beloved, in the laws of the land, and the manners of the age. Murder was not tolerated, servants were not slaves, and neither poison nor sleeping potions to be procured, like rhubarb, from every druggist. (Austen 1995: 174)

In the context of the novel as a whole, it is important to recognize that even a statement as seemingly forthright as this, coming from the narrator rather than from a character, may be deconstructed for evidence of ironic intent. However, I would maintain that Shelley's motives for subverting the popular Gothic tropes of Radcliffe and 'her imitators' remain fundamentally different from those of Austen. She was convinced that murder was indeed 'tolerated', and would have quoted the Peterloo massacre of 1819 to prove it. In addition to this, her handling of the Gothic ingredients of *Valperga* seems to suggest that most if not all of this kind of fiction tends to reinforce the power of patriarchy it claims to find so appalling. It is hardly surprising, therefore, that the novel she consequently wrote was to be nowhere near as appealing as its more traditionally Gothic counterparts, or for that matter, as the more orthodox kind of parody that Austen had produced.

Negotiating the boundary between the Italian historical novel and contemporary political commentary on Italy – and by clear implication England – no doubt gave Shelley her most satisfying *raison d'être* for the novel, while it presented Percy Shelley (acting as his wife's publishing agent) with a challenging task in damage limitation. He was at pains to reassure his publisher that the book was a harmless historical romance, and not at all politically dangerous. His motives were clearly for the best, but the consequent tendency to marginalize his wife's literary achievements should perhaps remind us that this was a time when his relationship with Mary had deteriorated into something approaching a stand-off, with Mary's step-sister, Claire Clairmont, unable to claim Shelley for her own, while Shelley himself was indulging in a fantasized passion for the young Emilia Viviani. It was not to be long before he began to gravitate towards another member of the Pisan circle, Jane Williams.

Thomas Love Peacock had sketched what is clearly a partial – but no less penetrating – analysis of the problem in *Nightmare Abbey*, published in 1818. Scythrop is Percy Shelley, and while the name of his partner, Marrionette O'Caroll, suggests a composite sketch of Harriet, Mary and Clare, the problem described remained very much the one Mary was having to negotiate:

> She loved Scythrop, she hardly knew why; indeed she was not always sure that she loved him at all: she felt her fondness increase or diminish in an inverse ratio to his. When she had manoeuvred him into a fever of passionate love, she often felt and always assumed indifference: if she found that her coldness was contagious, and that Scythrop either was, or pretended to be, as indifferent as herself, she would become doubly kind, and raise him again to that elevation from which she had previously thrown him down. Thus, when his love was flowing, hers was ebbing: when his was ebbing, hers was flowing. Now and then there were moments of level tide, when reciprocal affection seemed to promise imperturbable harmony. (Peacock 1969: 95)

Enough has by now been said to propose that another boundary negotiation is taking place in the pages of *Valperga*, one as characteristic of Shelley's literary output as it is absent from Scott's Waverley novels. *Valperga* is a *roman à clef*, a genre that invariably transports commentary into controversial critical and theoretical territory. Shelley, however, indisputably creates her historical figures in the likeness of the major players in her own life, rendering *Valperga*, along with the rest of her fiction, a text that may be considered in part as a formative document in the process of manipulating the evolving public perception of a 'Romantic movement' in England at this time. The *roman à clef* is a peculiarly perverse and intriguing blend of fiction with biography and autobiography, and at its worst it invites a reductionist reading redolent with gossip and scandal. Shelley's persistent engagement with the genre, however, cannot be excluded from an assessment of her work; in *Valperga* the personalizing strand of her narrative is an integral part of the process by which she negotiates the boundaries between past and present, between history and fiction, and between Italy and England.

The boundaries involved here are complex indeed, and despite the fact that it is an unfashionable critical enterprise, I shall now consider the relationships that exist between the characters in the novel, and the people in the Shelley circle upon whom they were – in varying degrees – based. The contemporary reader of *Valperga* would have little difficulty in recognizing ample helpings of Byron in the initial description of Castruccio:

> His beauty took a more manly cast; somewhat of pride, and more of self-confidence, and much of sensibility, were seen in his upturned lip; his eyes, dark as a raven's wing, were full of fire and imagination; his open forehead was shaded by the hyacinthine curls of his chestnut coloured hair. His face expressed extreme frankness, a frankness that did not exist in his mind; for his practices among the wily chiefs of Lombardy had robbed him of all ingenuousness of soul, although the traces of that which he had once possessed had not faded from his countenance. (Shelley 1997: 92)

Castruccio also has his Shelleyan side, and you did not have to be especially well-versed in the gossip of the day to discover a match between the fraught triangular relationship between Claire Clairmont, Percy and Mary, and the relationship explored in the novel between Euthanasia, Castruccio, and Claire cast as the feckless, unstable, gullible, hysterical Beatrice. There is of course much more; not least a characterization of William Godwin as Antonio dei Adimari, Euthanasia's scholarly, but blind and debilitated father. No evaluation of the novel can be complete without a consideration of this autobiographical ingredient. There remains, however, a persistent (and understandable) unwillingness on the part of critics to become enmeshed in the *roman à clef* maze. In a very helpful essay on *Valperga*, from 1997, Betty T. Bennett discusses the relationship between Shelley's characters and their historical originals (favouring Machiavelli over Sismondi as Shelley's primary source), but no mention is made at any point of the contribution the *roman à clef* has to make in this respect (Bennett 1997: 139–151). In the Introduction to his 1997 edition of *Valperga*, Stuart Curran (who opts for Sismondi as a primary source of historical information) likewise avoids all mention of the connections clearly being made by Shelley between her historical characters and the people who had such control over the life she led. Frankenstein, he suggests, is a combined portrait of the male egoism she encountered in Godwin and Percy Shelley; but the figure of Castruccio is compared to Napoleon. This is undoubtedly an important point to make, but it only begins to help us explore what lies at the heart of Mary Shelley's creative drive when we recognize the way in which both Byron and Shelley are being grafted onto the Napoleonic persona.

In his discussion of Shelley's approach to constructing a successful historical novel, Curran draws attention to her reading of Sir Walter Scott, and in particular her indebtedness to *Ivanhoe* (1819). Shelley drew freely on her reading of popular fiction for ideas when it came to the writing of her own novels and stories, but if one novel is to be singled out in the case of *Valperga*, then *Ivanhoe* is almost certainly the most important; but it remains necessary to go beyond the literary and historical sources if the novel is to receive a comprehensive analysis. Shelley's literary sources merge with the biographical facts of her life to produce her literary output, and in the process we see a blurring of the boundaries that existed between formal, public utterance, and private, reflective comment; between the creative self seen both as artificer and as the central subject of the work of art produced. In these circumstances, Shelley was destined never to be able to write popular fiction to order; neither Scott's historicizing nor Radcliffe's Gothicizing would be allowed to pass without a significant injection of her own critical assessment of the kind of writing they represented.

The one thing we should never forget or underestimate is the fact that Mary Shelley was born into an intellectual set that believed itself to be distinct from the rest of society; she was raised on the idea that it was the task of an informed, enlightened elite to educate the masses in the ways of political justice. The members of such a group must expect to be considered pariahs by those in power. Shelley grew up in a family coping with what was effectively a state of exile. Kept by her father for most of the time at arm's length, she observed him living in isolation from a world of political action where he should by rights have been engaged as a leading figure in the process of facilitating comprehensive reform. Percy Shelley had inherited this radical ideal from Godwin, and when, in 1814, Mary and Percy eloped (accompanied by Claire), they set off with the clear intention of establishing an enlightened community that would, before too long, include William Godwin among its number. Mary belonged within a circle that considered its existence – indeed, its most intimate affairs – to be a matter of national significance. For Mary to elope with the young man who seemed the reincarnation of her father's youthful political self was to overstep the accepted moral boundaries of the time, but it was to be entirely consistent with the beliefs she was born to; Godwin's *Political Justice* could be quoted in their defence (much to its author's dismay).

The couple, however, not only exiled themselves from society by their act; they also cut themselves off from Mary Shelley's immediate family as surely as Percy had long since exiled himself from his father. The proposed community of 1814 never of course materialized, but the goal remained a central feature of Percy Shelley's life's work, and his perception of it ran counter to Mary Shelley's aspirations, first as his mistress, then as his wife. She became an exile within the exiled group, reading the situation she was in as it might have been a novel: Percy's various infatuations, the complex shifting relationships between herself, Percy, Claire, Byron, Hogg, the Williamses, Mavracordato, Mrs Mason, Trelawney and sundry others, a group whose existence was predicated on 'a passion for reforming the world' (Peacock 1969: 47). All of this was then duly woven into her reading of history and her study of the writers and politicians who were represented there as having shaped the past.

The Shelleys were of course by no means exceptional in fostering such communitarian ideals, and consequently being lured into what may seem dangerously arrogant assumptions that the fate of the civilized world rested upon the outcome of their publishing and domestic arrangements. As a child, for example, Mary would have heard tell of Coleridge, Southey and Pantisocracy; as an adult she corresponded with Frances Wright, founder of the Nashoba settlement in Tennessee and friend of Robert Dale Owen, son of the socialist reformer, Robert Owen.

Over two generations, the Godwin/Shelley story was to be read as yet one more chapter of the story of the struggle for social and political justice that ran throughout history. Mary Shelley believed in the rightness of the struggle, but when she came to live with Percy Shelley and to know Byron, she was granted an insight into the way in which the struggle to achieve the power and influence needed to reform the world might become a source of corruption. It was a short, easy step from the high ideals of Godwin's *Political Justice* to the Byronic Castruccio; arrogant, cynical, and worldly. He is an easily recognizable stereotype possessed of a Shelleyan *alter ego*:

> Constant exposure to the sun and weather had tinged his cheek with brown; which, but for that, had been deadly pale; for care, and the strong emotions to which he was subject, had left their mark on his countenance; his eye had grown hollow, and the smooth lustre of his brow was diminished by lines, which indeed looked gracefully at his years, since they marked the progress of thought; but some, more straggling and undefined,

shewed that those passions whose outward signs he suppressed, yet preyed upon the vital principle; his eyes had not lost their fire, but their softness was gone. (Shelley 1997: 391)

If this Castruccio would but submit to be guided by the right woman, he would achieve great things. The Castruccio who would be Percy Shelley, however, is all too easily influenced by the powerful personality of his Byronic *alter ego*, even to the point where he becomes obsessed with Byron's woman, Beatrice/Claire. He thus becomes the false lover who conquers the castle of Valperga using knowledge of its surrounds gained when he was the childhood sweetheart of Euthanasia. He is described as disrupting the idyllic domestic order of the castle in a way that clearly suggests the violation of Euthanasia herself. It is at this point in the novel, as Castruccio's soldiers force an entry into Valperga while Euthanasia is led away from it, that the castle eventually assumes the full panoply of a Gothic fortress, but Shelley will not allow the reader to linger there and soak up the atmosphere; we are ejected along with Euthanasia in what is effectively a denial of the genre:

> The women clung about her, kissing her hands, her garments, and throwing themselves on their knees with all the violent gesticulation of Italians. They tore their hair, and called on heaven to save and bless their mistress, and to avenge her wrongs; – 'God bless you, good people!' cried their countess; 'may you never be reminded of my loss by any misfortune that may befal yourselves!'
>
> And, disengaging herself from their grasp, she walked on, while they followed crying and bewailing. She crossed the drawbridge, which was guarded at each end by soldiers; ere she put her foot on the opposite rock, Euthanasia paused for one moment; it seemed to her that all was irretrievably lost, when once she had passed the barrier which this bridge placed between her past and future life; she glanced back once more at the castle, and looked up to the window of her apartment; she had expected to find it desert and blank; but it was filled with soldiers, who stood looking from it on her departure; she sighed deeply, and then with quicker steps hastened down the mountain. (Shelley 1997: 297)

This is an intriguing reversal of the normal progress of the Gothic heroine, whom we would expect to see led – like Emily in *Udolpho* or Rowena and Rebecca in *Ivanhoe* – towards rather than away from the Gothic edifice.

By the end of the novel, the man who – unable to control his passion for Beatrice – has fallen in love (Frankenstein-like) with power itself, also becomes responsible for the death of Euthanasia. Faced with what are clearly several possible interpretations for this ending, it will help if we remind ourselves of the context of this novel within Shelley's career as a writer. The changes she made to the 1831 edition of *Frankenstein* clearly show her pulling back from the political implications of the 1818 narrative, and qualifying the political radicalism of the first version by providing a more sharply defined and controlling domestic context. Eight years before this, in *Valperga*, we may see how the fate of the heroine, though clearly symbolic of the fate of political liberty, is being linked to both the fate of subjected woman, and to Mary Shelley's sense of her own joyless future as the wife of Percy Shelley. It might be said that in this way Shelley returns to the theme of *Matilda*, though the fatal incestuous boundary she explored there between father and daughter is now become in *Valperga* at one and the same time the boundary between husband and wife, between men and women in society at large, and between liberty and slavery in the broadest political sense.

The boundary between what was the Shelleys' business and what was the world's business is thus destabilized by a novel which fictionalizes historical accounts, appropriates the past as the present, projects a critique of Italian political affairs onto an English scenario (in the process subverting the fashionable form of Gothic romance), and enrols the author's friends and neighbours in its cast list. In the end, readers cannot be sure if the text before them should be dealt with as matter for literary criticism, or considered as a test case for a cultural studies project. Destabilizing boundaries that frequently remain unchallenged elsewhere is a primary feature of the 'Gothic' text. Such boundaries include those between life and death, male and female, fiction and 'reality'; between the sublime and the beautiful, and the human and the monstrous. *Valperga* qualifies as a Gothic novel on most, if not all these criteria; it is certainly a novel that explores the way in which reading and writing negotiate a multiplicity of boundaries in the process of establishing meaning.

References

Austen, J. (1995) *Northanger Abbey*, Harmondsworth, Penguin Books.

Bennett, B.T. (1997) 'Machiavelli's and Mary Shelley's Castruccio: Biography as Metaphor', *Romanticism*, 3, 2, 139–151.

—— (ed.) (1980–88) *The Letters of Mary Wollstonecraft Shelley*, 3 vols, Baltimore and

London, John Hopkins University Press.

Crook, N. (1999) 'Sleuthing towards a Mary Shelley Canon', *Women's Writing*, 6, 3, 38–52.

Peacock, T.L. (1969) *Nightmare Abbey*, Harmondsworth, Penguin Books.

Scott, Sir W. (1996) *Ivanhoe, A Romance*, Oxford, Oxford University Press.

Shelley, M.W. (1997) *Valperga, or, The Life and Adventures of Castruccio, Prince of Lucca*, ed. S. Curran, Oxford, Oxford University Press.

Smith, J.M. (1996) *Mary Shelley Revisited*, New York, Twayne Publishers.

9

'Hallelujah to your dying screams of torture': representations of ritual violence in English and Spanish Romanticism

JOAN CURBET

The main concern of this chapter is sacred violence; or, rather, to define the function of representations of that violence and the limits that it encountered in the cultural discourses that emerged during the transition from the eighteenth to the early nineteenth centuries. In order to do so in the limited space of a single chapter, I shall confine myself to contrasting the perspective on religious ritualism that is offered by British authors writing about Spain with the representation of this phenomenon in Spanish culture. I hope that the following analysis will allow us to understand more clearly the thematic signficance of Catholic ritual violence within the Gothic tradition, and also enable us to reach some conclusions as to why the contribution of Spanish culture to this tradition was so scant, while Spain itself was such a fertile theme for literature in English.

In order to state my aims clearly, I shall begin by examining one obvious example of religiously sanctioned violence in one of the period's key texts, Charles Maturin's *Melmoth the Wanderer* (1820). The following extract, occurring towards the end of Chapter 11, presents the imagined execution of Alonso de Monçada, one of the main narrators in the text, as anticipated by him in one of his dreams, after he has been made a prisoner by the Inquisition:

> I saw myself in the garment of condemnation, *the flames pointing upwards*, while the demons painted on my dress were mocked by the demons who beset my feet, and hovered round my temples. The Jesuits on each side of me, urged me to consider the difference between these painted fires, and those which were about to enwrap my writhing soul for an eternity of ages. All the bells of Madrid seemed to be ringing in my ears.

JOAN CURBET

> There was no light but a dull twilight, such as one always sees in his sleep,
> (no man ever dreamed of sun-light); – there was a dim and smoky blaze of
> torches in my eyes, whose flames were soon to *be in my eyes* [...] The next
> moment I was chained to my chair again, – the fires were lit, the bells rang
> out, the litanies were sung; – my feet were scorched to a cinder, – my mus-
> cles cracked, my blood and marrow hissed, my flesh consumed like
> shrinking leather, – the bones of my legs hung two black withering and
> moveless sticks in the ascending blaze; – it ascended, caught my hair, – I
> was crowned with fire. (Maturin, 1989: 236)

This is certainly a text that is indebted to the Enlightenment tradition
of representing ritual and religious violence from a critical perspective.
The work of Voltaire, for instance, is full of such descriptions; the Portuguese *auto-da-fé* imagined in *Candide* (1759) or the execution of the
Calas family at the start of the *Traité de la tolérance* (1762) would be
two prominent examples of this, both of them also rooted very specifically in the culture of Catholicism. In the same tradition, this extract
insists on the role of the audience that religious ritual demands, and on
its active participation in the ceremony. It is not only the attendance of
the higher institutional authorities at the *auto-da-fé* that is emphasized here, but also the sonorous presence of both the preachers and
the shouting multitude, preceded by the ringing of the bells, all of
which 'seemed to be ringing in the ears' of the horrified narrator. And
it is precisely the subjective quality of the text, in its creation of a feverish, hallucinatory perspective, that takes it beyond Enlightenment critique. The sense of morbid fascination concerning the details of the
ritual and the subjective recreation of them that we see in this passage
would be lacking from similar descriptions by authors such as Voltaire.
Gothic writing separates itself from the tradition of the Enlightenment
by displaying a fascination with the very forms of horror that it criticizes and by renouncing a detached or objective description of them.
There is no suggestion of realism here: the fact that this is a dream
sequence (the light is 'a dull twilight, such as one always sees in his
sleep', and true demons 'hovered round' the speaker's temples) elimi-
nates any possibility of objectivity, and makes clear the masochistic
pleasure that the speaker exhibits in the detailed account of his imagined physical suffering ('my muscles cracked, my blood and marrow
hissed, my flesh consumed like shrinking leather'). Yet this is a sense
of fascination that does not prevent the text from retaining all its critical strength; on the contrary, the text is a subjective, nightmarish

162

recreation of a form of execution that nevertheless defines and criticizes the whole cultural tradition in which it is rooted, and which makes it possible: Spanish Catholicism. In the following pages, I shall consider the significance of the 'Gothic' sense of ritual violence in scenes such as the one quoted above and the importance of their role in the primitivist discourse on Spain; and, on the other hand, I shall examine the particular restrictions under which similar scenes could be represented in Spain at the close of the eighteenth and the start of the nineteenth centuries.

If Spain was perceived at the end of the eighteenth century as a primitive, non-enlightened space, this was also the very source of the fascination it exerted. Spain was not even included in the Grand Tour, and was therefore perceived as remaining, geographically as much as in terms of intellectual development, on the outskirts of Europe. The French contribution to this perception during the early nineteeth century can be found in the literary works of Prosper Mérimée and Théophile Gautier, who defined Spain as the romantic country *par excellence*. However, there was already in existence a major body of work produced by British intellectuals that had taken Spain as a major theme. For them, it was still a primitive country, one of those nations that possessed, as John Gregory put it, 'the bodily powers and all the animal functons in their full vigour'; a country in which where religion is 'universally regarded ... though disguised by a variety of superstitions' (quoted in Miles 1993: 43). Manifestations of religious devotion actually taking place in Spain at the turn of the nineteenth century could easily play on the duality between exaltation and fear: the processions involving flagellations, the worship of relics and the public exhibition of the prisoners and victims of the Inquisition were phenomena still widely practised throughout the peninsula in the late eighteenth century. From the perspective of the European travellers (and also of enlightened Spanish francophiles), these forms of popular ritualism exemplified an alienating tradition, appealing only to the irrational and the primitive response of an uneducated population. But, at the same time, they were beginning to be perceived, at the turn of the century, as 'picturesque', and as being representative of the Spanish *Volkgeist*, of which Catholicism and the sanguine, spontaneous expression of instinct were supposed to be essential aspects. The international perception of these forms of religion oscillated, therefore, between fascination and rejection.

Authors from a Protestant environment (or those who, like Maturin, had been in close contact with it) were alert to the deep connection between the Catholic insistence on sacrifice (the sacrifice of the physical body of Christ as represented by the Eucharist) and the forms of religious violence that were part of Spanish popular culture. In both cases, that culture endowed the sacrificed body, and its surrounding ritual, with a signifying power that it had not possessed in Protestant culture for nearly three centuries. According to historians of religion such as René Girard or Eugenio Trías, most forms of collective ritual enact a symbolic narrative including several episodes of a plot that culminates in a central sacrificial image. In Catholic culture (and more so as perceived by the European primitivist discourse), the key image is the sacrified body, either that of the penitent or that of the living Christ in the Eucharist. As Eugenio Trías has put it, this narrative is 'scenified as an action or as an operation in a ceremonial or ritual that befits it: fundamentally, [that action is] a sacrifice' (Trías 1996: 195). In a similar vein, the palaeographist and anthropologist René Girard states that 'the various procedures by which violence is regulated among men are all analogous ... All of them are rooted in religious celebration' (Girard 1998: 40). According to Girard, 'sacrifice reaches the very centre of the moral and social life of a society, but it does so through an extraordinary paradox ... It combines in itself, at once, the notions of guilt and sanctity, of illegitimate and legitimate violence' (Girard 1998: 36). Sacrifice thus lies at the heart of ritual and it remains at the centre of the ceremony even though the celebration may take different forms. The popular varieties of late eighteenth-century Spanish culture, operating on the margins of Enlightened Europe, deeply immersed in forms of religion that relied on collective celebration, were especially centred on sacrifice, which had to be ritualized violently in order to be effective and to acquire its central significant function.

It should now be evident why the representation of religious ritualism becomes so significant in Gothic writing: for it is precisely in the exaltation of the senses, in overcoming personal limits and in the experience of a significant transcendence, that some forms of Catholic popular ritual (using the sacrifice of the body as the central sign) become close, or analogous to, the experience of terror as represented in literature. As Fred Botting states, 'objects of terror and horror not only provoke repugnance ... but also engage readers' interest, fascinating and attracting them ... Terror, in its sublime manifestations, is associated with subjective elevation' (Botting 1996: 9). There is, then, a double movement of horror and fascination, of fear and transcendent exaltation, that characterizes Gothic horror just as it may characterize some popular forms of religious ritual in late eighteenth-century Spain. The same point is made by Robert Miles, when, in his discussion of the Gothic sublime, he remarks that the eighteenth-century discourse of nervous exaltation 'veils ... a masochistic subject-position and a predisposition to bliss, to pleasurable exaltation' (Miles 1993: 75). The masochistic position corresponds, in religious ritualism, to the position of the subject witnessing the bodily sacrifice either of Christ or of the flagellants. Moreover, the sacrifice itself, while involving the physical destruction of a body as a central sign (the transubstantiated Eucharist or the bodies of the flagellants), opens a space for an encounter with the sublime, and so also assumes a transcendent significance.

Was there a cultural space for a Gothic perspective on these matters in Spain itself at the turn of the century and, if so, where was it located? If we assume, following David Punter and Robert Miles, that the Gothic is a discourse produced by the Enlightenment, then we would have to look for evidence of such a discourse in the work of the Spanish Europhiles. This would include the writings of republican intellectuals such as José de Cadalso or José María Blanco-White, authors whose work brought them into conflict with their own cultural roots. But, paradoxically, the clearest example of a transition towards a Gothic viewpoint is to be found in the pictorial work of an artist who had started his career under the protection of the most conservative factions of the Spanish court: Francisco de Goya y Lucientes (1746–1828). Certainly, Goya's own progress from that of an unknown Zaragozan and a newcomer to Madrid in 1774, to an institutional position at Court in 1799 as Pintor de Cámara under Carlos IV, was made basically by following the neoclassic aesthetic conventions that dominated the Court, and by remaining completely uncritical of the monarchy. One of the main outcomes of this prestigious position was his increasing contact with groups of intellectuals who worked either in the court or around it during the years before the Napoleonic threat became significant. These included thinkers and essayists such as Gaspar Melchor de Jovellanos, Nicolás Fernández de Moratín and Tomás de Iriarte, all of whom had been thoroughly influenced by European Culture, and whose cosmopolitanism and intellectual distance from Spanish religiosity and traditionalism seemed to echo some of Goya's own preoccupations.

Some of the best work produced by Goya in the early nineteenth century reveals an assimilation of this critical discourse which clearly influenced his representation of Spanish culture. Thus some paintings of this period can be seen as documents of the Enlightenment in Spain, and especially of its critical revision of religious ritualism. Let us take, for instance, the painting entitled *Procesión de Disciplinantes* (*A Procession of Flagellants*), from 1812 (Figure 2). On first looking at the picture, we quickly become aware of a series of stark contrasts: between the darkness of the church building, from which the procession is emerging, and the clear skies on its right-hand side; between the mass of the processsion and the whitish, bloodied skins of the flagellants, who also carry a white San-Benito on their heads. Apart from the figure of the Virgin towering above the multitude, and the tortured bodies of the flagellants against the darkened group, individual features are lost within the dark mass constituted by the oppressive bulk of the church and the crowd of pro-cessionaries which cover the better part of the canvas. It is precisely in this negation of individual features, in their disappearance, that we find the key to the Enlightenment perspective informing the whole picture. In a simple but effective set of contrasts, the forces of traditionalism and of ancestral Catholic ritualism have displaced all possibility of clarity and

Figure 2 *Procesión de Disciplinantes* (*A Procession of Flagellants*) by Francisco de Goya (1812)

light to one side of the represented space, while putting in the forefront the tortured bodies of the flagellants.

Still, for all its suggestion of ideological conflict, this picture moves within the parameters of the Enlightenment, offering a clear reading of a tradition that is similar to that offered by José María Blanco-White in his *Spanish Letters*, published more than a decade later in 1822. The following extract from describes a procession akin to the one portrayed by Goya:

> These penitents came from the most abject strata of the lower classes. They were dressed in San-Benitos [*capirotes*], masks and shirts that offered naked backs, all white, to public view. Before joining the procession, they began wounding their backs, and soon they started hitting each other until the blood ran down their clothes. It is plain to see that religion did not have anything to do with these voluntary flagellations. In truth, there was an extended belief that this act had also an extraordinary effect upon the physical well-being of those who participated in it. (Blanco-White 1972: 228) (my translation)

The clear demarcation between 'religion' and 'superstition' that Blanco-White establishes here indicates the solidity of his Enlightenment perspective; yet it is precisely this critical distance that preempts any appreciation of the fascinating, deeply problematic strength of Catholic ritual. Both in this fragment and in Goya's *Procesión de Disciplinantes*, the rational disdain for popular superstition allows for a detached, critical reading of religious violence. However, the very possibility of establishing an objective discourse on the ritual and the sacrifice scenified in them forestalls the state of libidinal excitement brought about by the experience of fascination and fear. In order to reach a different perspective, we have to turn to other treatments of the subject made by Gothic literature and by Goya himself.

One good example of such a different perspective is furnished by another of Goya's paintings on the Inquisition: the earlier *Vuelo de Brujas* (1798) (Figure 3). Here the representation of superstition and its relation to ritualism and violence undergoes a radical shift. Inquisitorial practice and the punishment of the body are also at the centre of the picture, but here the possibility of a clear-cut, rationalist allegory is missing. The dominating darkness of the night, against which the central scene emerges, only allows for the perception of the situation as a vision or as a product of the imagination. The central group in the picture, carrying San-Benitos on their heads, and with the upper part

167

of their bodies naked, are holding the body of a fourth character, a man, close to their mouths, as if about to bite it. The suggestion here is clearly one of vampirism, yet the flames that decorate their San-Benitos indicate that they have been condemned by the Inquisition as sorcerers. The whole group is levitating above the ground; the bodies of the three wizards and their pointed San-Benitos create a vertical axis within the centre of the picture; the whole scene of cannibalism stands out in stark contrast against the night, and dominates the scene on the ground, where two other figures turn their faces away from the spectacle – one by covering himself with a cape, the other by crouching on the floor and hiding his face in his hands.

How is such a scene as this to be interpreted? The innovative force of the picture lies in its refusal to allow a full didactic, allegorical reading of it, whilst simultaneously hinting at such a reading. On the one

Figure 3 *Vuelo de Brujas* by Francisco de Goya (1798)

hand, the two characters on the ground seem to suggest an escapist attitude, a refusal to face the horrors of superstition combined with a fear of them. However, the rest of the picture does not allow for a relativization or a consideration of the ceremony as mere superstition. The central ritual, on the other hand, involves some crucial ambiguities: the sign of the Inquisition is on the sorcerers, who are likely to have been captured or tortured by it, but the key image of victimization is that of the body that is groping for help, and which is about to be bitten by the wizards. Where lies, therefore, the responsibility for this savage ritual? It might lie with the two figures on the ground, who allow the ritual to occur while hiding or recoiling in horror; but then the San-Benitos suggest that the wizards themselves are the victims of a higher institution. The sorcerers are therefore presented as both victims and executioners; a fact that cannot be perceived by those who recoil on the ground in horror, and whose fear might be taken both as consequence and as cause of the scene. The central image of cannibalism indicates that this is a chain of victimization and yet also communicates the impossibility of assigning clear responsibilities for the savage ritual. It is especially important to point out that this visionary painting predates by more than ten years the more clearly enlightened discourse of the *Procesión de Disciplinantes*: we cannot establish a distinction, therefore, between a figurative, almost classical Goya and another, 'Gothic' side of his work that would appear only after the Napoleonic wars and his self-imposed exile. Both before and after his major political problems and personal crises (the death of his eldest son, his separation from the Duquesa de Alba), Goya is constantly shifting between a visionary and a more didactic approach (corresponding to our first and second examples here) and between an enlightened and subjectivist perspective.

The distance between *Procesión de Disciplinantes* and the earlier *Vuelo de Brujas* is the distance between the didactic perspective of the Enlightenment and the Romantic fascination with the forces of superstition and irrationality. It is exactly the same distance that we find between the perspective of Blanco-White in the *Cartas de España* and that which is found in his short stories. It is far from coincidential that this oscillation between didacticism and the Gothic perspective is represented by Goya and Blanco-White, two francophile and Enlightenment thinkers, both of whom became exiles from a culture that they perceived as traditionalist and reactionary, but who experienced their exclusion from this same society as traumatic and crippling. Such an oscillation suggests conflict between the critical perspective and a deep fascination exerted by the object of this critique. The few instances of the Gothic that occur in Spain at the turn of the century are the work of specific, isolated individuals who operated in a state of extreme ambiguity towards their own culture.

Works such as *Vuelo de Brujas* show clearly show the process whereby the critique of religious traditionalism and 'superstition', exemplified by the central image of the sacrifice, comes into conflict, not with the didactic discourse of the Enlightenment, but with its claim to objectivity. In the Gothic, the critical discourse on religious ceremony coexists with the representation of subjective entrancement by it. Maturin's *Melmoth the Wanderer*, published a few years after Goya's painting, provides one of the best examples of such oscillation. In Maturin's novel, all the forms of ritualism that are not Protestant are assimilated under the common features of irrationalism and superstition; yet this ideological resistance to them does not prevent them from becoming objects of fascination. The narrative viewpoint offered by the whole of the novel itself, always hovering between the enlightened rejection of religious violence and its lavish, detailed description, is defined by this double movement. The success of such a narrative enterprise forces the reader to assume a voyeuristic viewpoint that requires the constant renovation of his or her interest, while distancing him or her from it. The novel itself offers the best possible image for the perspective that its reader has to adopt: the image of Immalee on her native island, urged by Melmoth to watch, with the help of a telescope, the barbaric sacrificial ceremony in which the idol Juggernaut crushes human beings before its advancing cart. Horrified, but led on to continue watching by Melmoth, Immalee is deeply affected by the bloody ceremony, yet remains unable to take her gaze away from it – a situation that corresponds precisely to that of the reader of Gothic literature, who is often forced to adopt the position of a voyeur. This insistence on a voyeuristic perspective is, in itself, already indicative of the close link existing between religious sacrifice and the libidinal drive towards violence, which Catholic culture (as understood by the European primitivist discourse) tends to enhance. As Melmoth himself says to Immalee at one point, the pious Catholics who welcome her in Spain are the same that, were she seen as retaining pagan beliefs, would shout their 'hallelujahs to your dying screams of torture' (Maturin 1989: 344). Maturin's novel returns again and again to this theme, tending to push the exploration of the subjective position to the point of sadism; always showcasing the participation of the subject in the ritual and the exaltation of instincts in the consummation of sacrifice.

The importance of the position of both the reader and the narrator as part of the participating audience in the ceremony, and the need to represent it from a subjective perspective, are essential aspects of the Gothic discourse on religious violence. Here, once more, the work of René Girard can help us to clarify the importance of these features. According to Girard, the central sign of the victimized body, which closes the sacred ceremony and gives it its significance, always finally unites all the members of the community at the sacrificial moment. This is, in Girard's view, a cross-cultural phenomenon. Girard claims that the ritual victim both represents and unites all the members of the community, who participate equally in the sacrificial act, far beyond their individual rationality and their individual isolation (See Girard's *La Violence et le sacré*, Chapter 4 especially). The subjective perspective offered by the Gothic involves a sense of fascination that superimposes itself on the ideological critique of Catholic Spain. At the same time, however, it helps to recreate from within the sense of escalating tension and loss of rationality evoked by a ceremony which often culminated in actual sacrifice. The result is an approach that could not have been reached from an Enlightenment position alone since the suggestion of the central sign (the sacrificed body) and the subjugating force of the ritual can only be described adequately by abandoning an objectivist perspective and by evoking the experiences of fear and fascination associated with the act of sacrifice.

There are some major moments in the English Gothic tradition that recreate this same sense of sacrifice as ceremonial, organized precisely according to a pattern of escalating tension and final culmination in the central sign of the tortured body. One of the final scenes of Matthew Lewis's 1820 novel *The Monk*, showing Ambrosio waiting for the moment of his execution at the hands of the Inquisition, can be seen as a prime example of this subjective recreation of sacrificial violence. Ambrosio's terror at being a prisoner makes him oscillate between the temptation offered by a Faustian pact and the embrace of a superhuman disdain for both Christian and satanic allegiance. While the prisoner is visited by Satan, his execution is being prepared outside:

the final moment is anticipated through the sounds infiltrating the cell from the outside; and the growing doubts of Ambrosio as the procession approaches his door are rendered in an escalating accumulation of sound effects. Ambrosio's execution has to take place at midnight because 'the horror of the flames being heightened by the gloom of midnight, the execution would have a greater effect upon the mind of the people'. As the moment approaches, the aural effects increase and begin to take their toll on Ambrosio, especially when 'the bell announced midnight ... the final sound for being led to the stake' (Lewis 1980: 436–437). From this moment onwards, there is an accumulation of sounds, organized in a mounting progression and offered to the reader from the over-excited perspective of Ambrosio: the 'archers were heard approaching', prompting him to sign the satanic pact offered to him; and, in the final moment, he 'heard the rattling of chains; the heavy bar fell', indicating that 'the archers were on the point of entering': it is at this point that the prisoner, signing the satanic pact, leaves the cell.

It would be inadequate to see this scene as a simple instance of the creation of an atmosphere of suspense towards the end of a novel: it can, however, be taken as an example of the way in which suspense can be superimposed, through the Gothic, on the subjective representation of religious violence, for a ritual that carries a religious significance is being enacted here. The passage offers the recreation, from the purely subjective perspective of the victim, of the preparation of the body that is going to be offered as a sacrifice. The cumulative force of all the preparations, perceived in the sounds that reach Ambrosio in his cell, is presented as a pattern of constantly growing effect. This corresponds precisely to the pattern of escalating tension that the ceremonial requires and which leads to the central moment, or the central sign, of the execution. The inherent Enlightenment critique of an execution by the forces of religious repression coexists here alongside the intense subjectivity with which the scene is presented, in which the gaze of the observer or the audience of sacrificial ritual is replaced by that of the reader. Obviously, this is not to say that Matthew Lewis consciously organized this scene following the specific form of ritual sacrifice; my point is rather that this scene must be seen as an indication of the strong identification that the Gothic discourse on Spanish Catholicism tends to make between religious violence and religious ritual, seeing the first in terms of the latter, and understanding the close links between both. It presents them, in fact, as two aspects of the same phenomenon: a sacrificial ceremony, deeply rooted in popular culture, which can only be adequately understood from a subjective perspective that hovers between rejection and fascination.

In European primitivist discourse, a context in which religious practice is closely linked both to representation and to violence will also produce a popular culture tending to express its sense of the sacred in similar terms. This was perceived by English observers and tourists such as Byron, who gave one of the most suggestive readings of the practice of bullfighting in terms that clearly indicates a relationship between popular entertainment and ceremonial sacrifice:

> The Sabbath comes, a day of blessed rest:
> What hallows it upon this Christian shore?
> Lo! it is sacred to a solemn Feast:
> Hark! heard you not the forest-monarch's roar?
> Crashing the lance, he snuffs the spouting gore
> Of man and steed, oérthrown beneath his horn,
> The thronged arena shakes with shouts for more,
> Yells the mad crowd oér entrails freshly torn,
> Nor shrinks the female eye, nor e'en affects to mourn.
> (Byron 1978: 43)

This fragment offers an intelligent interpretation of bullfighting as a form of (or a substitution for) religious ceremonial: the references to the 'Sabbath' and to the fact that the context is a 'Christian shore' on a day of 'blessed rest' immediately suggest the sacred nature of the celebration which includes a 'solemn Feast', in place of the Eucharist. The bullfight is a celebration of natural strength, but also of the death of the 'forest-monarch', whose entrails are 'freshly torn' in a bloody sacrifice. It is easy to recognize here all the features of ritual celebration that we find in the Enlightenment critique of sacred violence. But the most important feature of this representation, and one that brings it close to the perspectives on religious violence offered by Goya and Maturin, is the understanding of the fascination that it exerts on the crowd, and of the essential irrationalism that underlies it. It is this loss of individuality in the collective exaltation brought about by the sacrifice that, in turn, fascinates the speaker in this fragment. Ritual violence is recognized in all its horror, but so is its hold over the people who lose themselves in it, and who respond to its scenification of sacrifice.

Such a keen understanding of the popular roots of religious violence, and of its role in mediterranean culture, was not available to most Spanish authors working under the aegis of Romanticism, simply because the political conditions within which they operated tended to identify religious ceremonial not with the exploration of a fascination with violence, but with the ancestral glory and national independence of Spain. In contrast with the approach to religious ritualism shown in Goya's *Procesión de Disciplinantes* (also evident in Byron's representation of the bullfight in *Childe Harold's Pilgrimage*), it is not the troubling need for the scenification of violence or the sacrificial bloodletting that is inherent in the Spanish Romantic representation of religious ritual, but the continuation of a solemn and venerable tradition that has its roots in a mythified past.

Foremost among the causes that prevented the circulation and influence of European Gothic in early nineteenth-century Spain, was the persistence of strict censorship, which increased after the restoration of Fernando VII in 1814, and which continued until his death in 1833 (with the brief exception of the triennial liberal government of 1821–23). Even as late as 1820, no novels by Ann Radcliffe or Walter Scott had been translated into Spanish, and most of the authors who were directly involved in the progress of the Enlightenment (Voltaire and Rousseau especially) were strictly banned. In these conditions, the Gothic mode, which had its basis in the anti-Catholic, Enlightenment tradition, could not develop. The historical novel did not offer the same space for exploration of violence and fear, since its premise was the idealization of Medieval Christianity and its exaltation, in keeping with the traditionalism of the new Regime. The main historical novels of the following years were written under the influence of Walter Scott: *Los Bandos de Castilla* (1828) centred on the adventures of Alvaro de Luna at the start of the Reconquest, *La Conquista de Valencia* (1831) was about the Cid, and *Ni Rey ni Roque* (1835) focused on the war against the Turks in the sixteenth century. All of these texts share a tendency to the epic and the projection of the ideal of Spanish unity onto the past; the political project of Fernando VII, based on the absolutist alliance between the Church and the State, is reimagined in the context of Catholic feudalism.

A good example of this tendency is to be found in the epic poem *El Pelayo*, written by José de Espronceda in the early 1830s, and never completed: it is significant that, though Espronceda was deeply influenced by

Byron, he retained a thoroughly conservative approach in his approach to this matter. Even the choice of subject is at one with the dominant fashion that we have seen permeating the Spanish historical novel: *El Pelayo* offers a hyperbolic, mythologized image of the feudal lord who, in 988 BC, started the campaign against the Muslim empire in the peninsula. It is interesting, for instance, to compare the following passage with Goya's picture, or with Byron's own image of Spain in *Childe Harold*:

> The immense population gathers for
> The ceremony, looking after the world's Saviour [the Eucharist];
> Only a hymn resounds reverently,
> While deep silence reigns around it.
> A religious enchantment sublimates the breast,
> And fury is now changed into peace.
> The troops follow in humble dread,
> All baring their humble foreheads.
> The pomp is preceded by the sacred
> Shepherds, Ministers of the divine Christ,
> With golden colours richly overspread
> Over their candid linoleum vest,
> Ornamented with laurel and beauteous flowers
> Hanging from the mast with the Sign of the Cross,
> And there Rodrigo guides the rest with respect,
> Looking after the august, pious ceremony.
>   (Espronceda 1986: 25–26) (my translation)

A fragment such as this carefully avoids any discussion of the sacrificial content of the Eucharist, or the disappearance of the individual in the procession. On the contrary: the ceremony is described first in terms of the aural elements, the singing of the hymns punctuated by reverent silences; then follows a description of the priests and their colourful attire. The attitude of the troops and priests, both humble and reverent, suggests the existence of a harmoniously ordered medieval society, in which each social stratum complements the rest. Religious ceremony is here idealized and imagined as the centre of a carefully structured social order: at the birth of the nation is Catholic ritual, projecting its eternal, pure order onto the society around it. All the aspects of the text tend to recreate an idealized sense of the ceremonial, in which the Eucharist becomes disassociated from the notion of sacrifice and, instead, becomes the key element of a rigidly organized and stratified society.

This is a dominant tendency in Spanish Romantic poetry. In the narrative poem *Apuntaciones para un Sermón*, one of the most popular

Leyendas written by José Zorrilla, and published in 1840, the same effect appears. The poem describes the satanic profanation of a tomb in medieval Valladolid and the blasphemous exhumation of a dead body by the devils; the irreverent ritual, far from awakening a sensual response to the moment of ritual, leads to the very opposite phenomenon: the erasure of sacrificial violence and its substitution by an exaltation of dogmatic Catholicism. The medieval Spanish community described in the poem reacts spontaneously by piously genuflecting and praying, in orderly form, before the desecrated tomb. This allows the poet to contrast an idealized picture of devotion with the modern decadence of faith and the spread of free thinking:

> All Valladolid was kneeling down;
> And the empty tomb
> They came to see.
> They made the sign of the cross
> Before the hole;
> Because the crowd believed in God
> And their God they adored ...
> How unlike the impious multitude of today!
> (Zorrilla 2000: 421) (my translation)

Catholicism has become here (as in Espronceda) the focus of an imaginary and politically conservative medieval past and one that is averse to the influence of the Enlightenment. The few examples of a tradition akin to the Gothic in Spanish culture can be found only among those authors who were distinctly heterodox (such as the later Goya) or among exiles such as José María Blanco-White (1775–1841).

Ironically, Blanco-White had started his intellectual carreer as a brilliant Catholic priest; he was actually completing his studies in theology in Seville at the time when Goya was painting *Vuelo de Brujas*. From 1801 to 1805, Blanco-White was both an active preacher and an intellectual close to the circles and tendencies that were adapting the culture of the Enlightenment within Spain. Blanco-White's residence in Madrid from 1805 onwards (where he came into contact with francophiles such as Meléndez Valdés and Manuel José Quintana) later culminated in his voluntary exile from Spain, from 1812 onwards. In 1810 Blanco went so far as to propose popular revolution as the only source of political emancipation, both from French domination and from Spanish traditionalism. There was a strong reaction to this position both from the pro-monarchic and the enlightened intellectuals living in

Spain, which ultimately brought Blanco to see himself as heterodox, not only politically, but also in moral terms. The final sign of this rejection of his cultural roots took place in 1812, when Blanco-White converted to Anglicanism; the rest of his work, produced in Britain, bears the mark of this self-imposed exile.

The literary works of Blanco-White remained firmly set in the rationalist tradition; the only exceptions are a few short stories he wrote in his last years. The final scene in one of these short stories, *Fray Gerundio de Jerusalén,* represents the culmination of Blanco-White's anti-Catholicism, and provides one of the very few examples of true 'Gothic' prose written in Spanish before the 1850s. It is perhaps significant that, though some of the characters are Spanish, the scene of Catholic repression should in this case be set in Italy. The hero of the tale, Alberto-Ricardo, is about to commit suicide after a series of sentimental disappointments; his suicide is prevented by a monk who, leading him into a cloister, hears him confess. That monk, Fray Gerundio de Jerusalén, is in fact Alberto's father; he is also the political rival of the Inquisitor Mocénigo, the villain of the story. The last pages of *Fray Gerundio,* in which the Inquisition interrogates Alberto, offer one of the few representations of the Inquisitorial process written by a Spanish Romantic:

> The black curtains and the robes of the same colour used by the ministers obscured the light of four candles which had been placed so as to illumine the the accused, but so that only their faces and facial expressions could be clearly observed. The general darkness made their faces stand out, so that they seemed like images portrayed by some famous artist, about to jump out of the canvas ... All the while, the high-pitched voice of Alberto was heard speaking to his torturers; and that voice, even without breaking into a full squeal, suggested an intense pain that was quickly becoming unbearable. The silence that, for some moments, held the tribunal, gave way to a sustained cry, which concluded with a thud, like that of a person falling down. Even the rigid and dry features of the monk [Mocénigo] were altered, and his skin seemed to become more pallid. The bell rang again, and the president of the Tribunal, who had not taken his eyes off the prisoner, said to him: 'Confess, or prepare yourself to take the place that your companion will leave empty!' (Blanco-White 1975:144) (my translation)

The central image of the human sacrifice is here removed from the scene but this removal only increases the dramatic efficacy of the episode. For it is through arousal of the senses (the dark scenery, the whitish faces in the candlelight, the sounds of violence that are heard) that the atmosphere of fear is obliquely created. The whole of the scene is sustained by no more than a few visual and aural images: the illuminated faces of the prisoners standing out against a dominating darkness; the sounds of torture resonating in the room, and which are briefly but specifically detailed so as to suggest a rising intensity of pain. The situation is thus represented through a brief series of sensory contrasts: thick darkness against a ghastly light, silence against the sound of intense screams, and the few facial movements discernible in the pale faces of the prisoners. The narrator plays with terror and anxiety in order to engage the reader, but this very engagement depends upon the excitement brought about by the suggestion of physical pain. However, a fragment such as this, which is fully coherent with the Gothic discourse on religious violence, is also representative of the difficulties of articulating that discourse in Spanish: for it is, after all, a text written by an exile, and an exception within the extensive work of Blanco-White, both because of its use of a sensitive discourse instead of a rationalist perspective, and because it is written in Spanish and not in English, which was Blanco-White's usual literary language after 1812. It is not until the late 1850s, and the clearly post-Romantic work of Gustavo Adolfo Bécquer (who was working in a very different political climate), that we find another instance of Spanish 'Gothic' writing with the same capacity to offer a critical re-reading of the Catholic tradition.

My conclusion, offered here as provisional, affords a possible guideline for further discussion. The Gothic discourse on Catholic ceremonial violence seems to be based on two main characteristics. These are, on the one hand, a simultaneous fascination with, and rejection of, the central theme of ritual sacrifice; on the other hand, the tendency to approach it from a subjective perspective. The cultural tradition underlying ceremonial violence both informs its representation and is critically questioned by this very act of representation; yet it is impossible for the gaze that is projected onto the sacrifice to distance itself absolutely from it, or to see it as something entirely alien or external to the human subject that represents it. The key cultural space described in this discourse is Spanish Catholicism (especially as represented within the English Gothic tradition), but, paradoxically, the political conditions in southern Europe prevented such an approach from influencing most of the representations of the Catholic past made in Spain during the transition from the eighteenth to the nineteenth centuries. The Gothic perspective being directly linked to the cultural project of the Enlightenment, it was very difficult for it to take roots in a political environment that remained adverse to that tradition for the better part of 50 years after the French Revolution. These contextual conditions did not allow for a widespread re-reading of Catholic ritualism akin to those exemplified by Maturin, Lewis or Byron in the English tradition. The few Gothic elements that can be discerned in Spanish culture of this period (and which are seen in Goya's work, and in some isolated moments of Blanco-White's writings) can be taken as essential documents of the history of the Gothic, but also, in their very exceptionality, as key examples of the difficult progress of the Enlightenment in Spanish cultural history.

I would like to close this discussion with a brief reference to another of Goya's later works: *La Romería de San Isidro*, painted directly onto a wall in Goya's country house, *La Quinta del Sordo*, between 1820 and 1822, in the last years of his life. This belongs to the group of murals which include *Saturno devorando a sus Hijos* and *El Aquelarre* (Figure 4). It should be pointed out that, during these years, a liberal government was fitfully starting to modify the ultra-conservative politics of 1814–20. It is not possible, then, to see these murals as a response to the political climate; they have to be seen as reaching deeper into essential aspects of Spanish and Western culture. The entire group of pictures offers no instance of a daylight scene; instead, they are all dominated by the use of varying shades and degrees of darkness, which, in itself, becomes one of the dominating motifs of this cycle.

This is the last painting in which Goya represented a popular congregation gathered for religious purposes. If we compare it to the first of the three pictures we have examined, the evolution in the treatment of his subject is obvious. It is clear that any hint of a clear-cut allegorical or didactic purpose has been removed; any value that this painting may have as a commentary on a social reality is thus secondary. The term '*Romería*' designates, in Spanish, a religious procession or celebration in honour of the Saint or of the Virgin that includes the singing of popular songs and the walk towards the shrine or church inscribed to his or her memory. It is precisely such a procession that is depicted in Goya's mural painting. However, in this case there is no hint (as one might expect) of any religious implications; and there is not even any kind of easily interpretable contrast between light and darkness, as there is in *Procesión de Disciplinantes*. In the *Romería*, a clouded sky dominates a lansdcape of irregular hills, from which a thick group of

Figure 4 *La Romería de San Isidro* by Francisco de Goya (1820–22)

pilgrims descends; the scene fades into a blurred darkness towards the left and the right, while most of the scene seems offers a rough, unclear vision emerging from these blurs.

The key Enlightenment dichotomy of nature versus nurture is here subverted in a suggestive way: the culture of Catholic ritualism has allowed the darker, more primitive aspects of human nature to come out and to dominate the celebration. Ritual has been transformed into a dark carnival, and physical violence has been internalized: it is no longer represented by physical punishment but is expressed through the revellers, in the group centring the picture, whose faces are deformed by anguish. All references to the sacred theme that motivated the celebration have disappeared and have been substituted by the stark presentation of an irrationality that is motivated by human pain and is consubstantial with it. But this picture, unlike the others we have previously examined, offers no indication of the causes of this irrationality. With this final turn (as with all of his later work) Goya seems to be pointing, not towards a critique of human alienation brought about by culture, but towards a radical questioning of human rationality in itself; pointing, therefore, beyond the Gothic

aesthetic and towards an essential nihilism. As we have seen, the Gothic discourse on religious violence never became dominant in Spain. Arguably, though, one of the few artists to adopt that discourse, in expressing a widespread doubt concerning the very nature of humanity, influenced critical traditions that would continue to develop for the rest of the century and which would result ultimately in existentialism and Freudianism. But this was also a process that, like the development of the Gothic, would take place largely outside Spanish culture.

References

Blanco-White, J.M. (1975) *Luisa de Bustamante o la huérfana española en inglaterra*, Barcelona, Editorial Labor.
—— (1972) *Cartas de España*, Madrid, Alianza Editorial.
Botting, F. (1996) *Gothic*, London and New York, Routledge.
Byron, Lord (1978), *Byron's Poetry*, ed. Frank McConnell, New York and London, Norton.
de Espronceda, J. (1985) *Poesías completa*, Barcelona, Planeta.
Girard, R. (1998) *La Violence et le Sacré*, Paris, Hachette.
Lewis, M. (1980) *The Monk*, Oxford and New York, Oxford University Press.

Maturin, C. (1989) *Melmoth The Wanderer*, Oxford and New York, Oxford University Press.

Miles, R. (1993) *Gothic Writing 1750–1820: A Genealogy*, London and New York, Routledge.

Trías, E. (1996) *Diccionario del Espíritu*, Barcelona, Planeta.

Zorrilla, J. (2000) *Leyendas*, Madrid, Ediciones Cátedra.

10

Potocki's Gothic Arabesque: embedded narrative and the treatment of boundaries in *The Manuscript Found in Saragossa* (1797–1815)

AHLAM ALAKI

This chapter isolates two major point of focus in the complex and encyclopedic text of Potocki's *The Manuscript Found in Saragossa*: the formal feature of narrative embedding, and the cultural theme of the monstrous, uncanny or evil other.

The title of Potocki's *The Manuscript Found in Saragossa* suggests the nature of the tale. The 'found' manuscript is a standard Gothic motif in Radcliffe and Lewis, parodied by Jane Austen in *Northanger Abbey*. There is thus a definite structural connection between Potocki's work and the English Gothic tradition between 1790 and 1820. Potocki seems to have come to the Gothic via his interest in orientalism. The biographical evidence concerning what Potocki had read is not conclusive but it is clear from his use of the found manuscript convention that he was familiar with Radcliffe and Lewis and the major conventions of Gothic. When he visited London in 1792, Potocki is said to have been excited by this mode, which was then at its peak. The right time, place and people seem to have collaborated to ignite Potocki's intellectual curiosity in the Gothic. Orientalist societies that Potocki frequented were celebrating Beckford's Gothic work that analogically rewrites the structure of the *Arabian Nights* and which provided Potocki with both Gothic and Arabesque *mises en abîme* influences. According to Finné:

> Potocki devait se passionner pour ce genre littéraire qui atteignait son apogée, à l'époque de son passage à Londres, avec la publication des romans de Mrs Radcliffe, portée aux nues par la critique de l'époque. En outre, en 1786, avait paru *Vathek* de William Beckford. Le roman circulait dans toutes les sociétés orientalistes anglaises que Potocki fréquenta avec assiduité. (Finné 1970: 141)

(Potocki must have developed a passion for this literary genre, which was at its peak when he visited London during the period when Mrs Radcliffe's novels were being published (then being praised to the skies by critics). Moreover, *Vathek*, by William Beckford, published in 1786, was at that time circulating in all the English Orientalist circles of which Potocki was an assiduous member.) (my translation)

Potocki evidently decided to try his hand at this fashionable Gothic mode and hence, according to Finné's rather speculative account, the tale arose:

Ecrivain de génie, habile à découvrir et à exploiter les modes littéraires dont le succès était assuré, le Comte devait immanquablement écrire un roman qui comportât des éléments des *Gothic novels*. Le *Manuscrit trouvé à Saragosse* exploite, entre autres, toutes les 'ficelles' des romans noirs, sans comporter toutefois aucune des faiblesses qui déparaient souvent ceux-ci. (Finné 1970: 141)

(A writer of genius, skilful at discovering and exploiting successful literary trends, the Count was bound to write a novel containing some elements of the 'Gothic novel'. *The Manuscript Found in Saragossa* exploits, among other things, all the tricks of the *roman noir*, without containing the weaknesses that type of work usually exhibited.) (My translation)

It is clear, from Potocki's novel, that he was familiar with both the Gothic trends of his time, and the embedded structure of the *Arabian Nights* which divides stories into days. As Caillois argues:

Ces journées, qui sont alors des *Nuits*, prolongent les féeries de Cazotte et annoncent les spectres d'Hoffmann. Elles doivent sans doute aussi quelque chose au *Vathek* de Beckford, paru pour la traduction anglaise à Londres en 1786, pour le texte original français à Paris l'année suivante et dont Potocki a vraisemblablement eu connaissance lors de son séjour de 1791 à Paris et à Londres. (Caillois 1972: 29)

(Potocki's stories, written after the design of the *Nights* and divided into days, continue the tradition of Cazotte's tales and anticipate the spectres of Hoffmann. They also owe, without doubt, something to Beckford's *Vathek*, which was published in London in 1786, having been translated from the original French text which was not published in Paris until the following year. It is quite plausible that Potocki would have read either or both texts during his stay in Paris and London in 1791.) (my translation)

However, I shall argue that the idea of manuscripts with embedded stories precedes the emergence of the European Gothic tradition. This textual strategy links the oriental tradition with the Gothic, even if we go no further than Beckford's use of the *Arabian Nights* with its Arabesque embedding and Shahrazad's reading of manuscripts which she later uses to entertain and distract the king. Like many European writers of the era, Potocki seems to have been inspired by the *Nights,* first translated into French by Galland during the period 1704–17. Again, the biographical evidence we have about when and how he read it is uncertain and anecdotal. Caillois refers to a commentator who believes that the *Nights* inspired Potocki to write his tale:

> Pierre Wiaziemski raconte que la comtesse Potocka étant affligée d'une longue maladie, son marie prit l'habitude de lui lire les contes des *Mille et Une Nuits*. Quand il eut terminé, la comtesse réclama d'autres récits du même genre. Potocki alors aurait écrit chaque jour un nouveau chapitre qu'il lisait le soir à la convalescente. (Caillois 1972: 29)

> (Pierre Wiaziemski relates that Potocki's wife, the Countess Potocka, was afflicted with a prolonged sickness, during which her husband developed the habit of reading to her the tales of the *One Thousand and One Nights*. When he finished, the Countess demanded other stories of the same genre. Potocki therefore wrote each day a new chapter, which he read at night to his convalescent wife.) (my translation)

And Beauvois similarly argues that:

> If, as the legend would have it, the *Manuscrit trouvé à Saragosse* was first conceived as a sort of extension of *The Thousand and one Nights*, which the author used to tell to his sick wife, then one can easily see the persistence of the obsession with the Orient. (Beauvois 1984: 16)

These assumptions are speculative, yet we know for sure that Potocki was particularly interested in the oriental story collection of the *Nights*, which he clearly admired: 'in Morocco in 1791, he hunted without success for a manuscript of the *Nights*' (Irwin 1994: 255). Potocki mastered Arabic at some point in his life; visited the Orient and observed professional storytellers at work in the cafés; even experimented with composing tales in the oriental manner (Irwin 1994: 255, 256). In the light of this information, it is legitimate to assume that Potocki had read the *Nights*, which was the most popular oriental story collection of his epoch. The most famous translation of the *Nights* at that time was Galland's French translation of 1704–17, which was also the first translation of the *Nights* available within Europe. Potocki could have easily read this translation, as we know that he had mastered French – the language in which *The Manuscript* was written – when studying in Geneva and Lausanne.

Following the pattern of the *Nights*, *Saragossa* employs embedding, and the structuring of the text through days, as well as a distinctly Gothic mood. Similarly, Maturin's Gothic *Melmoth the Wanderer* opens with a discovered manuscript engendering nested stories. This also recalls *Don Quixote*, a story of a history that is other to itself, narrated from the manuscript of a Muslim historian, supposedly found in a leaden casket. The motif of the found manuscript has a double effect: on the one hand, it ostensibly enhances authenticity, for Potocki's Alphonse presents his story as a true autobiographical diary. On the other, the Gothic motif of the iron casket, which also appears in Beckford's *Episodes*, functions to suggest a cultural source of the uncanny. Manuscripts resurrected from their coffins pose questions, since a curiosity to discover the unknown or the forbidden generates new narrative levels within the existing story universe.

The motif of narrative curiosity is a trope that establishes the link between folk-tales and the Gothic tradition. In folk-tales such as *Blue Beard*, what is portrayed as the character's curiosity is actually the reader's narrative curiosity. The original moral of Perrault's *Blue Beard* makes it quite clear that the plot of the story is a device to engage the curiosity of the reader, not just the characters. The moral that Perrault offers at the end of his story is unequivocal:

> Curiosity is a charming passion but may only be satisfied at the price of a thousand regrets; one sees around one a thousand examples of this sad truth every day. Curiosity is the most fleeting of pleasures; the moment it is satisfied, it ceases to exist and it always proves very, very expensive. (Perrault 1979: 41)

Angela Carter, rewriting the theme of *Blue Beard* in her *The Bloody Chamber*, depicts the reader's narrative curiosity as mirrored by that of the young woman: she is forbidden to use the key to the prohibited chamber but tempted into so doing. The young woman's words describing the effect of her husband's tantalizations are really the reader's reflections: 'He dangled the key tantalizingly above my head, out of reach of my straining fingers'. What follows builds more excitement and pressure to discover the forbidden, as the husband tells her: 'promise me you'll use all the keys on the ring except that last little one I showed you. Play with anything you find ... All is yours, everything is open to you – except the lock that this single key fits' (Carter 1979: 21). The intimation that curiosity belongs to the reader, and not just the character, also informs Le Fanu's *Uncle Silas*, which again rewrites the *Blue Beard* plot, and which marvellously inquires:

> Why is it that this form of ambition – curiosity – which entered into the temptation of our first parent, is so specially hard to resist? Knowledge is power – and power of one sort or another is the secret lust of human souls; and here is, beside the sense of exploration, the undefinable interest of a story, and above all, something forbidden, to stimulate the contumacious appetite. (Le Fanu 2000: I, 2)

Sage demonstrates that the 'something forbidden' is one of the prime narrative characteristics of the folk-tale, as 'prohibition provides the forward drive' (Sage 2000: xvi). In his studies of folk-tales, Propp claims that two familiar features of the genre are an interdiction addressed to the hero, followed by a violation of this interdiction (Propp 1979: 26–27). The overwhelming curiosity of the figure of the king in the *Nights* represents the reader's narrative curiosity. Thus, when characters are curious, the reader's curiosity is being exploited. This functions to open up new dimensions in the text, especially through embedding.

The trope of narrative curiosity also relates Potocki's tale to a Faustian concept of knowledge, as Irwin argues:

> buried in all these stories, is the promise of secret knowledge. Alphonse Van Werden's interlocutors introduce him to a world of mysteries, initiatic secrets and buried treasures. Emina and Zubeida are subterranean creatures ... Their father, the Sheikh of the Gomelez, masterminds a vast plot, which mirrors and parodies the alleged and real conspiracies of the illuminists and other politico-occult groups of the eighteenth century. (Irwin 1994: 258)

Conspiracy is a key word in Potocki's tale, and the idea of the incongruous coexistence of diverse politico-occult groups and 'secret societies' – which is such an important theme in the 'horrid novels' of the 1790s – is also recurrent (Sage 1990: 16).

Moreover, the themes of the Gothic are reinforced in the Spanish setting of the novel. Saragossa, as a location, draws on a tension between one culture and another. In the fifteenth century, Spain was the location of a divided culture: Arabic Moorish Muslim and European Christian, plus a Jewish minority. Saragossa is remembered in the dreadful history of the Spanish Inquisition, as it was the location of a notorious Inquisition tribunal, and its marketplace was where punishments were carried out (Hillgarth 1978: 437). Potocki's narrative sets itself in this troublesome Southern European location, which draws on central European traditions but simultaneously, and Gothically, confronts cultural otherness.

The opening and the closing lines of the novel constitute the problem of the whole. The story begins with a French officer finding a manuscript in sinister Saragossa; it closes with his disappearance and with the appearance of Alphonse in the epilogue, who asserts the authenticity of the whole document. The spiral staircase that Alphonse descends in the beginning and ascends at the end is not just a focal or visual image of a subterranean journey. It thematically represents the uncanny labyrinths of the narrative, echoing the connection in Beckford between the subterranean antechambers of Hell and the potentially infinite embedding of his narrative in *Vathek* and *The Episodes*. Furthermore, Alphonse's return to his departure point corresponds to a *mélange* of structural effects from within the oriental and Gothic traditions, paradoxically creating both a cyclical image of continuity, and a dreamy sense of being in the same place all the time.

This elusive, self-conscious narrative informs the whole tale, the very pretext for which is based on a trick, as the reader finally discovers. In Potocki's story, as in *Don Quixote*, 'Todo era ficción y mentira' ('Everything was falsehood and fiction'). Alphonse, the sole remaining male descendant of the purest blood of the Gomelez, signifies a genetic treasure to the Gomelez, who face the danger of extinction. So the Sheikh of the Gomelez masterminds a plot to involve Alphonse with his own daughters, hoping that a noble offspring will result (which does eventually happen).

The metanarrative of the whole tale, the conspiracy to rob Alphonse of his genes, is set into the context of a divided society, in which 'heresy' is not tolerated, and purity of blood is the ultimate value. In what is an already bigoted society, this feudal strictness gives rise to a further level of masquerade. Hence, as I shall go on to argue, there is a contradiction between appearance and reality at two levels: in the narrative (through the use of structural embedding) and in the thematic (through the representation of otherness).

The readers, and Alphonse, have to wait until the very end of the story to realize the trick, which the Sheikh of the Gomelez explains when talking with Alphonse:

> We hoped that you would be converted to the Muslim religion or at least that you would become a father. On this latter point our hopes have been fulfilled. The children which your cousins bear in their wombs will be able to pass for descendants of the purest blood of the Gomelez. It was necessary for you to come to Spain. (Potocki 1995: 624)

This refers to the fact that the Spanish Inquisition created the concept of purity of blood, or *limpieza de sangre*; new Christians and conversos were therefore regarded as a danger to religious integrity and national security. In the above quotation, the Sheikh of the Gomelez comically subverts the *limpieza de sangre*, considering Arab Muslim blood to be the purest. On this level, embedded tales constitute a pretext, a meta-narrative,[1] orchestrated in order to distract Alphonse from the plot, as The Sheik confirms:

> We had to retain you longer among us and we feared that you would grow bored. That is why we thought up various distractions for you. Thus Uzeda had an old man of my band memorize the story of Ahasuerus, the Wandering Jew, which he took from his family chronicles and which the old man recited to you. In this case we were combining business with pleasure. (Potocki 1995: 625)

This masternarrative is a part of a perplexing frame of illusion, in conflict with the reality that the reader finally perceives. It acts as a parody of the division of Spanish society and the contradictions of an institutionalized intolerance that creates masquerades. Narration takes place retrospectively, which means that the narrator should already know the ending that had occurred previous to this moment in the plot. But the narrator tricks readers, maximizing the chaos between the 'real' and the 'fictive'. The pride and power that Alphonse loses at the level of the plot, he regains by deceiving readers at the time of narration. The reader effectively becomes a puppet at the mercy of a deranged, lying puppeteer.

The complexity of Potocki's tales, with their interactions that create contradictions, challenges the complexity of even the most labyrinthine tales of the *Arabian Nights*. Velasquez, the geometer, and therefore a representative of 'reason' in the story, says that he cannot find any coherence in the tales, nor can he distinguish the speaker from the listener:

> All the gypsy's stories begin in a simple enough way and you think you can already predict the end. But things turn out quite differently. The first story engenders the second, from which a third is born, and so on,

like periodic fictions resulting from certain divisions which can be indefinitely prolonged. In mathematics there are several ways of bringing certain progressions to a conclusion, whereas in this case an inextricable confusion is the only result I can obtain from all the gypsy has related. (Potocki 1995: 334)

The interactions between stories, and the variation in accounts of supposedly identical incidents, create numerous framing devices, and accentuate the principle of witnessing derived from Islamic law. There is always someone who wants to add a different (or forgotten) detail to the story. The fragmentation of contradictory accounts creates subordinated stories, which rebel against their frames. There is a master narrative and subnarratives: divided society and mutual conspiracy, and continuous contradictions between 'appearance' and 'reality' occur. The reader strives to rewrite each account logically to fit into the shattered whole. Like the splinters of a broken glass, each narrative fragment gives a ray of truth, but the image as a whole seems distorted to the eyes of the reader. This creates a power-struggle between reader and narrator, exposing the connection between the sublime and the deferral of authority created by the Gothic conventions of the manuscript found in a drawer. The deliberate foregrounding of the act of telling repeats itself to the reader; it is a part of the transmission of a relation between the sublime and the infinite narrative embedding. The narrative operation works in alignment with the theological question of 'who is witnessing the act?' It therefore functions at a deeper level than those questions of religious, cultural or sexual differences which work at surface level.

As with the testimony of witnesses, this tale needs both oral and written documentation to authenticate it, and to ensure its textual survival. Characters sometimes listen to stories narrated orally; at other times, they orally narrate what they read in books: this juxtaposes two authoritative narrative registers in a double act of narrative. The whole image is labyrinthine and puzzle-like, as Sumatsu points out:

> Tout comme le héros de l'histoire, le lecteur du *Manuscript trouvé à Saragosse* se laisse conduire les yeux bandés à travers un enchevêtrement inextricable: inquiet et charmé à la fois de cette passivité que le récit exige de lui, il n'espère plus qu'en une clarification finale. Qu'il y ait un rapport symbolique entre lecture et épreuve initiatique ne fait pas de doute, mais afin de l'éclaircir, ne convient-il pas d'explorer au préalable les détours du labyrinthe? (Sumatsu 1993: 29)

(Just like the hero of the story, the reader of *The Manuscript Found in Saragossa* is led blindfolded through an inextricable tangle; simultaneously worried and charmed by the passivity that the story imposes on him, he hopes for nothing more than a final explanation. There is a symbolic relationship between reading and the initiation test without doubt, but in order to solve the mystery, doesn't one first have to explore the twists and turns of the labyrinth?) (my translation)

Thibaud de la Jacquière's story, for example, is to be found in *The Book of Cabbalists*. It is later rewritten in Alphonse's diary (in Spanish), then read by the Spanish captain, and later rewritten, a third time, by the French officer (in French) and finally read by the novel's readers. Alphonse reads this story silently without narrating it to us, so we enter his mind to read the story, which he reads from a book. This is an intertextual reading because the reader experiences not only Alphonse's tale embedded in Potocki's novel, but also another tale of presumably another brain silently embedded in Alphonse's story.

Embedding in the orientalist context of the *Arabian Nights* promises textual infinity, since lack of closure signifies the constant deferral of final meaning or endpoint; in Beckford, and in Potocki's novel, this suggests the sublime, which paradoxically creates 'delightful horror', in Burke's phrase. The text evades death by opening endless gates to infinity through a series of sublime transformations and repetitions. Ending a story and beginning a new one, which offers a repeated image of closure (death) and resistance to closure (resurrection), provides textual 'immortality'. This resurrection recalls the uroboros image in Islamic art of the Arabesque based on repetitive interwinding of curious lines. The secret of the Arabesque (whether in art or in narrative) is its suggestion of resurrection through a perpetual repetition that overwhelms and blurs the vision: 'the main requisite for its composition remains the obligatory bifurcation and its ever-continuing course' (Kühnel 1977: 7). The theological infinity of the Arabesque translates into the notion of a vacuum. The horror associated with the labyrinth springs from its sublime nature: it is paradoxically interesting and threatening, as Faris explains:

> The labyrinth pattern suggests play and terror; it expresses both our control over our environment and our bewilderment within it; it represents orderly disorder, the systematic creation of a mystery more powerful than the creator, who may subsequently become lost in it. Because the labyrinth encompasses these opposing forces – order and confusion,

191

reason and passion, playfulness and fear – it can symbolize their combination in a work of art as well as their presence in the exterior world. (Faris 1988: 1)

Thus we can see how the orientalist and Gothic contexts overlap: the Arabesque of narrative embedding presents a situation in which the created is more important than the creator; the storyteller (architect) thus becomes lost in his or her own maze. In the *Nights*, for example, the reader forgets Shahrazad's presence while reading her interpolated tales. This dangerous state of theological and narrative vacuum reflects the uncertainty of *al-Aaraf*. *Al-Aaraf*, or the Islamic form of purgatory, is where the reader is placed, whether reading Potocki's work or other Gothic works employing similar conventions, such as Beckford's *Vathek*, or, later, Maturin's *Melmoth the Wanderer* or Edgar Allan Poe's stories of labyrinths. Readers are in purgatory, and characters in hell, or the opposite; or they both are simultaneously and paradoxically in both places. This idea of vacuum is central to the theme of otherness. Otherness contains the anxiety of absence of knowledge, which is the condition of purgatory. Potocki refers explicitly to purgatory in his tale. When Agyilar tells the Knight of Toledo: 'Our religion tells us there are other places to expiate one's sins', the knight answers: 'You are referring to purgatory' (Potocki 1995: 348). After his death, Aguilar's spirit visits Toledo, as promised, and knocks on his window:

> Toledo opened the shutter and said, 'Are you dead?'
> 'I am dead,' said a sepulchral voice.
> 'Is there a purgatory?' said Toledo.
> 'There is, and I am there,' said the same voice. (Potocki 1995: 350)

This purgatorial vacuum contains the narrative heterodoxicality of embedding, because it turns out to be an uncanny effect, and a conspiratorial joke. It finally corresponds to narrative levels by creating a hierarchy of levels like snakes and ladders.

The representation of the Spanish Inquisition in the novel is another example of the inversion of narrative levels, heterodoxy triumphing comically over the imposition of orthodoxy: so the reader is moving down the snakes of the mimetic, up the ladder of diagetic. The master plot is a conspiracy between the text and the knowing reader, against the naive reader, and that is where readers travel down the snakes instead of going up the ladders. Plot is transferred from the mimetic to the diagetic level (or the metadiagetic – telling in the second level; telling about telling), according to Platonic standards, which Lodge explains:

> In Book III of *The Republic*, Plato distinguishes between diegesis, the representation of actions in the poet's own voice, and mimesis, the representation of action in the imitated voices of the character or characters. Pure diegesis is exemplified by dithyramb, a kind of hymn. ... Pure mimesis is exemplified by drama. Epic is a mixed form, combining both diegesis and mimesis, that is, combining authorial report, description, summary and commentary on the one hand, with the quoted direct speech of the characters on the other. (Lodge 1990: 28)

Lodge comments further on 'telling about telling', by explaining that the rise of the English novel during the eighteenth century began with discovering new possibilities of mimesis in prose, including using characters as narrators, 'thus making the narrative discourse a mimesis of an act of diegesis, diegisis at a second remove' (Lodge 1990: 30).

Curiously, the story itself becomes the discourse, and acts as a masquerade against the naive reader. A Bakhtinian notion, the masquerade is a subversion of a particular mimetic set of circumstances. Masquerading is a cultural theme transferred to the metadiagetic level of narration in the idea of *al-Aaraf* (limbo or purgatory) as represented by textual infinity. In this way, the metadiagetic level returns the plot to a new mimetic level (imitation). Alphonse lives his story at the diagetic level (he is inside the story), then he narrates it at the metadiagetic level, but his narrative contains his adventures in Spain (doing, mimetic). Interestingly, there is a plot enclosed at the metadiagetic level, so it is like a paradoxical inverted maze, where the outer part is in the centre.

Alphonse narrates the stories of other characters using reported speech. But he preserves their words and register, giving them the authority of expression in the first-person narrative. Alphonse is therefore an agent of reporting, but not a reporting authority. Reported speech is paradoxical in nature, as Morson points out:

> To study embedded speech acts is to study the making – and still more interesting, the breaking – of frames. For the embedding speech does not simply transmit passively the speech it reports. Whether we are dealing with reported speech in a work of fiction, a child's narrative or a defence attorney's summation, we are dealing with the interaction of the two speech acts. There is retort as well as report. (Morson 1978: 415)

Reported speech is paradoxical because it translucently conveys the original utterance, yet wraps it in a personal subjective voice, as Morson remarks:

> Reported speech is embedded speech. The early formalists saw the embedded narrative and play with the framing of stories by stories as a model of narratology; Bakhtin and Voloshinov attribute analogous significance to the embedded speech act. In the same sense that for Skhlovsky the most 'typical' literary works were *Tristan Shandy*, *Don Quijote*, and *The Arabian Nights*, for Bakhtin the most typical speech act is indirect discourse, which 'bares' the 'meta' level present in every utterance. (Morson 1978: 414–415)

The merging of two voices, the original and the reporting voice, implies the integration of the two texts to form a unified plot against the reader. Reported speech itself is a source of embedding, not only because it multiplies narrative, but also because it is dialogic in nature. According to Bakhtin's metalinguistics, every word or utterance knows itself as such. Seager explains further: 'an utterance is *responsible*, answering and preparing to be answered, reframing and expecting to be reframed' (Seager 1991: 15).

Potocki's tale employs embedding that subverts the notion of singleness of level, which makes it a hybrid between Gothic horror and the *Arabian Nights*' principle of subordinating and embedding. Narrative 'boxing' comically subverts hierarchical control – by suggesting an infinity of subordination. Ideologically, hierarchical control in Spanish society works to undermine the solidarity of levels, which is linked to the context of feudal control and purity of blood guaranteed by law. Otherness is translated into Gothic notions such as the notorious Spanish Inquisition: a police force questioning the truth or falsity of one's race. The Inquisition is represented by Potocki (after Cervantes) as fabricating a Spanish society of masquerades and heresy in which nothing is what it seems to be. Avadoro, in Potocki's story, reports the speech of a man who refers to poor slaves: 'The negroes are slaves, or rather they were slaves, of my master, for on Spanish soil slavery is not tolerated any more than is heresy. From the moment their feet touched this sacred soil these blacks have been as free as you and I' (Potocki 1995: 430). These marvellous lines contain a profound irony: on Spanish soil one is free – free, that is, to believe what one is told to believe. The notion of otherness, Gothically placed close to heresy in the above quotation, needs further explanation.

The hybrid Hispano-Moorish setting of the story connotes otherness, which conveys a kind of framing by inclusion and exclusion. Both otherness and embedding connote obscurity and subordination. In both, the idea of a power-struggle operates because ideas or frames swallow each other and are swallowed by each other. Some critics propose that Potocki's tale demonstrates Enlightenment virtues of tolerance, and that it satirizes old-fashioned feudal codes of honour. But while this is true, Potocki's idea of otherness touches not only the thematic boundaries of morality and education, but also the formal frontiers of textual/social hierarchy.

The subversive concept of otherness exceeds (but includes) the traditional boundaries of religious, cultural, sexual or physical others. It creatively presents the text itself as an other, a masquerade, the embedding powers of which subvert its identity, and negate (yet paradoxically emphasize) its own existence. For example, the French officer (in the largest narrative frame) shows how the story is translated into French from a Spanish origin, which creates a double sense of otherness and alienation. Thus the text becomes twice removed from reality, which establishes obvious resonances between textual manoeuvres and the Gothic tradition. Moreover, the story oscillates between the written form (the Spanish manuscript) and the oral form (the dictation by the Spanish captain), and the written form again (the French documented text), and the oral form again, for Alphonse refers to his story not as a written text, but as speech: 'At the time of which I speak' (Potocki 1995: 5). An alienating distance is clear in the temporal design of the retrospective tale. There is one original story (plot) and there is another story (narration), which establishes a difference, or 'otherness' between oral and written forms.

Finally, otherness is evident in the multiplicity of temporal levels of the tale. At the level of action (plot) events take place, but stay untold (Sierra Morena,[2] Saragossa, 1739). At the level of characters narrating events, Alphonse listens, but says nothing to readers until later. Then there is the level at which Alphonse writes down these adventures; the time of the epilogue written by Alphonse (Saragossa, 1769); and the time when the French officer finds Alphonse's manuscript with all its stories, and gives it to the Spanish captain to translate it (Saragossa, 1809?); followed by the time at which the French officer writes down the translation; and then the time of the story written by the French officer, reproduced from the original manuscript.

Parallel to textual otherness in the fictional transmission of Potocki's tale, thematic otherness also appears in the text. Interestingly, for each person there is an other who is considered as hostile, heretic or extravagant. There are cultural others including Arabs, Spanish and Gypsies. Arabs are depicted as materialistic and greedy. The young Velasquez promises some Arabs a ransom if they return him to his father: 'The word 'ransom' has something about it which never fails to flatter Arab ears' (Potocki, 1995: 266). But Arab Muslims depict Christian Europeans also as others, and we read about the culture shock experienced by the Sheikh of the Gomelez in Madrid where women mix with men easily.

The religious other is depicted with Gothic rejection and fear, reflecting Spanish religious tension. Uzeda's Jewish grandfather shows an extremist view towards the Christian other, saying: 'Oh God of Israel and Jacob! ... An Asmonean of the purest blood of the Maccabees, a successor of Aaron, will be the page to the uncircumcised Antony?' (Potocki 1995: 246). Comically, his horror reveals the shibboleth of circumcision, the physical sign of otherness. Christians, such as the Duchess Manuela, express their horror at other religions. She tells Avadoro, her daughter's father: 'You can imagine ... how unhappy I am. My daughter died a pagan, my grand daughter must remain a Muslim' (Potocki 1995: 593). On the other hand, the Muslim Great Sheik of the Gomelez expresses his rejection of Christians, telling Alphonse: 'From my earliest childhood I was a fervent Muslim and a follower of Ali. I had been inculcated with a deep hatred of Christians. All these feelings were more or less innate and grew as I grew in the darkness of the caves' (Potocki 1995: 606–607). The reference to the 'darkness of the caves' confirms the Spanish intolerance to religious otherness. Others – heretics, or conversos, as they were called – suppressed their religious practices and lived in darkness. The gothic underground image appears also in the story of the second Dervish in the *Arabian Nights* (Haddawi 1995: 92–100). In Beckford's *Vathek* and *Episodes*, and in Maturin's *Melmoth the Wanderer*, similar underground scenes take place. This image brings the two traditions, the oriental and the European Gothic, together. Subterranean dwellings work on two different levels to connote narrative hierarchy (in embedding), and Spanish religious and social hierarchy. The idea of the underground carries theological implications, as Beauvois argues, because it represents the quest for the ideal: 'In this vain quest for the Absolute, the Ideal, the Synthesis of religions or philosophies, one is struck by the repetitive character of the mine theme, the subterranean chamber, the bowels of the earth' (Beauvois 1984: 17).

At the end of the novel, Mamoun tells Alphonse:

> Senor Don Juan, you find yourself here on lands whose deep places are hidden from profane eyes; lands in which everyone has a secret to keep. There are vast caves and extensive underground workings in the chain of mountains. They are inhabited by Moors who have never left them since they were driven out of Spain. (Potocki 1995: 583)

Like Cervantes in *Don Quixote*, Potocki here reveals how the Spanish Inquisition had created a society of masquerade founded on the taboo of heresy where nothing is what it seems to be. The reader learns this lesson after being fooled by everyone in the tale, including Potocki and Alphonse. The Spanish Inquisition offers a place where the Gothic meets with the carnivalistic. In this conjunction, subordination is parodied, since the act of subordination is itself subjected to the idea of infinity. Ironically, the plot or master narrative that constitutes the frame is a carnivalistic subversion of purity of blood: the story needs to be set up actively in a shattered society in which the Inquisition defended a feudal structure based on the purity of blood. Moors and Jews were forced to convert to Christianity or leave. Alternatively, they were forced to bury their otherness in a state of Gothic limbo. The Spanish persecution of Jews was pronounced. In *Don Quixote* we read:

> *Sancho Panza*: Since I believe firmly and truly in God and all that the Holy Catholic and Roman Church holds and believes, and am a mortal enemy of the Jews, historians should have mercy on me and treat me well in their writings. (Cervantes 1986, Book II, Chapter 8)

Spanish religious prejudice took an official form in 1480, when Isabella and Ferdinand issued the first commission for the Inquisition to eliminate Semitic culture from official Catholicism. To obtain forgiveness, the Inquisition gave a limited time in each city for people to confess their errors against the faith, and all the errors of others known to them. There might have been some exaggeration in depicting the Gothicism of the Inquisition, yet it was definitely a living threat in the minds of peasants, as Kamen argues:

> The Inquisitors came in the night in carriages specially fitted with rubber wheels that would make no noise; they listened at doors and windows to

hear what people were saying; they took away beautiful girls; their favourite torture – ... was to sit their victim down and drip boiling oil on his head until he died. (Kamen 1980: 294)

There are several punishments for the accused, as Hillgarth reports: 'He might escape with being scourged, never with less than a hundreds lashes – or simply with being paraded through the street naked to the waist, while the sentence was cried aloud. If he was less fortunate he would be condemned to the galleys' (Hillgarth 1978: 431). Sometimes the accused were gagged and paraded round the city on a donkey, beaten as they went, and then exiled, as happened to Catalina de Zamora. (Hillgarth 1978: 459). These carnivalistic punishments, which actually happened, remind us of their comic parallels in the *Arabian Nights*. In the cycle of the Hunchback, some of the barber's brothers are beaten and paraded around the city on a donkey before being banished. (Haddawi 1995: 206–289). Even silence in answering the questions of the Inquisition was considered a sin. Kamen notes that 'The council of the Inquisition was split over whether to treat quietism as a serious threat' (Kamen 1980: 293). From about 1687: 'the Inquisition began to prosecute quietists in Spain'. Potocki satirizes the Inquisition's hostility to silence. When the monk of the Inquisition notes that Alphonse has remained silent he threatens him thus:

> We are going to hurt you a little. You see these two boards. Your legs will be placed between them and they will be tied tightly with ropes. Then we will drive these wedges, which you see here, between your legs and they will be hammered into place. At first your feet will swell up, then blood will spurt from your toes and all your toe-nails will drop off. The soles of your feet will split open and from them will issue thick gouts of fat and mangled flesh. This will hurt you a great deal. Still you say nothing. But I am only talking of the standard torture so far. (Potocki 1995: 53–54)

The Gothic implications of the Spanish Inquisition become quite ridiculous, rather than terrifying, when read for the second time and once the realization dawns that they are only parts of a theatrical conspiracy. But even with the realization of its falsity, the text preserves horrible shadows of the actual Inquisition. Gothic novels are famous for depicting the horror of torture, emphasizing its impact on the imagination. The Gothic discourse of the false Inquisition, comic to the experienced reader, evokes real horror on a first reading. The whole effect of the two readings is paradoxical; it contains comedy, testing, pretence, plus a parody of the Inquisition, which nevertheless mystically retains its Gothic threat. Potocki creatively coins the concept of an 'inverted Inquisition' by showing how Muslims try to force the 'heretic' Christians into converting to Islam. Pacheco witnesses this inverted Inquisition between a demon and Alphonse:

> The demon held a book in one hand and a pitchfork in the other. He threatened to kill the young gentleman if he did not embrace the faith of Islam. Seeing this danger to a Christian soul, I made a great effort and think I was able to make myself understood, but at the same moment the two hanged men leapt on me, and dragged me out of the cave. (Potocki 1995: 95–96)

Alphonse does not see what Pacheco sees. In the place of the demon he sees the Sheikh of the Gomelez, and instead of the two men he sees the seductive Emina and Zubeida. Alphonse tells the hermit, negating Pacheco's report: 'Father, this demonical gentleman saw things that I did not see. One of us has been bewitched. Perhaps both of us were suffering from delusions' (Potocki 1995: 96). At the end of the tale, and following Alphonse's claim, readers are obliged to realize that the phrase 'both of us' refers to Alphonse and the reader, because Pacheco proves to be a paid actor. Here the Gothic theme of witchcraft vanishes into a narrative masquerade.

The Inquisition threw Spanish society into consternation, and introduced the idea of spies being everywhere. Juan de Mariana reported the fear of people during that age: 'they were deprived of the liberty to hear and talk freely, since in all the cities, towns and villages there were persons placed to give information of what went on' (Kamen 1985: 163). The records of the Inquisition are full of instances where neighbours, friends and family members denounce each other (Kamen 1985: 164). Avadoro also describes a scene of mutual spying, a familiar trope in the tale:

> I saw a man whose gait – now crawling, now scuttling – reminded me of Don Busqueros. I had him watched, and was told that he wore a false nose and was known as Dr Robusti. I did not doubt an instant that it was Busqueros, and that the wretch had slipped into the town with the intention of spying on us. (Potocki 1995: 586)

As we witness, Alphonse denounces his cousins' subterranean secret, despite all his promises, by exposing it to readers. A paranoid and divided Spanish society, very restricted and absolute, must be full of spies and masquerades. Many characters in this tale go under different disguises: Avadoro, Lonzato, Elvira, Frasqueta and her lover, the duchess of Avila, the Conde de Pena Valez and his sister, Laura Cerella, Rebecca, Blas Hervas, and Busqueros. Many of these disguises are not revealed as such to the reader. Physical dissimilarity, which connotes otherness, forms another ground for prejudice. For example, there are Gothic insinuations about black people: 'the little negro arrived to lay the table, and Thibaud saw that he was not a child, as he had first thought, but rather an old, coal-black dwarf with a hideous face' (Potocki 1995: 119). The word 'hideous' reminds us of similar descriptions of black people in the *Arabian Nights*, and carries, here, medieval Spanish views of otherness. Also, Orlandine lives in the Château de Sombre with physically disabled people, similar to those who appear in *Vathek*: 'the only human beings I ever saw were my governess, who was deaf, and a maidservant, who stammered so badly that she could well have been called mute, and an old gatekeeper, who was blind' (Potocki 1995: 115). The name of Château de Sombre itself, of course, is an allusion to the Gothic tradition.

Furthermore, Alphonse describes Pacheco as a mutilated other:

> I saw a person of yet more terrifying aspect than any I had seen up to then come to the cabin. It was a man still young-looking but hideously emaciated. His hair stood on end and from the socket of his missing eye blood was oozing. A slobbery froth dripped from his tongue, which hung out of his mouth. (Potocki 1995: 27)

On another occasion, Alphonse explains Lopez's idea of the other: 'He warned me that the officers of the Walloon Guards were all heretics, as can clearly be seen from their fair hair, blue eyes and pink cheeks; proper Christians have the complexion of Our Lady of Atocha' (Potocki 1995: 8). Here Lopez comically perceives the religious other as being physically different. Gypsy women, to Alphonse, are physical and sexual others. He sees two girls who look like his cousins, but says: 'They were not my cousins. They did not have their refinement although they were not as common and vulgar as the women of their race usually are' (Potocki 1995: 127). The words 'common' and 'vulgar' depict a medieval Spanish stereotype. Women are portrayed as devils. Zubeida and Emina try to convince Alphonse to renounce his Christian salvation to become a Muslim and marry them, at which he protests, saying: 'This seemed so much like a temptation of Satan himself that I almost believed that I could see horns sprouting out of Zubeida's pretty forehead' (Potocki

1995: 18). Moreover, Avadoro explains how prejudice exists between friends from different social classes:

> The Duchess of Sidonia seemed to fear the moment that she would have only a life rent to live on. On the other hand, every time the subject of the court and the court favours came up, the Duchess of Avila took on an even more haughty air than usual. I was amazed to realize that differences of rank remained a sensitive matter, even among close friends. (Potocki 1995: 570)

The Spanish upper classes despised the lower ones, as we see in the story of Diego Hervas. Cristofo Sparadoz treats Hervas arrogantly in the presence of mutual female friends, because of his humble origin as the grandson of a cobbler. Hervas comments indignantly:

> Maranon the cobbler was my maternal grandfather, who had brought me up, and I owed the greatest of obligations to him. But he was a blot on my genealogical tree ... It seemed to me that I would be much diminished in the esteem of the three ladies if they discovered that I had a cobbler for a grandfather. (Potocki 1995: 510)

But the disdain goes both ways, as envious lower classes ridicule the aristocrats. Maria de Torres talks about this phenomenon in the city of Segovia: 'Manufacturers of vicuna cloth lived in luxury; we could not emulate them, so we took our revenge by despising and ridiculing them' (Potocki 1995: 173). Thus, throughout the tale, Potocki depicts the relativity of otherness, and its comic, but also Gothic, implications.

To conclude, this chapter has shown how the formal feature of narrative embedding focuses the relation between the two traditions of orientalism and the English Gothic, put side-by-side in Potocki's text. But this relation does not only exist at the formal level; it is a part of the thematic structure of Potocki's novel as well. It is evident in the Gothic representation of Spanish society as a southern European Catholic and feudal culture, so that the Holy Inquisition becomes an object of satire and horror just as it does in Lewis's novel, *The Monk* (1796). The sense of the other is complex in Potocki's text because the text itself uses the Arab as an other, too. Thus Spanish society is seen as divided and it is this division which is represented in the peculiar conflation between the Arabesque tradition and the European tradition of the sublimely embedded narrative, because when looked at as a form of the infinite interlacing of the Arabesque, the indefinite nature of narrative subordination is a source of sublime and uncanny horror.

AHLAM ALAKI

Notes

1   In Shahrazad's case, the metanarrative also provides continuity and survival, but to the female kind, not the Gomelez tribe. Concerning this metanarrative, numerous Gothic stories fulfill the project of the *Nights*. In *Vathek* and *The Episodes* (1793–86), the characters fill their time by telling stories proceeding their eternal condemnation in the Palace of Fire.

2   In *Don Quixote* there is also a reference to the deserts of Sierra Morena which appear in Potocki's tale.

References

Almansi, G. (1975) *The Writer as Liar: Narrative Technique in the Decameron*, London and Boston, RKP.

Beauvois, D. (1984) 'Jean Potocki's Voyages: from Mythic Orient to Conquered Orient', trans. W.L. McLendon, *L'Hénaurme Siècle: A Miscellany of Essays on Nineteenth-Century French Literature*, Heidelberg, Carl Winter.

Caillois, R. (1972) 'Introduction', in J. Potocki, *Manuscrit trouvé à Saragosse*, Paris, Gallimard.

Caracciolo, P.L. (ed.) (1988) *The Arabian Nights in English Literature: Studies in the Reception of The Thousand and One Nights into British Culture*, Basingstoke, Macmillan.

Carter, A. (1979) *The Bloody Chamber and other Stories*, London, Vintage.

Cervantes, M. de (1986) *The Adventures of Don Quixote De La Mancha*, trans. Tobias Smollett, with an introduction by Carlos Fuentes, London, Andre Deutsch.

Le Fanu, J.S. (2000) *Uncle Silas*, ed. Victor Sage, London, Penguin Books.

Faris, W.B. (1988) *Labyrinths of Language: Symbolic Landscape and Narrative Design in Modern Fiction*, Baltimore, The Johns Hopkins University Press.

Finné, J. (1970) 'Jan Potocki et le Gothic Novel', *Revue des langues vivantes*, 36, 141–165.

Haddawy, H. (trans.) (1995) *The Arabian Nights*, New York, W.W. Norton & Company.

Hillgarth, J.N. (1978) *The Spanish Kingdom 1250–1516*, Vol. 1, Oxford, Clarendon Press.

Irwin, R. (1994) *The Arabian Nights: A Companion*, London, Penguin.

Kamen, H. (1985) *Inquisition and Society in Spain in the Sixteenth and Seventeenth Centuries*, London, Weidenfeld and Nicolson.

—— (1980) *Spain in the Later Seventeenth Century, 1665–1700*, London and New York, Longman.

Kühnel, E. (1977) *The Arabesque: Meaning and Transformation of an Ornament*, trans. Richard Ettinghausen, Graz, Verlag Für Sammler.

Lodge, D. (1990) *After Bakhtin: Essays on Fiction and Criticism*, London and New York, Routledge.

Mathers, P. (1959) *The Book of the Thousand Nights and One Night*, vol. 3, Suffolk, The Folio Society.

Morson, G.S. (1978) 'The Heresiarch of *Meta*', *PTL*, 3, 414–415.

Perrault, C. (1979) *The Fairy Tales of Charles Perrault*, trans. A. Carter, New York, Avon Books.

Potocki, J. (1995) *The Manuscript Found in Saragossa*, trans. I. Maclean, London, Penguin Books.

Propp, V. (1979) *Morphology of the Folktale*, Austin and London, University of Texas Press.

Sage, V. (ed.) (1990) *The Gothic Novel: A Casebook*, London, Macmillan.

—— (ed.) (2000) 'Introduction', in J.S. Le Fanu, *Uncle Silas*, London, Penguin Books.

Seager, D.L. (1991) *Stories within Stories: An Ecosystematic Theory of Metadiagetic Narrative*, New York, Peter Lang.

Sumatsu, C. (1993) 'Le Récit labyrinthique: fantastique et procédés narratifs dans *Le Manuscrit trouvé à Saragosse* de Jean Potocki', *Etudes de langue et literature françaises*, 62, 29–41.

11

The Gothic crosses the Channel: abjection and revelation in *Le Fantôme de l'Opéra*[1]

JERROLD E. HOGLE

Since the 1980s, we have come to understand, more than we ever have before, the cultural work that has been and is still being done by so-called 'Gothic' fiction in the West. Thanks to several scholars, we now see that the archaic spaces and haunting ghosts or monsters in this mode of narrative, theatre and film provide methods of 'othering' that have definite ideological and social, as well as psychological, functions. In the Gothic from the later eighteenth century on, as David Punter has revealed most explicitly, the 'middle class' in particular (the principal audience for Gothic fictions) 'displaces the hidden violence of present social structures, conjures them up again as past, and falls promptly under their spell' with feelings of both fear and attraction towards the phantasms of what is displaced (Punter 1980: 418). Starting in England with Horace Walpole's *The Castle of Otranto* in 1764–65, at least in the sense that it was the first prose narrative to be subtitled 'A Gothic Story', this mix of previous genres enables a growing bourgeois hegemony to be both haunted by and distanced from what Punter calls the 'hidden barbarities' that have helped make it possible (1980: 419) – and hence, as Leslie Fiedler has noted, the repressed uncertainties the middle class feels about its own legitimacy (Fiedler 1966: 129) – by projecting such anomalies into the relatively safe horrors of seemingly old and alien spectres, buildings and crypts. Indeed, as the Gothic develops through wide variations from the times of Walpole and Mary Shelley to its lurid re-emergence at the *fin de siècle* (the 1890s, the decade of Bram Stoker's *Dracula,* Oscar Wilde's *The Picture of Dorian Gray,* Charlotte Perkins Gilman's 'The Yellow Wallpaper', and Henry James's *The Turn of the Screw*), it keeps confronting the middle-class spectator, and its frequently class-crossing protagonists, with estranged, hence 'othered', hence monstrous or wraith-like symbols of the contradictions (and thus the potential dissolutions of identity) that keep threatening, and threatening to expose, the unstable and mixed foundations of the very cultural positions that authors, inhabitants and readers of the Gothic nearly always want to claim for themselves. In this process, to be sure, the Gothic has helped to generate the depictions of archaic mental levels and depths that have come to characterize Freudian psychoanalysis, that exceedingly middle-class construct which arose during the last *fin de siècle* and has, not surprisingly, become an effective lens for reading Gothic fiction throughout the twentieth century. Yet this level of psychological symbolism, we now see, arises out of, disguises and manifests a much broader cultural process whereby the Gothic both buries and exposes, to quote José Monleon, many kinds of 'otherness that li[e] next to', or even reside within and beneath, the supposed 'core of the bourgeois world' (Monleon 1990: 34).

In fact, the reasons for the Gothic's particular revival at the turn of the nineteenth into the twentieth century surely include what Judith Halberstam sees as a pervasive cultural drive to 'condense various racial and sexual threats to nation, capitalism, and the bourgeoisie [all] in one body' such as a Jekyll-and-Hyde, a Dorian Gray, or a Count Dracula (Halberstam 1995: 3). That era, not entirely unlike our more recent *fin de siècle* with its more diffuse revivals of the Gothic from *Rocky Horror* cults to *The X-Files*, was a time of potentially collapsing biological, sexual, racial, class, national and even interplanetary boundaries. Consequently, several authors reasserted the Gothic's capacity to 'produce the negative of the human' for public consumption – the 'abhuman', as Kelly Hurley has termed it (1996: 3–4) – so that such 'novels' could use that 'othering' to 'make way for a [re]invention of [a cultural norm: the essential] human as white, male, middle class, and heterosexual' at a time when the desired certainty of this standard was being called into question by rapid changes, particularly in the urban centres of the UK, continental Europe and America (Halberstam 1995: 22).

Gothic fiction has thus been more recently revealed by several critics (Halberstam and Hurley among them) as a long-standing exemplar of what Julia Kristeva calls the production of 'the abject' and the process of 'abjection'. For Kristeva what we primarily 'throw off' and 'throw under' (the literal meanings of 'ab-ject'), so that we can seem to have coherent adult identities that gain acceptance within the most standard ideologies of middle-class selfhood, is a primordial state of total betwixt-and- betweeness, our condition at birth in which we are half-inside and half-outside the mother's body and thus both half-alive and half-dead as we long both to return to and to leave behind the state of our being prior to birth (see Kristeva 1982: 3–55). Recent analysts of the Gothic, including Kristeva herself at brief moments, have shown that this heterogeneity so basic to us yet cast off by us is actually cultural and intersubjective as much as it is visceral, personal and mental, quite vividly so in texts ranging from *Frankenstein* and the American-Gothic tales of Edgar Allan Poe and Gilman to *Dr Jekyll and Mr Hyde*, *Dracula*, and H.G. Wells's *The Island of Dr Moreau*. Grotesque figures that oscillate between the supposedly human and inhuman in these texts are used as locations for 'throwing over there' fundamental interactions between supposedly different social, racial, sexual and evolutionary conditions, all into repellant yet strangely desirable embodiments – or really *dis*embodiments – of the abject who are then made to seem 'thrown under' the normative existence that the would-be dominant classes and their ideologies keep working to enforce. Such Gothic figurations thereby act out Slavoj Žižek's definition of the 'sublime object' created by capitalist ideology: the simultaneous embodiment and concealment of a 'traumatic social division' or set of class 'antagonism[s]' at the heart of Western culture as both are placed at a fictional distance from and by those who wish to pretend they are free of them (Žižek 1989: 45). We Westerners use the Gothic to transform those anomalies so close to us into an ominous, removed and impenetrable depth, a fictional 'otherness' far less threatening (even as a manifestation of a psychological 'unconscious') than the actual social conflicts and blurrings of cultural distinctions that are abjected onto it. Gothic fiction, it turns out, albeit in changing ways, has continuously crossed generic boundaries, moving between forms of 'high cultural' and 'low cultural' symbol-making, in order to help us all deal with many crossings of cultural boundaries that are really prior to and hidden in the foundations of the social separations and hierarchies we keep trying to reassert.

Such boundary-crossing in this kind of fiction, I want to stress here, has been quite international as well as cultural and has been so in ways that expose with striking precision what the cross-generic and class-crossing Gothic can simultaneously abject and reveal in the dynamics of Western middle-class culture. As I have already begun to argue elsewhere (Hogle 1996), one of the texts that continues the Gothic tradition quite fully and deliberately just after the turn of the last century is the original novel version of *Le Fantôme de l 'Opéra* (*The Phantom of the Opera*) by Gaston Leroux (hereafter *Le Fantôme*, to distinguish it from its adaptations), which was published in Paris in 1910 with several allusions to earlier Gothic texts (especially those of Poe and Stoker) and has reappeared, however greatly altered, during our own *fin de siècle* (the 1990s) in several reincarnations including and inspired by the Andrew Lloyd Webber musical play that first opened in London in 1986. *Le Fantôme*, though it has been far less studied than other 'monster' tales that have been adapted nearly as often, enacts the abjective functions of the middle-class Gothic more extensively than anyone has ever noticed before now. It imports a host of elements from American and English Gothic tales particularly into the vast underground crypt that the title character, Erik the 'Opéra ghost', occupies in the deepest cellar below the actual neo- Baroque Paris Opéra designed by Charles Garnier in the 1860s and opened during France's Third Republic as its primary centre of national musical culture in 1875. In bringing so much anglophilial Gothic material to bear on French locations and even recent French history – including the real falling of the Paris Opéra chandelier due to an electrical defect in 1896 (Perry 1987: 21) – Leroux plays up, more clearly than his adaptors, the grounding of a quasi-antiquated 'high culture' on a repressed depth of underlying levels filled with much that has come to be thrown off and thrown down as 'low culture'.

After all, Erik, as both an original contractor for the Opéra's construction (almost an artisan) and the chief inhabitant of its deepest foundations, turns out, like Gaston Leroux himself, to be the product of an unsettling but frequent cultural shift from a low-middle-class/provincial status at birth (in Rouen) to a quasi-upper-middle-class, even semi-aristocratic urban standing, symbolized by this phantom's possession of a well-placed opera box from which he can watch performances in the grandest evening wear of the day. This fluidity of social placement alone, along with several other contradictions, in this living spectre makes him an apt repository for objecting many mixed and anomalous conditions, each of which is really one basis of high culture's visible ascent buried beneath it and haunting it with the foundations of itself that it will not admit. As Leroux's novel proceeds, numerous 'high-brow' features associated with citified, nationalistic,

JERROLD E. HOGLE

occidental and quasi-aristocratic opera turn out through Erik to be rooted in and invaded by the provincial and rural, the Germanic and Scandinavian (even in his name), the 'oriental' (considering the 'dark arts' he once learned in Persia and India), and the 'low-brow' carnivalesque, given Erik's history as a freak in travelling county fairs where he learned the sort of ventriloquism and legerdemain that he now uses to make a senior diva on the Opéra stage suddenly appear to croak like a frog (see Leroux 1959: 471, 248, 402–403, 494, 151–155). The original *Fantôme de l'Opéra* carries out all the major tendencies in *fin de siècle* Gothic and even in much of Walpole, supremely using the Gothic's drift between high-class and lower-class forms of fiction, to present a stunning exposé and concealment of the very mixed states and socio-economic roots at the core of early twentieth-century pretensions to cultural supremacy, especially in France, the centre of Paris, and its famous and gaudy Opéra Garnier.

To say this much, however, as I really have already, is not to reveal the extent to which this crossing of the channel by the originally English 'Gothic' ends up pointing, in *Le Fantôme*'s abjections, to the contradictions and anxieties at the heart of the 'new Europe' that was beginning to emerge after the extreme conflicts of the 1890s seemed – but only seemed – to be settled during the fourth decade of the Third Republic just prior to World War I. I want to argue here that Leroux's importation of the Gothic, used by him many times but nowhere more than in *Le Fantôme de l'Opéra*, allows him and his readers both to confront and to disguise from themselves, as they choose, the nagging antagonisms, persistent guilts, and still-haunting mixtures of distinct social levels that were buried just beneath the surface of Parisian and urban European life as its cultural and political unconscious, along with its psychological one, all at the dawn of the twentieth century. The survival of this story in adaptations, even when they change it greatly (as they have) to abject anomalies and anxieties of their *own* times, stems from its ability to use Gothic abjection to throw off and yet obliquely face – acts we still need and want to repeat – some of the most difficult ironies of life of the supposedly 'new Europe' throughout the twentieth century. *Le Fantôme de l'Opéra* continues to haunt us with many of the functions that the Gothic has long performed in our culture, but it haunts us particularly with cultural interconnections that Europe and America have wanted to efface or seem to destroy in constructing 'high' culture's distinction from what is 'low' ever since the nineteenth century.

To be sure, some of the transformations that occur as Leroux makes the Anglo-American Gothic more French only slightly alter tendencies that were already apparent in English or American tales of this kind. Unlike nearly all the adaptations of it, *Le Fantôme* gives its grotesque title character, not so much a set of deformities affecting the skin of his face (as in those several films where he has been splashed by acid), but the face of a skull covered by an epidermis so thin that it is visible only in its parchment-like yellowness, adding even more qualities of decay to a walking embodiment of death (see Leroux 1959: 253–256). This sort of Gothic monstrosity links the kind of living dead we see in Stoker's vampiric Dracula to the long Franco-Germanic tradition of the *danse macabre* in religious art – as in a classic example from France in 1485 Figure 5; Warthin 1977: 12) – where skeletons invade the false security of insouciant high-livers to remind them of the immanence of death and the final wages of sin. Indeed, Erik does precisely that in the novel, especially when he appears as Red Death at the Opéra's masked ball by descending the grand staircase, not in a skull-*mask* as in the adaptations that use this scene (starting with the 1925 silent film with Lon Chaney (Figure 6; see Julian 1982), but as the only figure at this mixture of

Figure 5 'The physician and the youth' panel from the *Danse Macabre* sequence in the Cloister of the Innocents in Paris, based on a reproduction from a 1485 rendering by Guyot Marchant

opera and carnival in the novel who is *un*masked, a true living death with a face that has remained a skull from birth and so can serve as a 'sight', like the skeleton in the *danse macabre,* that abruptly 'provoke[s] the soul to the most funereal thoughts' (Leroux 1959: 57; all translations from this text are mine). At the same time, though, Leroux is both reviving the haunting skeleton that indicates the hidden primal crime in Walpole's *The Castle of Otranto* (Walpole 1996: 106–107) and directly echoing Poe's 1842 American tale 'The Masque of the Red Death'. By recalling the latter especially, *Le Fantôme* is alluding without question to the ironic attempt of would-be 'knights and dames', in Poe's Gothicized words, to seclude themselves from the bloody and multi-featured 'contagion' of the wider social world in a very exclusive 'masquerade' in a 'castellated abbey' that turns out to harbour what it would exclude as already locked deep within itself (Poe 1981: 253). This decomposing multiplicity starts to appear in 'The Masque', even before the figure of

Figure 6 The Masked Ball scene in Universal's 1925 silent film *The Phantom of the Opera,* with Lon Chaney

Red Death comes to embody these tendencies in one scapegoat form, in the wild mixture of the 'beautiful' and the *'bizarre'* – 'not a little of that which might have excited disgust' in upper-class people (as Poe's narrator puts it) – all in the 'writhing' figures of the masked knights and dames themselves, who are consequently inhabited by virtually everything they would throw off, culturally and physically, in their resplendent preserve (Poe 1981: 254–257).

Le Fantôme de l'Opéra thus extends the Anglo-American Gothic penchant for oblique cultural commentary in its own haunting of operatic exclusivity by the teeming and disease-like carnivalesque, the 'low' and the plebian, that it tries to contain, control and keep out, just as the Paris Opéra actually did in an annual *bal masqué* after real carnivals were banned from the heart of Paris in 1870 (Stallybrass 1986: 177). As it happens, the association of the skull with the low and primitive as opposed to high culture became firmly established in West European and American thinking between the times of Poe and Leroux. It is this very ideological contrast that we see in *Coombs' Popular Phrenology* of 1865 (Figure 7; Levine 1988: 222) when it sets the 'high brow' of a William Shakespeare against a 'low brow', as embodied in the slant-headed skull of a dug-up New Zealand aboriginal chief, with all the imperialistic and racist assumptions that such a construct carries with it. Leroux's use of a skull-face for his Gothic monster-ghost repeats the fear of 'degeneration' and 'decadence' in figures such as Dracula from the 1890s so well studied by Elaine Showalter (1990), Martin Tropp (1990) and Kelly Hurley (1996), but it does so by combining the very French *danse macabre* with the social implications of the English and American Gothic, all as further coloured by the post-Darwinian associations of the skull with a lower-class devolution towards the troglodytic childhood of humanity. The great irony in *Le Fantôme*, of course, is that Leroux's Erik combines tendencies associated with degeneration at the time (such as the childish and unrefined writing style in his threatening notes to the Opéra managers; Leroux 1959: 62–63) with extreme high-cultural sophistication, as in what Christine Daae – the young singer from the country whom he coaches and desires – has to admit to be his 'sublime', if eccentric, musical genius (1959: 259). It is as if the cultural ideologies attached to the skull (especially the otherings in them) keep showing through features of the highest class in theatre and culture, such as Shakespeare came to embody in the nineteenth century far more so than he did in his own day. One of the great

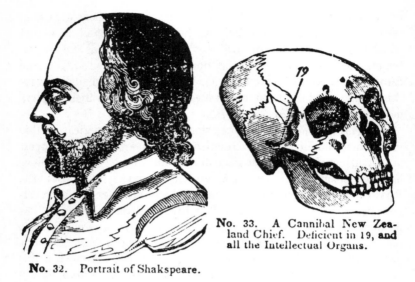

No. 33. A Cannibal New Zealand Chief. Deficient in 19, and
all the Intellectual Organs.

No. 32. Portrait of Shakspeare.

Figure 7 Illustrations 32 and 33 in Coombs's *Popular Phrenology* of 1865

threats posed by Leroux's phantom is how much he reveals an insepa-
rable mixture of cultural levels which may really be, but can never be
admitted as, characteristic of the many class-climbers who attached
themselves to the Opéra, much as Erik has himself in his movements
from country, carnival and cellar into a high-priced box in Paris's most
central and gaudy institution of high culture.

Even here, however, this French use of the Gothic does not deviate
greatly from English and American uses of the form, partly because of
Le Fantôme's own debts to French writing of the early nineteenth century. The resemblance of this novel's underground world to features of
the Freudian unconscious, already not terribly surprising in a book
published only ten years after *The Interpretation of Dreams*, reveals
Leroux's debts to the French variation on the Gothic best known then
and now as the *conte fantastique,* the strongest avatar of which was
Smarra, or the Demons of the Night, published in 1821 by Charles
Nodier (by then a translator and adapter of John Polidori's *The
Vampyre*, published in England in 1819). Many of the *contes fantas-
tiques*, especially *Smarra* with its explicitly underground, highly
sexual, and mother-centred dream-world (see Kessler 1995: 14–21),

helped bring about the conceptualization of the psychoanalytic unconscious later in the century. There is no doubt Leroux is drawing on this tradition when he has Erik construct his rebuilt cellar around an exact replica of his mother's bedroom, into which he places Christine after luring her down to his lair in a descent she later describes as leading her soul 'to the threshold of a dream' (Leroux 1959: 245). Yet Leroux's novel further alludes, on the one hand, to the social histories and critiques presented in the novels of Victor Hugo, especially *Notre Dame de Paris* from 1831 (long recognized as a precursor of *Le Fantôme de l'Opéra*), and, on the other hand, to the stinging portraits of bourgeois hypocrisy in the ironic novels and novellas of Honoré de Balzac. In *Le Fantôme*, as a matter of fact, I find several direct reminders of Balzac's *Sarrasine* (1830), that complex novella highlighted in Roland Barthes' influential *S/Z* of 1970. There the financial and hidden cultural base of a social-climbing family with a multi-chandeliered mansion turns out to be the fortune amassed by an old figure in the house who seems 'to have come out from the underground' with a 'cadaverous skull' barely covered by the 'thin, yellow skin of his face' and who turns out to have been the *castrato* Zambinella, once celebrated throughout Europe's opera houses for the range of his singing voice (Barthes 1974: 225–230), a range very like the one that causes Leroux's Erik to be identified sometimes as a man and sometimes as a woman by those who hear him sing over six octaves without seeing him up close (Leroux 1959: 384–385). This combination of echoes in the original *Fantôme* makes its flirtations with the unconscious, undeniable to be sure, rest quite firmly on layers of suggestion about the multiple and concealed underpinnings of middle-class life, so much so that the sense of historical progression towards the dominance of the *bourgeoisie* celebrated by Hugo at the expense of his lovesick hunchback in *Notre Dame* (see Hugo 1923: 80–87) is definitely haunted by a Balzacian unconscious of social hypocrisies and suppressions, even crossings of class and gender boundaries, on which that dominance and its accoutrements of 'high culture' are based. In this respect Leroux's book vividly continues the similar interplay of the psychological and the deeply cultural that has always been a part of the English Gothic, particularly in the 1890s, even though it does so in some peculiarly francophilial ways based on earlier French transformations of the Anglo-American Gothic into dark psychological fantasies or descriptive devices within bourgeois hyperrealism.

The Gothic crosses the channel more completely, I believe, in the ways *Le Fantôme de l'Opéra* explores the 'new Europe' of its day more widely. Consequently, in the rest of what follows, I want to draw out the boundary-crossing revelations and overtones that lie in those explorations, however undergrounded and abjected they are in the novel, into a 'political unconscious' sublimated within Gothic or semi-Gothic characters, actions and settings. In his extensive use of the real Paris Opéra and its actual history, for example, Leroux both unearths and conceals several ironic foundations of a central city that had by 1910 become a model of urban redevelopment throughout much of Europe. Granted, in its attempt to subsume many architectural styles (including oriental ones) within its neo-Baroque and very insistent façades and interiors, the Opéra was designed, first for the Second Empire and then for the purposes of the Third Republic, to be the supreme announcement of France's 'imperial power ... and the participation of the urban middle-class audience in the imperial enterprise' (Lindenberger 1984: 238). Yet its construction and placement were parts of a monarchical master plan that destroyed, and even buried, as much as or more than it built. After his election following, and for many his betrayal of, the 1848 revolution, the Emporer Napolean III (nephew of Napoleon Bonaparte) appointed the Baron Haussmann 'Prefect of the Seine' in charge of redesigning the centre of Paris as a celebration of the Second Empire, which inevitably meant the razing of many structures and street-patterns left over from more *anciens régimes*. The 'broad, tree-lined boulevards and avenues radiating [from a center] like wheel spokes' in the Paris of today are among the lasting results of this sweeping redesign and the 'draconian powers of demolition' that Haussmann and his builders were granted in order to achieve it (Perry 1987: 8).

One consequence was the demolition of some slums initially, to the point of forcing 'the teeming working classes ... to the edges of the city' (Perry 1987: 8). Among the reactions to this reconstruction was a foreign republican's 1858 bombing of the Emperor's procession directly in front of the old opera house, which killed or wounded 150 and came close to wounding Napoleon III himself (Perry 1987: 8), all of which is at least somewhat recalled in the incendiary threats posed by Gaston Leroux's 'Opéra ghost'. That shock led very soon to Haussmann's call for a grander Opéra at a new Paris site, partly so that there could be greater security at the times the Emperor attended and partly so that the new Opéra could be a more manifestly imperial and cultural 'focal point in [the Baron's] Paris plan' (Perry 1987: 8–9). Hence he and his associates 'began to lay down new thoroughfares which radiated outward in seven straight lines from [a] large square, [which soon became what it still is today:] the *Place de l'Opéra*' (Perry 1987: 9). In doing so, they established the opera house that would rise at the centre of that square as the high bourgeoisie's and imperial aristocracy's own version of the palace at Versailles, Louis XIV's enormous and glittering neo-Classical residence begun in the 1660s from which the streets of *its* city were redesigned to radiate as well. To make way for this new 'palace of the people' displaying *haut bourgeois* supremacy, the 'rabbit warren of old buildings and alleys standing in the ways of Haussmann's scheme was ruthlessly flattened', arousing extensive 'criticism in the National Assembly' at the time and forcing even more of the poorer and working classes to the margins of a city that has kept on trying to keep them out of its centre, except as workers and peddlers, ever since (Perry 1987: 9). In an effort to 'strengthen his dictatorship and to place Paris under an emergency regime', as Walter Benjamin has written, Haussmann increasingly 'estranged Parisians from their [own] city' (Benjamin 1978: 159–160).

While thus creating 'the *quartier* that has become the commercial center of modern Paris' (Perry 1987: 9), Haussmann even went so far, quite notoriously, as to plan the removal and stop all the further digging of charity graveyards in the central city, threatening all the remains they held (Pinkney 1958: 145–148). Much of what these graveyards contained, though this process was only begun, were slated to be gathered together and moved, somewhat in the way the poor had already been herded, to outlying burial sites very like, and sometimes including, the Paris catacombs established in the eighteenth century. These former limestone-quarry passageways just outside the heart of Paris still show what such a removal project meant at its most extreme by the time of Leroux's birth in 1868: extensive and winding dirt halls below ground, open for public tours at selected hours, in which bones upon bones relocated from former gravesites are piled head high for great distances along the walls. The skulls are laid in lines atop the bone-piles, seeming to stare at the visitors from their perches on the stacks of assorted parts from many different and unidentified bodies. As a result, for readers of *Le Fantôme de l'Opéra* to tour the Opéra Garnier and these catacombs on the same day, as I did in 1996, is for them to confront a broadly cultural 'return of the repressed' in this novel and

JERROLD E. HOGLE

in the history of Paris before and after 1848. When Leroux's skull-face set on top of a nearly skeletal body, itself little more than a pile of bones, invades the Paris Opéra from quarters deep in some underground passages, it is, among many other things, a haunting at the core of Haussmann's 'new Paris' by the skeletons of the lower classes (from the middling bourgeoisie down) who have been removed from the heart of the city, 'othered' as undesirable residents there, and sometimes reburied at the outskirts to make space for the breadth and depths of the Paris Opéra, along with so much else that still surrounds the cultural centre it was designed to be.

Indeed, given that such 'others' are wanted in the heart of Paris only as artisans and labourers – as those who dig out the foundations and cellars of new structures the way Leroux's Erik supposedly helped to do in the 1860s and '70s (Leroux 1959: 497) – the irony of high culture both depending on these people and casting them outside the city centre, especially as piles of bones and skulls, is very much a part of what is horrifying in the original *Phantom of the Opera*. When Leroux finally named his favorite poet to another journalist, it was, not surprisingly, Charles Baudelaire (Leroux 1984: 997), that master of the post-Romantic macabre, champion and translator of Poe, and portrayer of the city's undersides, who died a paralytic (for some a 'degenerate') in 1867, the year before Leroux was born. As it happens, one of the most vivid poems on the repressed foundations of urban life in Baudelaire's *Les Fleurs du mal* (1857, revised 1861), a collection frequently focused on the 'living dead' of Paris, is 'Le Squelette laboureur' ('The Skeleton at Work'):

> Bêchant comme des laboureurs,
> Des Ecorchés et des Squelettes.
> De ce terrain que vous fouillez,
> Manants résignés et funèbres,
> De tout l'effort de vos vertèbres,
> Ou de vos muscles dépouillés,
> Forçats arrachés au charnier,
> Dites, quelle moisson étrange,
> Tirez-vous, et de quel fermier
> Avez-vous à remplir la grange?

> (Digging like labourers,
> The skinned and the skeletons.
> From that earth that you turn
> Working resigned and funereal

216

With all the effort of your vertebrae,
Or your fleshless muscles,
Tell us, what strange harvest,
Convicts dug from a charnel,
Do you seek, and for which farmer
Must you fill up the grange?)
(Baudelaire 1936: 208–210, ll. 11–20) (my translation)

Although Baudelaire's speaker is here addressing, on one level, skeletal emblems he sees in an antique (and quite religious) book, his fleshless figures recruited explicitly from the bone-piles of a charnel house are also ceaselessly digging at the command of an unknown being for a 'harvest' entirely alien from them, partly because they are not really on a farm. In that effort they are very like the emaciated 'spectres' of the 'Seven Old Men' in another *Fleurs du mal* poem, 'all come from the same hell', who accost the viewer in the 'swarming city' that is thus increasingly revealed as a hell-on-earth at its deepest levels, a morass of the death-bound and increasingly homeless destitute, a 'great sea monstrous and without shores' (Baudelaire 1936: 182–187, ll. 3, 30, 1, 52). Echoing such images in his skeletal digger of foundations, Leroux points implicitly to this urban *symboliste* underworld, intimately connected to what lies above it, that through Erik brings to the surface, for the all-too-blinded middle-class gaze (Baudelaire's target as well), the poor, the labouring, the exiled, the wandering, the criminalized, the 'othered', the dying and the dead.

It is no wonder that when Christine first descends beneath her Opéra dressing room towards the phantom's lair on the underground lake – the lake actually produced by the draining of marshy land during the real Opéra's construction (Perry 1987: 10) – she reaches him as the ultimate figure after observing a host of shadowy 'black demons in front of boilers', all of them 'work[ing] with shovels and pitchforks' as if they were the 'souls of the dead' who had already crossed the mythical River Styx (Leroux 1959: 237–238). These figures, made racially black by Christine's unstated assumptions about how 'low' they are, are the workers in the Opéra's physical infrastructure, underground labourers in an imperial building's hidden but necessary depths. The farther beneath the surface anyone goes in *Le Fantôme*, the more the urban labouring classes become connected to the encrypted deathliness of Erik that is their all-too-immediate destiny in the post-Haussmann modern city that Baudelaire exposes and Leroux's phantom recalls. This rising of the culturally repressed as characters and readers descend is even more ironic when we remember that Erik's prime ambition in Leroux's novel is to become so high bourgeois, partly through marriage with Christine, that he can walk on boulevards above ground arm-in-arm with his wife as others of that class fashionably do on weekends after evenings in their Opéra boxes (Leroux 1959: 411). The very aspirations of the new-European *bourgeoises* who read this Gothic novel could hardly be more intimately linked 'at bottom' to what they would most abject: the labourers prone to earlier deaths on whom they depend so that they can be entirely dissociated from the physical work that they both need and ignore to achieve the class standing they seek.

At the same time, I would further suggest, *Le Fantôme de l'Opéra* is equally haunted by – and consequently abjects – the anomalies in a specific political history upon which the new Paris, the new French Republic, and the new Europe of the new century were quite deliberately grounded, precisely by efforts to keep that history underground. As it happens, Leroux's phantom constructs his subterranean lair largely out of the remnants of the Paris Commune. Commune vestiges could indeed be found beneath the Opéra Garnier, as Leroux himself discovered in his own journeys into the cellars (Leroux 1959: 14–15). The hidden passage behind Christine's dressing-room mirror, the main avenue to and from this novel's underworld, is therefore designated by Erik as 'my way of the Communards' (Leroux 1959: 393), since he supposedly found it in the early 1870s as an already-constructed leftover from the Commune's brief occupation of the Opéra from March to May of 1871. This construction occurred, as did some of Erik's initial efforts there, during the suspension of the Opéra's building process from 1870–71 because of France's war with Prussia, the Prussian Siege of Paris, and the short defiance of both the French National Assembly and the foreign invaders by the Commune as it occupied several buildings, using the Opéra especially as a storehouse, prison and centre of communications (Leroux 1959: 404–405; Williams 1969: 4–7; Perry 1987: 12–13). In the early 1880s, when the novel takes place, Erik is thus reusing and helping to demonize the fragmented workings of the Commune that recall *the* most disruptive and disrupted time in the history of Paris from 1848 to 1910, a time when national and class conflicts produced the fullest suspension of high-bourgeois-based political structures that any Parisian could remember by the turn of the century. Moreover, Leroux's phantom combines some wildly different postures in transfiguring the memory of the

Commune as he does. To a slight extent, as a quasi-anarchist, he is an 1880s revisitation of the outcast and downcast in 1871 who employed the Opéra to take prisoners, send messages, and threaten war with buried munitions so that groups of marginalized people could take more sanctioned control of the centre of the State. Yet Erik also casts off the political agenda and social values expressed by the actual Commune. Particularly as he extorts 20,000 francs a month from the Opéra management (Leroux 1959: 63), he is more of an insatiable creditor and freelance entrepreneur using pieces of the Commune for his own profit to support an acquisitive, rising-middle-class, albeit underground, lifestyle. To his symbolic combination of many other conflicted positions, the Erik of the original novel adds this wildly oxymoronic condition whereby he both returns the threat of the Commune from its repression by an Opéra touted as a hallmark of the Third Republic's ascent *and* embodies – to what we might call a bare-bones degree of nakedness – the grasping drive of the class-climber, usually hidden from immediate view, to be both a creditor and an investor against the wishes of the very Commune he now recalls.

As it turns out, this Gothic paradox reflects quite precisely the way the Commune was in fact demonized (extending the tendencies in a sketch of the period by Honoré Daumier; Figure 8) as a means by which the Third Republic and its supporters could define themselves against the 'otherness' that the 'way of the Communard' was made to represent. Erik's erasure of Commune ideology to emphasize only its threats echoes Leon Gambetta's efforts in Parisian pamphlets and newspapers throughout the 1870s to establish the rise, in his words, of 'a new social stratum' (for him the 'enlightened Republican bourgeoisie') by urging this group to explicitly set itself off from those 'utopians and dreamers [who have been] showering the masses with unrealizable promises', a description in which he knew his readers would recognize the Paris Commune as propaganda had already recast it (Elwitt 1975: 54). For Gambetta such extremists could be easily linked to 'brutal revolutionary action' and 'horrible social wars' inimical to 'working out' what he construed as the 'legitimate consequences of the French Revolution' (1975: 54–55).

At the same time, for Henri Allain-Targé, an even more active opponent in the press of the socialist schemes epitomized by the Commune (especially after Karl Marx extolled it on hearing how it had been violently routed in May of 1871; Williams 1969: 47–57), such movements

Figure 8 *Appalled by the Heritage* (1871)
a caricature by Honoré Daumier

were so alien to 'true' European values that they were really suitable
only for Orientals, specifically 'Asiatics' or 'Moslem and slavic peoples'
in Allain-Targé's words (published 22 August 1881, and translated in
Elwitt 1975: 270). He 'othered' them within the same French orientalist ideologies that several of Leroux's characters scapegoat onto Erik,
making him the sort of 'abject' cross-fertilization of the oriental and
occidental that all 'pure race' middle-class Republicans want to throw
off from themselves completely. Whether they are disguised behind this
orientalism or alluded to more directly, it is not simply the truths or history of the Commune that are abjected in *Le Fantôme de l'Opéra*;
instead Leroux's Opéra ghost both conceals and echoes the middle-class
use of the Commune as the 'abnormal' monstrosity against which the
bourgeois Republic fashioned its supposed normality, all of which shows
that it was deeply bound up with exactly what it tried most to dissociate
from itself. That is why the original phantom is both a partial re-enac-
tor of a hollowed-out Commune and the most nakedly acquisitive of

bourgeois social-climbers all at the same time. The bourgeoisie of this era in France depends upon recasting pieces of the Commune that it has emptied of their original ideological content, and it additionally relies, through the Commune, on an undergrounded monstrosity connected to threats from the past (like Mary Shelley's creature made from parts of corpses or Robert Louis Stevenson's 'troglodytic' Mr Hyde) to bury the most extreme drives of naked bourgeois acquisition from view, as though they are not really part of the above-ground Republic that they actually motivate at all times.

Leroux's use of his Gothic phantom as this kind of abjecting 'deviant', however, does not stop at embodying and obscuring broad conundrums of French history and politics. Erik and his underground also throw off and down states of betwixt-and-betweeness deeply pervasive in Western culture that challenge specifically Third Republic standards of sexual normality and ethnocentricity beyond the general prejudices of orientalism alone. On one set of levels, Leroux's phantom has features that would have been immediately associated by Parisian readers of 1910 with male–female indistiction or hermaphrodism, as in the range of his voice; onanism, since he is all by himself 'down there' in the dark with the sort of 'haggard' appearance associated in nineteenth-century sexology with persistent masturbation (Figure 9; Mosse 1985: fig. 1, opp. p. 96); and inclinations in the direction of homosexuality, as when a Persian policeman and the Vicomte Raoul de Chigny (Christine's childhood sweetheart) 'fall into an embrace' upon nearing Erik's lair in their pursuit of him or when Erik himself enters Raoul's bedroom at night, coming at least to the foot of his bed and arousing in the younger man a vague desire 'to know everything' by seizing that beckoning body in the dark (Leroux 1959: 379, 271–273). For at least three decades by 1910, hegemonic writing in western Europe, as George L. Mosse has shown, had placed all these avenues for sexual desire – right along with what was classified as 'oriental', 'degenerate' and 'decadent' – in one generalized and mythic location thought to contain, as a composite 'abject', all the threats to European 'nationalism and respectability posed by the rapid changes of the [urban] modern age' (Mosse 1985: 45, 31). Leroux's Erik is another version of that conglomeration of 'others', indeed a blatant antithesis of the ideal masculine body and self that were held up, in France as much as Germany around 1900, as simultaneously the 'national stereotype and the middle-class stereotype' (Mosse 1985: 16). 'Nationalism and respectability', which the

Figure 9 'The Consequences of Masturbation'
an illustration included in R.L. Rozier's *Des
habitudes secrets* (*The Secret Vices*)

Paris Opéra (among other venues) was employed to represent at the
turn of the century, after all, strove to assign 'everyone his place in life,
man and woman, normal and abnormal, native and foreign [one but not
the other]; any confusion between these categories threatened chaos
and loss of control' for many people at the time of great upheaval (Mosse
1985: 16), just as Leroux's seemingly abhorrent and anarchist phantom
does by incarnating and abjecting an astonishing array of confusions
among categories.

The original Erik is most entirely betwixt and between, however, in
the way he seems both semi-Jewish and entirely Aryan at a time when
the problem of anti-Semitism in France had been raising its ugly spectre with unusual force for more than twenty years. On the one hand,
Erik as a demonically obsessed and sometimes vindictive music master
teaching a young woman with uncertain potential to sing like a diva
would have reminded readers in Leroux's day immediately of Svengali,
the lascivious Austrian Jew – one of the most anti-Semitic creations in
literary history – who mesmerizes the title character into public vocal
brilliance in George du Maurier's 1894 novel *Trilby* (Figure 10; du

Maurier 1931: 249), that English literary sensation by a French expatriate which was quickly and widely adapted for the stage (Kelly 1983: 87, 119–123). On the other hand, the phantom of Leroux is explicitly revealed to be a Gentile native of France born near Rouen, however much his long-faced and haggard figure (like Dracula's as well as Svengali's) resembles the cartoon stereotype of the Jew at the time (Halberstam 1995: 91–99) that had grown in prominence with the large migration of Jews into France after the pogroms in Russia of the early 1880s (Goldstein 1985: 535). This ambivalent use and rejection of anti-Semitic images becomes even more arresting when we realize that Leroux's *danse macabre* description of his phantom bears a striking resemblance to his own newspaper accounts of the 'skeletal' figure of

Figure 10 'Au clair de la lune' one of George de Maurier's illustrations for his novel *Trilby* (1894)

223

Alfred Dreyfus (the subject of many political cartoons at the time (Figure 11; Zola 1996: fig. 10, opp. p. 175), whom Leroux describes as arriving in 'a phantom landau' for his retrial in Rennes (*Le Matin*, 2 July 1899, 2) after his conviction for treason in 1894 had sent him to hard labour on Devil's Island. As we now realize in our cultural memory of Emile Zola's 'J'accuse' (1898) denouncing the pervasive anti-Semitism behind the false accusation and railroading of the defendant, the Dreyfus Affair was still a focal point in 1910 for 'the Jewish Question', the most openly unresolved cultural quandary in middle- and upper-class France and much of western Europe.

Like Zola, Leroux himself was quite capable of using the demonizing of Jews for literary effect, as he surely does in making his phantom *so* like Svengali and Dreyfus, yet also condemning anti-Semitism roundly in his articles of 1899, where he adds up all the episodes in the Affair and calls them 'these unbelievable, fantastic, maddening,

Figure 11 'The Sponge': an 1899 ink drawing by H.G. Ibels, a pro-Dreyfus cartoonist, commenting on the case of Alfred Dreyfus, which began in 1894

monstrous or stupid, bloody or ridiculous stories that have constituted the History of France over the last hundred years' (my translation from Leroux's article in *Le Matin*, 19 August 1899, 1). In the sweeping generality of these words, Leroux even sees how much the Dreyfus case became a scapegoating focus for the growing 'hostility ... of 1894 between the governmental Republicans and the socialists and the radicals on the extreme Left' who soon increased their expanding support by taking up Dreyfus' cause against both the French army and the *haut bourgeois* ruling class (Cahm 1996: 11–12). Given these additional ingredients in the conflicting images borrowed to depict him, Leroux's Opéra ghost augments the many confusions of categories he harbours, not by simply being somewhat Jewish symbolically, but by being a quasi-wandering Jew *and* a home-grown Gentile, a rightly demonized other *and* an unfairly persecuted scapegoat, and a seemingly left-leaning rebel against the most established power-brokers *as well as* an obsessive pursuer of the standard, climbing, middle-class self. Ultimately Leroux shows the underside of urban Europe in 1910, its very heart, to be the *exact* interaction of tendencies that it tries to make distinct, and he does so by abjecting those tensions onto a Gothic spectral monster who seems to be the frightening exception to most rules instead of what he actually embodies (or dis-embodies): the fundamental shifting between cultural positions that the rules attempt to regulate and bury from sight.

By abjecting so many crossings of boundaries onto its title character, then, the original *Le Fantôme de l'Opéra* makes the maximum symbolic use of the crossings of generic and class boundaries basic to the Gothic as a highly mixed form *and* the crossing of international boundaries that the Gothic has achieved more and more after the eighteenth century. The result, though, as we have seen on many different levels in Leroux's novel, is the continual association of numerous abjected cultural anomalies *with* the desired 'normality' of bourgeois aspiration. Unlike Mr Hyde or Dracula, Erik the Opéra ghost is an 'other' who is really normal to an extreme within rising middle-class ideology, definitely *not* working class, completely dead, communistic, hermaphroditic, homosexual, or Jewish even as overtones of these 'others' are abjected onto him and conflated into the abject features of this spectral figure mirroring us back to ourselves. As we readers of the novel peel away his layers, we find greater and more intricate crossings of boundaries the deeper we go. Erik is clearly an interplay among many 'different' beings 'othered' by the dominant middle class at his time; *then* a revelation that these otherings may be more projections by class-climbing people (including the author) than realities endemic to any aberrant condition; *then* a demonstration of how such projections create 'abjected' others that obscure their ideological roots and purposes; *then* an exposure of how the bourgeois 'normalcy' that gains its ideological distinction from such objections is intimately and continuously connected with what it throws off (as in the Opéra's masked ball); and *then* a suggestion that this *entire complex* of culturally motivated self-constructions-by-abjection (all parts of which appear in Erik at once) is what must be abjected most and made most anomalous – using the most established otherings available – so that the supposed 'high-cultured' selfhood that is fashioned in this process can sublimate its roots symbolically and effectively.

Conventional middle-class aspiration, Leroux's *Fantôme* reveals, so needs its otherings to establish its difference from them that those very confusions of categories turn out to be the deepest foundations of this sense of identity in the new Europe of the early twentieth century. Such a linkage, which here rises from the repression of it in the depths of high culture, means that the construction of the modern, bourgeois, hegemonic, Anglo-European self is usually an attempt to distill an illusory 'purity' with precise boundaries out of an actual underpinning of class-crossing positions, multi-cultural interconnections, and conflicting attitudes in which apparent opposites by middle-class standards are interactively basic to the vision of existence that wants to define itself by abjecting these betwixt-and-between roots beneath or beyond its own location. The capacity of the Gothic to help us either avoid or face this cultural unconscious comes to a revealing apotheosis in *Le Fantôme de l'Opéra* precisely by crossing the English Channel enough to draw peculiarly French ironies, concealments and unresolved quandaries of recent history into the anomalous symbolic 'technologies' of Gothic fiction, as Judith Halberstam has so aptly termed them (1995: 33).

All of this is both 'thrown down' and visible in *Le Fantôme*, we should note, *not* because its author was, let us say, a post-Commune radical exposing the duplicities and abjections of his own class (as Baudelaire did) so as to directly overturn its supremacy. Leroux, in fact, was so committed to 'a stable bourgeois system fortified against both aristocratic reaction and social revolution', the goal of the Third Republic (Elwitt 1975: 10), and thus was so opposed to communistic movements, that he quite readily expressed his fears in the 1920s (before he died suddenly in 1927) that 'if [such] imbeciles [as the Bolsheviks of the Russian Revolution] persist, they will force us to choose between two tyrannies, that of Caesar and that of the concierge', between whom Leroux would 'love Caesar more' if there came to be no middle ground (quoted in Lamy 1977: 18). Still, this same Gaston Leroux saw himself as a balance of tendencies in his writing. 'I have taken on the skin of an *hônnete homme* [the bourgeois standard self]', he had written by 1904, 'and [I] am at the same time an assassin' not completely unlike the incendiaries in Paris about whom he both worried and reported (Leroux 1985: 7). Well aware of the problems and hypocrisies in class-climbing and self-definition-by-othering in his own boundary-crossing life, he chose to confront his middle-class readers in his Gothic or near-Gothic fictions with horrifically disguised versions of their own abjections, a great many of them in *Le Fantôme de l'Opéra,* as though these very readers could and should be haunted, as he surely was, by the contradictory conditions and anxieties that surrounded (and still surround) them even as they strive to rise beyond that awareness.

He went so far with Erik, we now find, as to make him incarnate that particular striving right alongside its inescapable connection with crossed or blurred, rather than strict, cultural boundaries. Now even his own slippage between *hônnete homme* and 'assassin' was effectively projected into his title character, as well as villainized to the point of concealment when incarnated in the extremes of the phantom's most violent acts. In thus making the line between bourgeois 'right' and 'wrong' so difficult to draw – and hence in crafting Erik as both a half-sympathetic and an abhorrent character – Leroux allows us, even today, both to confront and to keep abjected at arm's length the mythic process of middle-class self-construction in Europe and America, so much so that he has left us a powerful re-enactment of that process which we can choose to see or ignore as such. We keep coming back to this story, increasingly as a myth that transcends any one version, in part because it presents us with some key features of our most basic cultural mythmaking, the production-by-abjection of a bourgeois identity still under construction even in the newest 'European community'. At the same time, given Leroux's ambivalence about the 'assassin' side of his efforts, we also see this myth worked out conventionally and Gothically enough that all the mixings of categories in its 'political unconscious' can be ignored if that is what we decide, much as the

JERROLD E. HOGLE

real Paris Commune can be kept away from our direct gaze and demonized as simply a violent 'other' in this novel the way it was in the republican press of Leroux's own time. From this major example, we now know even more about the cultural work that the Gothic performs – the good, the bad and the ugly in that ongoing process – primarily because a French reworking has taken to very French extremes an Anglo-American Gothic breaking of boundaries to the point of making those crossings, not just the method of symbolization, but the fundamental meaning at the unsettling core of *Le Fantôme de l'Opéra*.

Note

1   For very particular assistance with this chapter, my heartfelt thanks go to Avril Horner, Terry Hale, Ari Anand and Kathy Fitzgerald.

References

Barthes, R. (1974) *S/Z: An Essay*, trans. Richard Howard, New York, Hill and Wang [1970].
Baudelaire, C. (1936) *Flowers of Evil*, trans. G. Pillon and E. St Vincent Millay, New York, Harper's [1861].
Benjamin, W. (1978) *Reflections: Essays, Aphorisms, Autobiographical Writings*, ed. P. Demetz, trans. E. Jephcott, New York, Harcourt.
Cahm, E. (1996) *The Dreyfus Affair in French Society and Politics*, London, Longman.
Elwitt, S. (1975) *The Making of the Third Republic: Class and Politics in France, 1868–1884*, Baton Rouge, Louisiana State University Press.
Fiedler, L. (1966) *Love and Death in the American Novel*, New York, Dell.
Goldstein, J. (1985) 'The Wandering Jew and the Problem of Anti-Semitism in Fin-de-Siecle France', *Journal of Contemporary History*, 20, 521–551.
Halberstam, J. (1995) *Skin Shows: Gothic Horror and the Technology of Monsters*, Durham NC, Duke University Press.
Hogle, J.E. (1996) 'The Gothic and the "Otherings" of Ascendant Culture: The Original Phantom of the Opera', *South Atlantic Quarterly*, 95, 821–846.
Hugo, V. (1923) *Notre-Dame*, trans. anon., London, T. Nelson [1831].
Hurley, K. (1996) *The Gothic Body: Sexuality, Materialism, and Degeneration at the Fin de Siècle*, Cambridge, Cambridge University Press.
Julian, R. (dir.) (1982) *The Phantom of the Opera* with Lon Chaney, producer C. Laemmle, screenplay E.J. Clawson and E. Sedgwick, Universal, VideoYesteryear # 871, New York, Video Images [1925].
Kelly, R. (1983) *George Du Maurier*, Boston, G.K. Hall.
Kessler, J.C. (ed. and trans.) (1995) *Demons of the Night: Tales of the Fantastic, Madness, and the Supernatural from Nineteenth-Century France*, Chicago, University of Chicago Press.
Kristeva, J. (1982) *Powers of Horror: An Essay on Abjection*, trans. L.S. Roudiez, New York, Columbia University Press.
Lamy, J.C. (1977) 'Gaston Leoux, ou le vrai Rouletabille', in G. Leroux, *Histoires epouventables*, Paris, Boudinaire, pp. 15–70.

Le Matin: derniers telegrammes de la nuit, Paris, 1887–1909.

Leroux, G. (1959) *Le Fantome de l'Opéra*, Paris, le livre de poche [1910].

—— (1984) *Oeuvres*, ed. Francis Lacassin, Paris, Editions Robert Laffont.

—— (1985) *Du Capitaine Dreyfus / Au Pole Sud*, ed. Francis Lacassin, Paris, Union generale editions.

Levine, L. (1988) *Highbrow/Lowbrow: The Emergence of Cultural Hierarchy in America*, Cambridge MA, Harvard University Press.

Lindenberger, H. (1984) *Opera: The Extravagant Art*, Ithaca, Cornell University Press.

du Maurier, G. (1931) *Trilby: A Novel, with the Author's Illustrations*, London, Dent [1894].

Monleon, J.B. (1990) *A Spectre is Haunting Europe: A Sociohistorical Approach to the Fantastic*, Princeton, Princeton University Press.

Mosse, G.L. (1985) *Nationalism and Sexuality: Middle-Class Morality and Sexual Norms in Modern Europe*, Madison, University of Wisconsin Press.

Perry, G., with J. Rice (1987) *The Complete* Phantom of the Opera, New York, Henry Holt.

Pinkney, D.H. (1958) *Napoleon III and the Rebuilding of Paris*, Princeton, Princeton University Press.

Poe, E.A. (1981) *The Annotated Tales of Edgar Allan Poe*, ed. Steven Piethman, New York, Doubleday.

Punter, D. (1980) *The Literature of Terror: A History of Gothic Fiction from 1765 to the Present Day*, London, Longman.

Showalter, E. (1990) *Sexual Anarchy: Gender and Culture at the* Fin de Siècle, New York, Viking.

Stallybrass, P. and White, A. (1986) *The Politics and Poetics of Transgression*, London, Methuen.

Tropp, M. (1990) *Images of Fear: How Horror Stories Helped Shape Modern Culture, 1818–1919*, Jefferson, McFarland.

Walpole, H. (1996) *The Castle of Otranto: A Gothic Story*, ed. W.S. Lewis and E.J. Clery, Oxford, Oxford University Press [1765].

Warthin, A.S. (1977) *The Physician of the Dance of Death: A Historical Study of the Evolution of the Dance of Death Mythus in Art*, New York, Arno [1931].

Williams, R.L. (ed.) (1969) *The Commune of Paris, 1871*, New York, John Wiley.

Žižek, S. (1989) *The Sublime Object of Ideology*, London, Verso.

Zola, E. (1996) *The Dreyfus Affair: 'J'accuse' and Other Writings*, ed. Alain Pages, trans. Eleanor Lavieux, New Haven, Yale University Press.

12

'A detour of filthiness':
French fiction and Djuna Barnes's
Nightwood

AVRIL HORNER

The French have made a detour of filthiness – Oh, the good dirt! Whereas
you are of a clean race, of a too eagerly washing people, and this leaves no
road for you. (Barnes 1985: 123[1])

The inclusion of a chapter about an American novel in a book on European Gothic writing might seem somewhat anomalous. However, in
this chapter I shall argue that Djuna Barnes's most famous work,
Nightwood, which was written in Europe and published in 1936,
engages with French literature in a number of ways in order to develop
its own transatlantic Gothic agenda. I shall therefore try to retrieve
Djuna Barnes's *Nightwood* as a Gothic text and, in so doing, trace its
derivation from a French tradition of Gothic or quasi-Gothic writing.
This tradition begins with the *roman noir* and the *roman frénétique*,
which flourished respectively between 1790 and 1820 and between the
1820s and 1830s.[2] It continues with the work of authors such as Eugène
Sue, whose novels were widely translated across Europe, and Lautréamont, whose emphasis on sadism and cruelty recuperates the radical
agenda developed by de Sade some 80 years earlier. This disquisition on
darkness influences, in turn, the work of 'decadent' *fin-de-siècle*
authors such as Huysmans, whose cynicism and interest in excess are
reflected in the novels of later writers such as Louis-Ferdinand Céline
and Georges Bataille.

What we therefore see in *Nightwood* is an expression of anomie
coloured by its author's exposure to a particular French literary tradition, described by Kristeva as 'a black lineage'. Exemplified for Kristeva
by the works of Lautréamont and Artaud, this lineage is one in which

'inhumanity discovers its appropriate themes, contrary to all lyrical traditions, in horror, death, madness, orgy, outlaws, war, the feminine threat, the horrendous delights of love, disgust, and fright' (Kristeva 1982: 137). Barnes's embrace of such a lineage is inflected by her situation as a modernist. Like many of her contemporaries, she took to heart the radical experimentation with language which was central to the French symbolist movement and which constituted its most important legacy to modernism. It is curious that T.S. Eliot, who was himself profoundly influenced by French symbolism, ignored the impact of French writing on Barnes's work in his famous introduction to *Nightwood*. In so doing, he set in place a critical tradition which presents the novel as a bizarre and eccentric text owing more to English Renaissance drama than to French literature. Resisting this reading, recent feminist interpretations of *Nightwood* have retrieved it as an important American modernist and/or lesbian text. Mary E. Galvin, for example, in her book *Queer Poetics: Five Modernist Women Writers*, describes Barnes as a writer who:

> consistently presents lesbian sexuality as central to her urban settings and her depiction of her times; the 'otherness' her characters experience is integral to the modernist scene. (Galvin 1999: 102)

This championing of Barnes as an American lesbian modernist has had its uses. The current resurgence of interest in her work has coincided with the emergence of queer theory, which has been used to interpret her writings in a manner more sophisticated than that of earlier critics such as Field, who tended to conflate the works with a gossipy version of the life (Field: 1983). Nevertheless, there is still much work to be done on Barnes's debts to French literature.

However, before exploring the impact of certain aspects of French culture on Barnes's writing of *Nightwood*, we perhaps need first of all to establish briefly the novel's Gothic credentials. Lewis Gannett commented in 1937 in the *New York Herald Tribune* that 'It is a book of Gothic horror, not of Elizabethan tragedy' (Field 1983: 215) – thus taking issue with T.S. Eliot's claim in his 1937 introduction to Barnes's novel that its 'quality of horror and doom' related it to Elizabethan drama (Eliot 1937: 7). Leslie Fiedler also included *Nightwood* in his 'neo-gothic' category in *Love and Death in the American Novel* in 1966 (Fiedler 1992: 490) and Ellen Moers defined it as 'modern female Gothic' in *Literary Women* (Moers 1976: 108). In seeing *Nightwood* as a Gothic text, however, these critics have remained exceptions. In part, this neglect of the novel's Gothic elements may be due to the inclusion of *Nightwood* within the modernist canon: the early masculinist critical construction of modernism as a movement of 'high', experimental culture, which eschewed the melodramatic, the popular and the Gothic, has meant that texts canonized within modernism tend to be read in a certain way. Thus while Barnes has been coupled with Joyce and *Nightwood* with André Breton's *Nadja*, the novel's Gothic elements have been largely ignored. These include: the representation of Paris as a dark and labyrinthine space; the presentation of the Volkbeins' Viennese home (complete with ancestral fake portraits and a 'thick dragon's blood pile of rugs from Madrid' (p. 17)), as a Gothic house; a continual questioning of normality as benign; and, above all, a blurring of the boundaries between night/day, masculine/feminine, sacred/profane, real/surreal and human/animal. Furthermore, whilst Felix Volkbein is linked explicitly with the figure of the Wandering Jew (p. 20), Robin – through her restless night-time predatory wanderings during which she 'feeds off' her café victims – is implicitly associated with the figure of the Vampire. In particular, the novel's strange closure, which shows us Robin's union with a dog in a ruined chapel, both recalls the Gothic novel's fondness for the sacrilegious act and expresses the insight that modernism's anxieties concerning the fragmentation of the self are essentially Gothic.[3] Nevertheless, the critical resistance to seeing *Nightwood* as a Gothic work has persisted. Bonnie Kime Scott notes that the novel 'has been called, alternatively, surrealistic, Eliotic, Dantesque, fugal, Elizabethan, *even gothic*' (my italics) (Scott 1990: 23) and Diane Chisholm also argues for the novel's debts to surrealism rather than the Gothic tradition (Chisholm 1997: 185). This ambivalence concerning the strong Gothic legacy evident within *Nightwood* perhaps also derives from a rather limited conception of the nature of Gothic. Given the complex development of the Gothic mode over 250 years, it is clearly too reductive simply to equate it with suggestions of the supernatural or with the use of tropes such as the haunted house, the young female victim and the Bluebeard figure. Rather, it is now best defined in the spirit of Angela Carter who argues that the Gothic:

> grandly ignores the value systems of our institutions … (and) deals entirely with the profane … Character and events are exaggerated beyond reality, to become symbols, ideas, passions. Its style will tend to be ornate, unnatural – and thus operate against the perennial human desire to

believe the word as fact ... It retains a singular moral function – that of provoking unease. (Carter: 1974: 133)

This broad definition, together with David Punter's claim that Gothic authors are writers who 'bring us up against the boundaries of the civilized, who demonstrate to us the relative nature of ethical and behavioural codes' (Punter 1996: 183–184), allows us to locate *Nightwood* firmly within the genre of the Gothic – for the novel does nothing if not provoke 'unease' and 'bring us up against the boundaries of the civilised'.

Written mainly in England during the early1930s, *Nightwood* nevertheless draws heavily on French literary and cultural legacies. This is not surprising, given the fact that Barnes lived in Paris – often seen as *the* modernist city – between 1921 and 1931, a period frequently presented as the defining moment of high modernism. Barnes felt what one biographer has described as 'an intense alienation from both family and nation' (Herring 1995: 85) and she looked to English and European culture for intellectual inspiration. Like other American expatriates, such as Ezra Pound, Ernest Hemingway and Gertrude Stein, Barnes was a writer whose residence in Paris had a catalytic effect on this desire to embrace Europe and European consciousness. It is, of course, impossible to know exactly what Barnes read during those eleven years in Paris but it seems likely that she would have absorbed much French, as well as English and American, literature. Certainly she was an eclectic reader. We know from her diaries and letters that during the 1930s she read the work of Proust, Fielding, Dostoevsky, certain Renaissance authors (including Sir Thomas Browne, Robert Burton and Donne), William James, Céline, Luther, Pascal, Montaigne, Bergson and Emily Brontë (Herring 1995: 139, 194–195, 219). Such reading patterns probably owed much to the fact that as a child she was exposed to a very wide range of literature, including much in translation. James Scott's interviews with Barnes revealed that her childhood evenings were often spent, along with other family members, listening to her grandmother, Zadel, read aloud from a broad selection of European and American authors; favourite writers included Dostoevsky, Dickens and Proust (Herring 1995: 38). Barnes even claimed that her own name, Djuna, 'came from Eugène Sue's *The Wandering Jew*, where there is an Indian prince called Djalma, which became spliced with Thurn's word for moon, "nuna"' (Herring 1995: 32). Given that Barnes had very little formal education, the literary diet made available at home through both her grandmother's and her parents' reading would have been the main influence on her as a creative child and adolescent. There is no doubt that this intellectual legacy helped shape the content and form of her work, although the emotional legacy of an unorthodox childhood – one scarred by a strangely intense and probably incestuous relationship with her grandmother – has aroused more interest and has been better documented (Dalton 1993; Herring 1993).

An early acquaintance with the works of Eugène Sue thus formed part of Barnes's intellectual legacy. Sue's *The Mysteries of Paris* (1842–43) was translated into several languages, including English, and remained immensely popular throughout the nineteenth and early twentieth centuries. It almost undoubtedly informs her portrayal of Paris in *Nightwood* as a dark and labyrinthine city, more reminiscent of the capital before Haussmann's transformation of it between 1852 and 1870 than during the period in which *Nightwood* is set (the novel opens in 1880 but its main focus is on Paris in the mid-1920s). Indeed, several elements of *Nightwood* can be tracked back not only to Barnes's time and friends in Paris (Matthew O'Connor being based on Dan Mahoney, an infamous resident of Paris during the 1920s, for example), but to the city as represented by nineteenth-century authors such as Dickens, Zola and Eugène Sue. In Sue's *The Mysteries of Paris*, the rural idyll of Bouqueval Farm offers a place where goodness, health and love flourish, in contrast to the capital, which is the scene of numerous cruelties, sadistic acts and criminal deeds. As in the work of Victor Hugo, the surface morality of Sue's novel hides a fascination with the criminal, a downwardly mobile figure who both lives outside the confines of bourgeois life and threatens it. Despite the hero's claim that 'the good and wicked, great and small, submit almost always to the influence of higher, nobler spirits' (Sue n.d.: 390), the moral ambiguity of Sue's novel resides in the fact that the relish and energy with which urban scenes of depravity and cruelty are described result in far more convincing scenarios than those offered by the rural idyll of Bouqueval Farm, meant to indicate a better life. In this sense, *The Mysteries of Paris*, whilst continuing to express a Romantic anxiety about the city as a place of exploitation and depravity, nevertheless positions itself as an early decadent city novel through its prurient and consistent interest in urban evil. *The Mysteries of Paris* and *Nightwood* both portray Paris as an urban Gothic space in the sense defined by Alexandra Warwick:

'The city is seen as uncanny, constructed by people yet unknowable by the individual' (Mulvey-Roberts 1998, 288–289).

Paris, Vienna, Berlin and New York as we see them in *Nightwood* are 'unknowable' in this sense; they are labyrinthine spaces where freedom exists more as an intellectual concept than an actuality. Guido Volkbein, a Jew of Italian descent and Robin's father-in-law, finds no peace of mind in his pseudo-Gothic mansion in Vienna, where anti-Semitic feeling runs rampant (as, in fact, it did during the 1920s4). Barnes's portrayal of the circus as an exotic event in Paris and New York enables the reader to experience the modern city through the eyes of the unconventional and the marginalized, categorized as unclean and abject by the bourgoisie who wish their cities to be clean, tidy and ordered. The perspective offered by such a spectacle – like that provided by carnival – is allowable, however, only within carefully defined city limits and definitions. Neither do the anonymity and sexual freedom offered by the city result in emotional fulfilment and liberation. The liberty to conduct a lesbian relationship in Paris means little to Nora since her lover, Robin, uses that freedom precisely to challenge Nora's desire for a monogamous love by finding other lovers in Parisian bars and cafés and by eloping with Jenny Petherbridge. In Barnes's novel, cities are informed by Sue's Paris and Dickens's London, worlds in which suffering and exploitation are commonplace and where freakishness and the grotesque indicate both the limits of, and a challenge to, urban order and bourgeois values. The idea of the city as the acme of urbane sophistication and cultural integrity is thus profoundly challenged by Barnes, as it was by Dickens and by nineteenth-century French novelists such as Sue, Balzac and Zola.

Interestingly, early readers of *Nightwood* were quick to point to the European legacy evident in the novel and, in particular, to parallels with certain French authors. For example, Rose C. Feld, reviewing the novel for the *New York Herald Tribune* in 1937, compared Barnes to Baudelaire whilst Theodore Purdy, in the *Saturday Review* during the same year, noted T.S. Eliot's 'failure to perceive that the atmosphere of decay in "Nightwood" stems from the fin-de-siècle Frenchmen rather than from the Elizabethans'; in the same year, the anonymous reviewer for the *Times Literary Supplement* likened Barnes to Céline (Marcus 1990a: 195–204). Later, in 1945, Joseph Frank claimed that *Nightwood* was constructed on the same principles as Proust's *A la recherché du temps perdu* (Field 1983: 145). Given this reception, it is strange that

AVRIL HORNER

critics have engaged very little with the French dynamic of *Nightwood*. There are three notable exceptions to this statement. Jane Marcus, in her influential essay 'Laughing at Leviticus: *Nightwood* as Woman's Circus Epic', interprets the novel as exploring the political unconscious of the rise of fascism. Constructing Barnes as a subversive writer, she briefly draws attention to Barnes's debts to Rabelais, Victor Hugo and Eugène Sue (Marcus 1990b: 221–250). Diane Chisholm, in her article 'Obscene Modernism: *Eros Noir* and the Profane Illumination of Djuna Barnes', presents Barnes as an avant-garde author, carefully situating the novel in the context of modernism, obscenity and surrealism and paying particular attention to the parallels between *Nightwood* and Breton's *Nadja* (Chisholm 1997: 167–206). Erin G. Carlston, in her book *Thinking Fascism: Sapphic Modernism and Fascist Modernity*, charts *Nightwood*'s links with French *fin-de-siècle* decadence and a particular strain of what she calls 'romantic Catholicism' which she sees as ushering in the rise of fascism (Carlston 1998: 42–85). It is evident from these quite different readings that Barnes's 'detour' into a French 'filthiness' has divided these critics: whereas Marcus and Chisholm represent her as radical and subversive, Carlston sees her as an author who moved from a flirtation with fascism in the thirties to a final rejection of it in the 1950s. This recuperation of Barnes as either excitingly left- or dangerously right-wing suggests something about both the elusive nature of *Nightwood*'s 'meaning' and the continuing ambivalence of the American imagination in the face of a Gallic 'black lineage'. The French, of course, have a better track record than the Americans for accommodating dark desires – as Barnes's words, used as the epigraph to this chapter, indicate. Through its representation of 'Frenchness', the American novel has often embraced decadence and iniquity – aspects of human behaviour supposedly excluded from the agenda of the New World – by projecting them on to a European other (the writings of Henry James offer an obvious example). These elements, as Ahmed Nimeiri has pointed out, are signalled in *Nightwood* 'by such metaphors as the night, the forest, the beast and "filthiness"'. Hence, as Nimeiri notes, Matthew O'Connor's admiration of the French as a people who can accept both night and day as 'two travels' and who are able to make 'a detour of filthiness' (Nimeiri 1993: 106–107).

In this respect, a key text for any evaluation of the impact of French literature on Barnes's creative imagination must surely be Lautréamont's *Les Chants de Maldoror* (1868–69) (translated as *Maldoror*).

This strange Gothic text, described in the *New Oxford Companion to Literature in French* as celebrating 'the unbridled predatory misdeeds of a prowler monster whose shape is as indefinite as his age' (France 1995: 447), reaffirms the values of Eugène Sue's world, in which evil usually triumphs over good. It also continues the Sadeian tradition of portraying cruelty in order to explore the dynamics of power and control (Blanchot 1949; de Jonge 1973). Certainly both de Sade and Lautréamont relish the creation of nightmare scenarios as a way of probing the seductions of power in order to ask questions about the relationship between the governance of personal desires and the governance of peoples and nations. It is not surprising, then, that de Sade and Lautréamont were embraced by Surrealists such as André Breton and critics such as Maurice Blanchot, since their anti-Christian and anti-humanist agendas seemed to offer a very modern reaction to realism, rationalism and the optimistic faith in progress characteristic of modernity. Again, it is not surprising that such a reaction provoked fresh allegiance in the wake of World War I (Chisholm points out that de Sade enjoyed a revival in literary circles in Paris in the early 1920s; 1997: 201). However, whereas there is an explicit Sadeian element in *Nightwood*, signalled by the fact that at one point in the novel we find Robin Vote reading 'the memoirs of the Marquis de Sade' (p. 73), the connection with *Les Chants de Maldoror* is more tenuous – although given Barnes's own interest in surrealist thought, it is likely that she would have come across Lautréamont's work. Indeed, the parallels between Lautréamont's novel and *Nightwood* are, to say the least, highly suggestive. Certainly, like both de Sade and Lautréamont, Barnes uses Gothic paraphernalia in order imaginatively to challenge the definition of desire as it socially constructed.

Maldoror is a disturbing work that eschews linear logic in favour of a nightmare scenario in which – as in the writings of de Sade – one episode of sadistic cruelty follows pell-mell upon another. Its anti-hero, Maldoror, is the perpetrator of these acts, which include rape, incest, bestiality and murder. In diabolic fashion, he sets himself against God, who is portrayed in the spirit of Goya's Saturn as a divinity who eats those he has made and who is careless of, and impervious to, man's suffering. Indeed, like the novel's anti-hero, Lautréamont's God seems to derive pleasure from both causing and watching human agony. Its excesses, like those of the Gothic genre which it both mimics and parodies in places, give *Les Chants* a blackly humorous air. However, as

Alex de Jonge, one of Lautréamont's most perceptive critics has suggested, the French author's use of sensationalism is harnessed to an intellectual end; as in the work of de Sade, the indulgence of excess is used to shock and to challenge cultural conventions:

> In forcing man's attention on his instinctive love of cruelty, no less real for being inadmissible, Maldoror appeals to man's repressed and secret self. Desires that normally have to be sublimated by culture into notions such as crime and punishment, law-enforcement, the obscene rituals of social justice and authoritarianism, are exposed by Maldoror for what they are: institutions created by society to permit its leaders to exercise their natural, instinctive desire to treat their fellows as their slaves, without abdicating from their role as do-gooders and pillars of the community: to behave, in short, like miniature versions of the eating God. (de Jonge 1973: 51)

Hence, of course, Maldoror's similarity to Milton's most famous character: 'most think that he is tortured by incommensurable pride, as Satan was, and that he would like to be God's equal' (Lautréamont 1973: 31). Milton's Satan and Lautréamont's Maldoror share the same intellectual impulse: a desire to expose the tenets of Christianity and Western civilization to a searing critique. In Lautréamont's text, however, there is no salvation for the deity. Indeed, de Jonge suggests that Lautreamont's work anticipates the Foucauldian insight that we are all trapped within an episteme which limits our self-understanding and knowledge: the only way out, intellectually, is to smash the metaphorical bars of the cultural prison thereby erected (de Jonge 1973: 15). To this end, Lautréamont eschews the world of daylight for the world of night, daytime logic for night-time imaginings, *civitas* for wildness, civilization for barbarism; in terms of style he draws attention to the text by baring the device and by poeticizing his language through linking words by shape and sound rather than by meaning. The resulting experimental nature of his writing gives it a very modern air, although clearly he draws on the works of Maturin, Poe, Scott and Eugène Sue in creating his strange fictional world. Indeed, in choosing his *nom de plume*, Isidore Ducasse presumably turned to Sue's historical novel, *Lautréamont*, published in 1837, the hero of which is described by de Jonge as 'a brutal, insolent officer, with a black and cynical sense of humour and distinctly mephistophelian characteristics' (de Jonge 1973: 29). Lautréamont's writing identity is thus textually haunted by that of an earlier rebel against law and order, just as is that of Barnes. For I want to suggest here that what have been perceived as the more bizarre elements of *Nightwood* derive from a French literary tradition in which *Maldoror* is an important element. In portraying same-sex love, bestiality and incestuous desire, Barnes is not simply writing a 'confessional' novel, which is how *Nightwood* has often been interpreted. Rather, she is also engaging with a European tradition, intellectually iconoclastic and quasi-Gothic in temperament, which seeks to deconstruct the morality of Western civilization in order to expose its hypocrisy and institutionalized cruelty.

This is certainly the aim of Lautréamont's text, which unsympathetic readers dismissed as full of freakishness, salacious acts of cruelty and gratuitous violence. The novel follows the wanderings of the malicious Maldoror, whose restlessness relates him to Melmoth and the Wandering Jew, and whose predatory instincts and thirst for blood relate him to Dracula:

> Heaven grant that his birth be not a calamity for his country, which has thrust him from its bosom. He wanders from land to land, hated by all. Some say that he has been a victim of some special kind of madness since childhood. Others believe that he is of an extreme and instinctive cruelty, of which he himself is ashamed, and that his parents died of grief because of it. There are those who maintain that in his youth he was branded with an epithet and that he has been inconsolable for the rest of his existence because his wounded dignity perceives there a flagrant proof of the wickedness of mankind, which manifests itself during their earliest years and grows continually. This epithet was *The Vampire!* (Lautréamont 1965: 30–31)

As I have already intimated, Robin Vote is also a vampiric figure, albeit a less obvious one, in so far as by night she preys sexually on the café inhabitants of Paris, draining her partners of love and energy. A wandering, emotionally estranged being, dislocated from her environment, Robin embodies a misanthropic cynicism. Eschewing the values of her unconventional companions as well as those of the bourgeoisie, she is an anarchic force even within the liberal and tolerant environment of *Nightwood*'s Paris. She is linked with the marginality of the circus people and with the social liminality of the Jew and the sexually 'deviant' (just as Dracula is linked with the Jew, the Gypsy and homosexual desire). Like Maldoror and Dracula (who is associated with wolves and bats), she sometimes seems closer to animals than to people – a feature emphasized by her silence (she speaks fewer than ten times in the novel). Arguably, she has an avatar in Maldoror, whose most ful-filling sexual encounter is coupling with a female shark (and, since Maldoror fantasizes himself as 'the son of a female shark' (Lautréamont 1965: 15), the deed also has a quasi-incestuous dimension). Indeed, Maldoror places dogs above humans in the hierarchy of living things:

> When you are in bed and you hear the howling of the dogs in the fields, hide yourself beneath your blankets, don't make a jest of what they are doing: they have the insatiable thirst for the infinite, like you, like me, like the rest of human beings with our long, pale faces ... I, even as the dogs, feel a yearning for the infinite. (Lautréamont 1965: 15)

Maldoror even sees himself as half beast, half human, with the 'protrud-ing bones of [his] emaciated face, resembling the bones of some great fish' (Lautréamont 1965: 15). Similarly, Robin's connection with ani-mals in *Nightwood* reaffirms the breakdown of the boundary between beast and human represented throughout Barnes's novel. We first meet Robin in a room which looks like 'a jungle' (p. 56); she is described by the narrator as 'a woman who is beast turning human' (p. 59) and later, by the doctor, as 'a wild thing caught in a woman's skin' (p. 206).

This dissolution of the boundary between human and animal takes a particularly nasty turn in *Maldoror*, however, when Maldoror's dog, imitating his master, rapes a beautiful young girl, the daughter of Providence:

> Carrying out that order appeared to be difficult for the bulldog. He thought his master had commanded him to do what had already been done, and this wolf with the monstrous muzzle contented himself with violating the virginity of that delicate child in his turn. From her lacerated stomach the blood ran again down her legs and upon the meadow. Her cries mingled with the animal's yelps. The child held up the golden cross that she wore about her neck that he spare her; she had not dared to pre-sent it before the savage eyes of him who first conceived the idea of prof-iting by the weakness of her age. (Lautréamont 1965: 137)

The peculiar closure of *Nightwood*, which culminates in a strange union between Robin and Nora's dog, seems to rework this passage in a more benign manner:

> Sliding down she went; down, her hair swinging, her arms held out, and the dog stood there, rearing back, his forelegs slanting; his paws trem-bling under the trembling of his rump, his hackle standing; his mouth open, his tongue slung sideways over his sharp bright teeth; whining and

waiting. And down she went, until her head swung against his; on all fours now, dragging her knees. The veins stood out in her neck, under her ears, swelled in her arms, and wide and throbbing rose up on her fingers as she moved forward.

The dog, quivering in every muscle, sprang back, his lips drawn, his tongue a stiff curving terror in his mouth; moved backward, back, as she came on, whimpering too now, coming forward, her head turned completely sideways, grinning and whimpering. Backed now into the farthest corner, the dog reared as if to avoid something that troubled him to such agony that he seemed to be rising from the floor; then he stopped, clawing sideways at the wall, his forepaws lifted and sliding. Then, head down, dragging her forelocks in the dust, she struck against his side. He let loose one howl of misery and bit at her, dashing about her, barking, and as he sprang on either side of her he kept his head toward her, dashing his rump now this side, now that, of the wall.

Then she began to bark also, crawling after him – barking in a fit of laughter, obscene and touching. The dog began to cry, running with her, head-on with her head, as if to circumvent her; soft and slow his feet went. He ran this way and that, low down in his throat crying, and she grinning and crying with him; crying in shorter and shorter spaces, moving head to head, until she gave up, lying out, her hands beside her, her face turned and weeping; and the dog too gave up then, and lay down, his eyes bloodshot, his head flat along her knees. (pp. 237–239)

Interestingly, the raped child in *Maldoror* holds up her cross before the dog 'that he might spare her', knowing that it would be useless to present it to the 'savage eyes' of Maldoror (who will later treat Mervyn, his young male victim, worse than a dog). Similarly, Robin's encounter with Nora's dog, whilst strangely disturbing, seems less threatening than most of the human encounters described in the novel which reveal the 'naturally' exploitative and manipulative manner of human behaviour. The behaviour of dogs, by contrast, ranges from an honest animality to the intellectual/spiritual 'longing for the infinite' assumed traditionally to be the prerogative of human beings. Thus the Gothic agenda is the same for both episodes: to submit to scrutiny the power of the Church and the intellectual legacy of the Enlightenment which enables the categorization of every thing and every living thing into hierarchies, a supposedly 'objective' process which in fact conceals an agenda whereby particular aspects of life can be denigrated or abjected. An apparently 'innocent' activity, such categorizing underpins particular ideologies and social hegemonies, justifying certain barbarous acts, such as genocide or ethnic cleansing.

On one level, then, Robin, like Maldoror and Dracula, is the wild stranger who brings chaos into the city space and who threatens 'normal' hierarchies. And in the spirit of the Gothic text, Robin's final flight is into the wilderness. Dracula's last resting place is within the rocky wildness of the Carpathian mountains; Frankenstein's monster flees to the Northern Arctic wastes to die. *Nightwood*'s closure gives us Robin finally taking refuge on Nora's wild estate, where the ruined chapel indicates a lost faith and a crumbling civilization. The use of Gothic tropes in Barnes's work, however, is not simply derivative; like Lautréamont, she parodically adapts the Gothic mode in order to challenge convention, conservatism and institutionalized cruelty. Lautréamont's defence of the supernatural and of horror – 'do not despair, for in the vampire you have a friend despite your opinion to the contrary' (Lautréamont 1965: 48) – is, finally, a defence of the right to attack the vile body of modernity. It is a sentiment with which Barnes would have been in sympathy.

The same fierce antagonism to contemporary society marks the novels of Huysmans and Céline. Although their works are less obviously Gothic than those of Lautréamont, their penchant for excess and their conviction that suffering is the natural condition of humanity place them in the same French tradition of intellectual disaffection. Moreover, even a cursory reading of Huysmans's *A Rebours*, published in 1884 (translated as *Against Nature*), and Céline's *Voyage au bout de la nuit*, published in 1932 (translated as *Journey to the End of the Night*), suggests their influence on *Nightwood*. For example, the *fin-de-siècle* extravagances of des Esseintes's house at Fontenay in Huysmans' *Against Nature*, including a jewel-encrusted tortoise and an organ from which one can draw off various alcoholic drinks in relation to the notes on its keyboard (Huysmans 1998: 35–40), find an echo in the eccentricities of Robin and Nora's apartment in the Rue du Cherche-Midi, which contains:

> circus chairs, wooden horses bought from a ring of an old merry-go-round, venetian chandeliers from the Flea Fair, stage-drops from Munich, cherubim from Vienna, ecclesiastical hangings from Rome, a spinet from England and a miscellaneous collection of music boxes from many countries (p. 85)

Similarly, des Esseintes's predilection for unusual sexual partners (which include Miss Urania – an androgynous American circus acrobat

– as well as a female ventriloquist and a strangely dressed young man) is reflected not only in Robin's sexual eclecticism but also in Barnes's portrayal of the circus in Paris and New York as curiously fascinating and erotic. Whilst Jane Marcus is no doubt right to suggest in 'Laughing at Leviticus' that the depiction of the circus as well as the opera in *Nightwood* indicates Barnes's Rabelaisian spirit and her desire to embrace low as well as high culture, it is worth remembering that there is in French art, as Nicholas White points out, a tradition of representing circus performers as objects of desire (as in the work of Degas, Rops and Seurat) which both Huysmans and Barnes exploited (Huysmans 1998: 208–209).[5] But perhaps the most striking similarity between Huysmans's novel and *Nightwood* is the strange conjunction of Catholic and Sadeian thought evident in both works. Whilst the works of Baudelaire and Edgar Allan Poe are evoked in *Against Nature* 'on account of their similar poetics, their mutual interest in the study of mental illness' (Huysmans 1998: 156), it is de Sade's ambivalent attitude towards religion which fascinates des Esseintes, in particular his desecration of 'a Divinity which he hoped would be willing to damn him, while yet declaring, as a further act of defiance, that this Divinity did not exist' (Huysmans 1998: 132). Not surprisingly, then, des Esseintes's drift towards Catholicism is clearly informed by a relish for suffering as well as beauty (as, indeed, was that of Huysmans himself). The religion that appeals to him is, by his own confession:

> a Catholicism gingered up with a little magic, as occurred under Henri III, and a touch of sadism, as happened at the end of the last century. This special brand of clericalism, this depraved, artfully perverse mysticism towards which, at certain times of day, he was drawn, could not even be discussed with a priest, who would not have understood it, or who would have promptly, and with horror, rejected it. (Huysmans 1998: 176–177)

This same ambivalence towards Catholicism is represented in *Nightwood*, where it is linked with Robin's furtive recourse to beautiful churches in Paris and with Matthew O'Connor's masturbating during mass (although this does not stop him describing himself as 'as good a Catholic as they make' (pp. 217–218)). For Erin G. Carlston, Barnes's debts to Huysmans link her with the rise of fascism, for she sees in the alliance between *fin-de-siècle* decadence, Catholicism and dandyism an alternative to Marxist or liberal positivism which ended in the rise of Hitler (Carlston 1998: 59). In order to sustain such a reading, however, Carlston has to ignore the self-reflexive irony of *Nightwood*, conveyed mainly through the musings of Matthew O'Connor who, Felix thinks, although he lies, is 'a valuable liar' (p. 49). O'Connor, who gave his 'kidney on the left side to France in the war' (p. 31), has come face to face with 'the Beast' in the wood of the night and expresses his cynical understanding of human nature in a series of elliptical philosophic musings. He knows that cruelty derives from unresolved fear and that at a social level this expresses itself in war: 'he berserks a fearful dimension' (p. 119). He also understands that the French embrace of 'filthiness' leaves 'a path for the Beast' (p. 123): that the fascinated interest shown by the French in horror and the abject is also symptomatic of a susceptibility to the agenda of fascism which embraces irrationality and cruelty. There is an understanding, however, that risking excess can engender insight : 'You beat the liver out of a goose to get a *pâté;* you pound the muscles of a man's *cardia* to get a philosopher' (p. 127). Or, in Kristeva's words, 'the danger of filth represents for the subject the risk to which the very symbolic order is permanently exposed, to the extent that it is a device of discriminations, of differences' (Kristeva 1982: 69). The American, in avoiding the risk, also eschews greater knowledge and understanding: 'The French are dishevelled, and wise, the American tries to approximate it with drink. It is his only clue to himself. He takes it when his soap has washed him too clean for identification' (p. 131). The American obsession with cleanliness, then, suggests a puritan nation which, whilst resistant to the dangerous seductions of fascist philosophy, demonstrates a cultural narrowness, naivety and intolerance that belie its political agenda of individual freedom (and which can result in McCarthyism). In this respect, whilst Carlston's critique of Barnes as a decadent writer (whom she links with Huysmans, Oscar Wilde and Céline), is extremely useful in properly contextualizing *Nightwood*, her claim that O'Connor's narrative position 'can rather easily be aligned with certain predominant impulses in fascist writing' (Carlston 1998: 67) is tenable only if one ignores the irony in O'Connor's monologues. If one reads them as ironic, however, they lead us to conclude that any description of *Nightwood* as a quasi-fascist text has already been pre-empted by O'Connor's own critique of American and French consciousness in relation to 'filthiness' and 'the Beast'. In order to accept Carlston's argument, readers have to close their ears to the element of Gothic parody in *Nightwood*.

I am not, however, trying here to recuperate Barnes as a radical, left-wing thinker. Rather, I would link Barnes's *Nightwood* with Céline's *Journey to the End of the Night,* an equally problematic text. Kristeva has described Céline's novels as expressing 'A yearning after Meaning together with its absorption, ingestion, digestion and rejection' (Kristeva 1982: 136). She has also defined his work as 'apocalyptic' in so far as it embraces 'suffering, horror and their convergence on abjection' (Kristeva 1982: 154): indeed, for her, 'his whole narrative stance seems controlled by the necessity of going through abjection, whose intimate side is suffering and horror its public feature' (Kristeva 1982: 140). Even sexual desire is presented as a form of 'debilitated suffering' (Kristeva 1982: 148). Such a nihilistic vision appealed to intellectuals of both the extreme Left and the extreme Right during the 1930s since, whilst not always agreeing on the causes of alienation (although capitalism became a shared scapegoat in the aftermath of 1929), the same feelings of disaffection from modernity's myth of progress informed opposite ends of the political spectrum.[6] Whilst *Nightwood* has continued to attract divided readings (as those offered by Marcus and Carlston illustrate most recently), *Journey to the End of the Night* has, in retrospect, frequently been seen as sounding a protofascist note which was later to develop into a virulent anti-semitism, tainting Céline's literary reputation and besmirching his life. It is therefore worth recalling that in 1932, Paul Nizan, then a Communist militant, reviewed *Journey* as offering a sinister, but recognizable, portrayal of the world: 'il arrache tous les masques, tous les camouflages, il abat les décors des illusions, il accroît la conscience de la déchéance actuelle de l'homme' ('he tears off all masks, all disguises, he destroys all illusory façades, he seduces us into believing in the total decline of humanity') (my translation) (Suleiman 1971: 45). Indeed, the novel even evoked a Christian defence by René Schwob (Noble 1987: 22). Both works resisted, and continue to resist, definitive readings. In this respect, Carlston's claim that *Nightwood*'s 'resistance to any totalizing "cultural vision" or interpretation' (including her own) is 'both wily and forceful' and her suggestion that its 'complexity' is 'dangerous' (Carlston 1998: 84–85) – as if the novel had a malignant life of its own independent of the reader – betray a strange nervousness. Such a reaction reveals more, perhaps, about a continuing American anxiety in the face of the 'black lineage' of French intellectual pessimism than it does about Barnes's most famous work.

Barnes's letters reveal that she read Céline's *Voyage au bout de la nuit* soon after it was published (Herring 1995: 219) and, indeed, the anonymous reviewer for the *Times Literary Supplement* likened *Nightwood*'s 'sickness of the soul' to 'M. Céline's otherwise quite different book "Voyage au Bout de la Nuit"' (Marcus 1990a: 200). There are certainly some striking parallels between Céline's novel and *Nightwood*. Both novels are structured through the restless picaresque activity of characters who feel emotionally dislocated from their home cultures, with Bardamu journeying between France, French Colonial Africa and the United States and Robin moving between Paris and New York. The self-reflexiveness of both works derives from their self-conscious and experimental use of language which destabilizes the realist dimension of the two novels; in this respect, they are clearly written within the modernist framework. Although Céline's *Journey* is not obviously Gothic, its fascinated delineation of horror and excess, together with what Nicholas Hewitt has described as 'the considerable presence of ghosts' in the text (Hewitt 1987: 75–84), give it a quasi-Gothic air.[7] Moreover, Céline's Bardamu and Barnes's O'Connor are alienated, cynical narrators who see the world as a place of hypocrisy which reeks of lies, suffering and mortality:

> When the grave lies open before us, let's not try to be witty, but on the other hand, let's not forget, but make it our business to record the worst of the human viciousness we've seen without changing one word. When that's done, we can curl up our toes and sink into the pit. (Céline 1997: 28)

In addition, the trauma of World War I hangs like a pall over both texts and whilst Catholicism is present as nostalgic whiff of incense, God is not. The pessimism of both novels is relieved, however, by a Beckettian humour which allows for despair to be expressed aphoristically: 'love is only infinity put at the disposal of poodles' (Céline 1997: 14); 'We are but skin about a wind, with muscles clenched against mortality' (p. 122). (O'Connor's definition of life as 'the permission to know death' (p. 122) even seems to anticipate the title of Céline's novel, *Mort à crédit*, published in 1936.) Characters survive rather than live in such worlds, which are as black as hell yet portrayed by their authors with what Céline described as a 'comic lyricism': the result is what Kristeva has defined as '(a) laughing apocalypse' or 'an apocalypse without god' (Kristeva 1982: 206). Both texts use the darkness of the night as a metaphor for anomie and despair and both use 'the Beast' to suggest the savagery at the heart of human darkness. Indeed, Céline's Baryton sees the twentieth century as a monster slouching towards annihilation:

> 'I saw the human mind, Ferdinand, losing its balance little by little and dissolving in the vast maelstrom of apocalyptic ambitions! It began about 1900 ... mark that date! From then on, the world in general and psychiatry in particular have been one frantic race to see who could become more perverse, more salacious, more outlandish, more revolting, more creative as they call it, than his neighbour ... A pretty mess! Who would be first to throw himself into the arms of the monster, the beast without heart and without restraint! ... The beast will devour us all, Ferdinand, it's a certainty and a good thing too! What is this beast? ... A big head that goes where it pleases! ... Even now its wars and its flaming slobber are pouring in on us from all sides! ... ' (Céline 1997: 371)

O'Connor equates knowledge of the Beast with the knowledge of the worst that humans can perform and therefore with a true understanding of the human condition:

> The French have made a detour of filthiness – Oh, the good dirt! Whereas you are of a clean race, of a too eagerly washing people, and this leaves no road for you. The brawl of the Beast leaves a path for the Beast. You wash your brawl with every thought, with every gesture, with every conceivable emollient and savon, and expect to find your way again ... There is not one of us who, given an eternal incognito, a thumbprint nowhere set against our souls, would not commit rape, murder and all abominations. (pp. 123–124; 128)

The 'detour' into 'filthiness', then, that we see so clearly in the work of de Sade, Lautréamont, Céline and Barnes represents a willingness to confront the abject as Kristeva defines it in *The Powers of Horror*: 'what disturbs identity, system, order. What does not respect borders, positions, rules. The in-between, the ambiguous, the composite. The traitor, the liar, the criminal with a good conscience, the shameless rapist, the killer who claims he is a savior ... ' (Kristeva 1982:⁴). Drawing on the work of anthropologists and Freud's *Totem and Taboo*, Kristeva explores the key role of filth in the construction of social identities:

> It is as if dividing lines were built up between society and a certain nature, as well as within the social aggregate, on the basis of the simple logic of *excluding filth*, which, promoted to the ritual of *defilement*, founded the 'self and clean' of each social group if not of each subject ... Defilement is what is jettisoned from the *'symbolic system'*. It is what escapes that social

rationality, that logical order on which a social aggregate is based, which then becomes differentiated from a temporary agglomeration of individuals and, in short constitutes a *classification system or a structure*. (Kristeva 1982: 65)

To explore the relative nature of 'filth', and to question its categorization, is thus to question the construction of social orders and the basis on which individual subjectivity is founded. It is to probe at the very boundaries of what it means to be human: 'filth is not a quality in itself, but it applies only to what relates to a *boundary*' (Kristeva 1982: 69). The frailty of both collective and individual identities is thereby instantly exposed. That way madness – or at least the risk of it – lies; hence the interest in dislocated states of mind evident in the work of both Barnes and Céline. Such writing also exposes the fact that social morality derives from cultural constructions of the abject rather than philosophic objectivity. The inevitable conclusion that social-value systems are arbitrary and primitive results in both aggressive challenges to convention and profound cynicism. Thus, within the fictional worlds of Céline and Barnes, the usual taboo system is reversed so that darkness equals enlightenment, transgression equals liberty and the embrace of 'filth' signals intellectual integrity (for Bardamu war is to be rejected as 'filth' rather than to be welcomed as a noble venture and for Robin Vote promiscuity is true freedom). Or, as de Jonge notes of Maldoror's unsociable antics, 'Truth and freedom will be only achieved through basic transgression' (de Jonge 1973: 49). However, whereas exploration of the abject through transgression cannot be culturally tolerated as social deed, it can be tolerated as literary text: 'Because it occupies its place, literature may also involve not an ultimate resistance to but an unveiling of the abject: an elaboration, a discharge, and a hollowing out of abjection through the Crisis of the Word' (Kristeva 1982: 208).

This 'unveiling' is what links the work of the French authors briefly discussed here and whose writings seem to have influenced Barnes' creation of *Nightwood*. It should be clear, therefore, that I disagree with Chisholm, who locates Barnes's 'grotesquely pessimistic' eroticism solely within the modernist moment of surrealism, which she sees as outdoing 'its Romantic and Sadean precursors by using eros to invoke and release the revolutionary energies concealed in the detritus of industrialist-capitalist society' (Chisholm 1993: 187, 172). Rather, I see Barnes as aligning herself with a particular French intellectual tradition whose authors all share an obsession with '(a)bjection, or the journey to the end of the night' (Kristeva 1982: 58). (The exception here, perhaps, is Huysmans who turned, like des Esseintes, to Catholicism for consolation in the face of nihilism.) Moreover, in so far as their writings thereby face the void of meaninglessness, they also engage with Gothic notions of sublimity. 'No Beast is there without glimmer of infinity' in Victor Hugo's words (Kristeva 1982: 1). It is not surprising, then, to find that, in its turn, *Nightwood* influenced other writers of the Gothic, including Carson McCullers and William Faulkner, both of whom admired her writing style and her portrayal of the grotesque (Herring 1995: 299). It also seems to have left its mark on Jeanette Winterson's *Sexing the Cherry* and Carter's *Nights at the Circus*. The French 'detour' into 'filthiness', then, found its way across the Channel and the Atlantic via the *'Colonie américaine'* in Paris. European Gothic has a way of spiriting itself into even the cleanest of Anglo-Saxon beds.

Notes

1   All quotations are from this 1985 edition of the novel; page references will appear hereafter in the text. I would like to thank Paul Callick for first drawing my attention to Lautréamont's *Madoror* and Ursula Tidd for suggesting the link with Huysmans's *A Rebours*. I would also like to express my warm appreciation of help received from Ursula Tidd and Geoff Harris, who both provided detailed feedback on the final draft of the chapter. Any errors or misjudgements that remain are, of course, my own.
2   For more on the *roman noir*, see Hale 1998.
3   See Horner Zlosnik 2001 for a fuller justification of Barnes's novel as a gothic text.
4   See Pulzer 1964 for the reasons for this.
5   It is perhaps also worth noting that the Hoffmannesque element in *Nightwood* noted by Marcus might well derive from Barnes's reading of *Against Nature*, in which the Coppelia of Hoffmann's *The Sand Man* is invoked.
6   See Sternhell 1983.
7   Hewitt argues that the portrayal of so many *'fantômes'* in the novel are Céline's way of representing Barmadu's alienation from contemporary society: 'Bardamu as the "fantôme burlesque de la médecine bourgeoise", demonstrates a profound and sensitive awareness on Céline's part of the historical significance of the First World War, whichushered in a new and increasingly rebarbative society and contrived to invalidate so many of the positive myths by which men live' (Hewitt 1987: 84).

References

Barnes, D. (1985) *Nightwood*, London, Faber & Faber [1936].
Blanchot, M. (1949) *Lautréamont et Sade*, Paris, Gallimard.

AVRIL HORNER

Carlston, E.G. (1998) *Thinking Fascism: Sapphic Modernism and Fascist Modernity*, Stanford, Stanford University Press.

Carter, A. (1974) *Fireworks*, London, Faber & Faber.

Céline, L.-F. (1997) *Journey to the End of the Night (Voyage au bout de la nuit)*, trans. Ralph Manheim, London, John Calder [1932].

Chisholm, D. (1997) 'Obscene Modernism: *Eros Noir* and the Profane Illumination of Djuna Barnes', *American Literature*, 69:1, 167–206.

Dalton, A.B. (1993) '"This is Obscene": Female Voyeurism, Sexual Abuse, and Maternal Power in *The Dove*', *Review of Contemporary Fiction*, 13:3, 117–139.

Eliot, T.S. (1937) 'Introduction', in D. Barnes, *Nightwood*, London, Faber & Faber, 1–7.

Fiedler, L. (1992) *Love and Death in the American Novel*, New York, Anchor Books.

Field, A. (1983) *The Formidable Miss Barnes: The Life of Djuna Barnes*, London, Secker & Warburg.

France, P. (ed.) (1995) *The New Oxford Companion to Literature in French*, Oxford, Clarendon Press.

Galvin, M.E. (1999) *Queer Poetics: Five Modernist Women Writers*, Westport, Greenwood Press.

Hale, T. (1998) 'Roman Noir', in M. Mulvey-Roberts (ed.), *The Handbook to Gothic Literature*, London, Macmillan, pp. 189–195.

Herring, P. (1993) 'Zadel Barnes: Journalist', *Review of Contemporary Fiction*, 13:3, 107–116.

—— (1995) *Djuna: The Life and Work of Djuna Barnes*, London and New York, Viking.

Hewitt, N. (1987) *The Golden Age of Louis-Ferdinand Céline*, Leamington Spa, Hamburg, New York, Berg Publishers.

Horner, H. and Zlosnik, S. (2001) 'Strolling in the Dark: Gothic Flânerie in Djuna Barnes's *Nightwood*', in A. Smith and J. Wallace (eds), *Gothic Modernisms*, London, Macmillan, pp. 78–95.

Huysmans, J.-K. (1998) *Against Nature (A Rebours)*, trans. M. Mauldon, Oxford, Oxford University Press [1884].

de Jonge, A. (1973) *Nightmare Culture: Lautréamont and Les Chants de Maldoror*, London, Secker & Warburg.

Kristeva, J. (1982) *Powers of Horror: An Essay on Abjection (Pouvoirs de l'horreur)*, trans. Leon S. Roudiez, New York, Columbia University Press.

Lautréamont (1965) *Maldoror (Les Chants de Maldoror)* trans. G. Wenham, New York, New Directions Publishing Corporation [1868–69].

Marcus, J. (1990a) 'Mousemeat: Contemporary Reviews of *Nightwood*', in M.L. Broe (ed.), *Silence and Power*, Carbondale and Edwardsville, Southern Illinois University Press, pp. 195–206.

—— (1990b), 'Laughing at Leviticus: *Nightwood* as Woman's Circus Epic', in M.L. Broe (ed.), *Silence and Power*, Carbondale and Edwardsville, Southern Illinois University Press, pp. 221–250.

Moers, E. (1986) *Literary Women*, London, The Women's Press [1976].

Mulvey-Roberts, M. (ed.) (1998) The Handbook to Gothic Literature, Basingstoke, Macmillan.

Nimeiri, A. (1993) 'Djuna Barnes's Nightwood and "the Experience of America"', *Critique: Studies in Contemporary Fiction*, 34:1, 100–112.

Noble, I. (1987) *Language and Narration in Céline's Writings*, Basingstoke, Macmillan.

Pulzer, P.G. (1964) *The Rise of Political Anti-Semitism in German and Austria*, New York and London, John Wiley & Sons.

Punter, D. *The Literature of Terror (Vol. 2) The Modern Gothic*, London, Addison Wesley Longman.

Scott, B.K. (1990) *The Gender of Modernism: A Critical Anthology*, Bloomington and Indianapolis, Indiana University Press.

Sternhell, Z. (1983) *Ni droite ni gauche: l'idéologie fasciste en France*, Paris, Le Seuil.

Sue, E. (n.d.) *The Mysteries of Paris* (*Les Mystères de Paris*), Sawtry, Cambridgeshire and New York, Dedalus/Hippocrene (Dedalus European Classics).

Suleiman, S. (1971) *Paul Nizan: pour une nouvelle culture*, Paris, Editions Bernard Grasset.

Index

INDEX

INDEX